Nicholson's Guide to the
Thames

From source to sea
Edited by Paul Atterbury

Robert Nicholson Publications
3 Goodwin's Court, St Martin's Lane, London WC 2

We should like to thank the following:—
Admiralty Librarian.
Abingdon Borough Council.
Barbara Atterbury.
Miss M. Bates, Thames Barge Sailing Club.
Biological Records Centre.
R. C. Bolland.
E. J. Brettel, Thames Conservancy
Engineers Dept.
British Council for Archaeology.
British Rail Board Dept of Historical Relics.
British Trust for Ornithology.
P. D. C. Brown, Ashmolean Museum.
Alan Burchard, Wiltshire Archaeological &
Natural History Society.
R. A. Canham, London Museum.
Central Council of Physical Recreation.
City of Oxford Information Centre.
Corporation of London City Engineer's
Office.
Corporation of London Information Centre.
Council for Nature.
Countryside Commission.
Deserted Medieval Village Research Group.
Doulton & Co.
D. S. Dunsmore, Association of Master
Lightermen & Barge Owners.
H. L. Edlin, Forestry Commission.
L. A. Edwards, Waterways Research Centre.
Geological Society of London.
Gloucestershire County Council.
H. Godwin Arnold, ARIBA.
Greater London Council—in particular the
Parks Dept, the Public Information Dept,
the Dept of Architecture and Civic Design
and the GLC riverside boroughs.
Guildford Museum and Muniment Room.
E. C. Gunkel, Gravesend Central Library.
W. Lindley, Secretary of the Watermen,
Lightermen, Tugmen & Bargemen's Union.
National Maritime Museum.
John O'Callaghan, GLC Public Information.
Ordnance Survey.
Patricia Perrott.
Ponies of Britain.
Port of London Authority.
Prittlewell Priory Museum.
Public Library Service—in particular the
reference libraries of Richmond, Battersea,
Chiswick, Fulham, Westminster, Greenwich,
Woolwich, Erith, Dartford, Gravesend,
Reading and Oxford.
Ramblers Association.
Reading Museum and Art Gallery.
Royal Yachting Association.
Salter Brothers.
S. H. Sharpley, Forestry Commission
Research Information Section.
Miss Joan Small, BA.
Thames Amateur Rowing Council.
Thames Conservancy.
Thames Division of the Metropolitan Police.
Thames Valley Tourist Association.
E. W. Tilley.
F. M. Underhill, FSA.
W. A. Webb, Passenger Vehicle Operators
Association.
Ben Weinreb.
H. J. Wilson, London Anglers Association.
B. G. Wilson, Clerk to the Company of
Watermen and Lightermen.
J. Wymer.
Wiltshire County Council.

Introduction

The Thames has long been a fascination and a challenge to authors and publishers. This book is designed to answer the need for an accurate and concise guide to the whole of the river, from source to sea. It covers the casual day trip as well as the more serious business of sailing, fishing and other activities. Above all, the river is presented in practical map sections with all related information on the same page. A team of ten people have been at work on the book for several months. The editor, Paul Atterbury, carried out the marathon, and sometimes adventurous task of walking or boating the whole 215 miles of the river.

No advertising is carried. No one can buy a place in the guide. Every entry is here on its own merit.

I hope this book gives pleasure and fulfills its practical aims. I would welcome any suggestions that might add to the value of future editions.

Robert Nicholson

Editor: Paul Atterbury
Research: Jane Eley and Andrea Line
Natural history: Mrs Pearl Small
Fishing: Bill Howes
Typography: David Perrott
Design Consultant and
Cover design: Romek Marber
Drawings: Paul Sharp and Roger Nicholson
Photography: David Perrott and Andrew · Whittuck

Maps based upon the Ordnance Survey map with the sanction of the Controller of HM Stationery Office, Crown Copyright reserved.

Filmset in Monotype Univers by Siviter-Smith, Birmingham. Printed offset lithography by NV Grafische Industrie, Haarlem, Holland.

We are particularly grateful to Bert Bushnell Ltd, Boat Builders and Hirers, Ray Mead Road, Maidenhead, Berks for providing the research boat.

Contents

Symbols

Key to symbols used throughout map sections. See also 'Explanation of maps and text', page 16.

X Meals served
♀ Licenced
BB Accommodation

Ⓢ Boatyard or service point
△ Camping site
⁚∴ Archaeological site
⸬ Footpath

4 History

The river Thames was known by the Romans as Tamesis below Dorchester, while the part running on to the source seems to have been called Isis. At Dorchester, the Thame, a tributary, enters the main river. It is thought that the name Tamesis derived from the amalgamation of Thame and Isis, in their Celtic forms Taom and Uis. From Taom-Uis, which means the pouring out of the waters, the name Tamesis was formed, and this in turn became Thames.

Geographically the Thames holds the key to the centre of England. 215 miles long, it crosses much of the centre of England, from East to West. The Romans recognised its importance. Watling Street, the Fosse Way, Ermine Street and the Icknield Way were all built to cross the river. These crossings were usually fords, traces of which remain, but bridges were built at London and Staines. Many of the earliest settlements were close to the river. London, founded by the Romans, grew into a great trading centre and port. By the C19th it was the largest port in the world.

Goods were shipped from the capital inland along the river by horse-drawn and sailing barges, and by the early C19th the Thames was linked to the central canal network, and so to other parts of Britain. The importance of the river as a transport vehicle diminished after the coming of the railways.

The economical and geographical importance of the river led to a growth of fortified buildings along the banks. The Romans had a vast military fortification at Dorchester, and another on the site of the Tower of London. The Angles and Saxons, entering the country through the mouth of the Thames, built their fortified settlements on the Kent and Essex banks. The Norman plan to build castles at strategic points throughout England included Windsor and the Tower of London. The Tudors extended the line of fortresses under the threat of invasion from France and Spain. Tilbury Fort and The Royal Dockyard at Woolwich were built, and Sheerness was established as a defence outpost. Despite these precautions the Dutch sailed up the Medway in 1667. Consequently Tilbury Fort was enlarged, and Sheerness became a regular garrison. During the C19th General Gordon built Cliffe Fort, Coalhouse Fort and Shorne Fort. These were used in both World Wars, as coastal and anti-aircraft batteries.

During the Middle Ages the river was for many people a source of livelihood. Great monasteries were established, and mills were built using the river power. From earliest times the Thames held an abundance of fish. Trout and salmon could be caught readily. The latter were once so common that they were eaten by the poor. The river was also thick with eels. These would swim up the river in such numbers that they could be caught with sieves and buckets, and were made into a form of cake. In Essex there was a thriving shrimping and cockling industry. Since the early C19th pollution has gradually driven the salmon and most eels from the Thames.

To catch the fish and power the mills, weirs were built, often in places hindering navigation. From earliest times there was constant warfare between the fishermen and millers, and the bargemen. Some weirs, known as flash locks, had movable sections to allow barges to pass through. But even then the bargemen would have to wait for the fierce rush of water to subside before passing the weir. Then he would have to wait on the far side for the depth of water to build up again. Legislation tried unsuccessfully to control the building of weirs, and so allow the river to fulfil its important role as a highway. Navigation did not improve until the Pound Lock, the first modern lock on the Thames, was built at Swift Ditch, near Abingdon in 1630. The building of the modern locks accelerated, and by the end of the C18th navigation had ceased to be a laborious and hazardous business.

In the lower reaches smuggling was a very important source of livelihood. There was a lively trade in contraband along the Kent and Essex coasts until well into the C19th.

The Thames has often been the scene of festivity. In the C17th and C18th Frost Fairs were held in London whenever the river froze. There were stalls, performing bears, fairground amusements and ox roasting on the ice. The last Frost Fair was held in 1814. The removal of the old London Bridge which had the effect of a dam, and the building of the embankments in the C19th narrowed the river, and deepened and speeded the flow of the water. The tidal river can no longer freeze. However in 1963, the non-tidal Thames froze as far as Teddington.

Since the early C19th, the river has become the scene of regattas in the summer. The Henley Regatta is now an international event.

From the Norman period the City of London exercised control of the river as far as Staines. Above this point it was in the hands of various riparian owners. In 1857 the Thames Conservancy gained control of the river below Staines. In 1866 their jurisdiction was extended as far as Cricklade, giving them control over the navigable part of the river. In 1909 the tidal river, from below Teddington, was put under the control of the port of London Authority. These boundaries persist today.

The future development of the Thames will be decided by the building of a barrier across the mouth of the river. After the 1953 floods, the Waverley Committee recommended that a permanent structure be placed across the river, making it non-tidal. This structure could be a permanent dam with locks for shipping, or a retractable barrier. Since 1928 the dam versus barrier dispute has drifted on, the large number of vested interests making a decision seemingly impossible. And all the time the costs have been rising: £11 million in 1958 has now become £39 million.

The effects of the dam/barrier would be widespread. From a commercial point of view there are advantages and disadvantages. The non-tidal river would mean quicker travelling times for barges, which at present are dependent on the tides. Equally the restricted access from the estuary could be a serious delaying factor. At present the commercial life of the river is its most important aspect. There are over 4000 barges in the Thames, which are responsible for unloading the ships and transferring the cargoes to their destinations, either via the inland waterway system, or to a suitable road/rail terminal. The barges can only thrive if the waterway system is used to its fullest extent. At present far too much is carried by road, with the obvious results on the national economy. The dam/barrier would help to overcome this, as the speeding-up of the barges would draw custom back to the rivers and canals. Both the Association of Master Lightermen and the Watermen, Lightermen, Tugmen and Bargemen's Union are in favour of the dam, as the barrier would hinder the commercial interest.

The recent closure of the Brentford Docks has aroused much anger, yet this is part of a long-term plan to move the commercial part of the river away from the centre of London. The steadily increasing size of ships has reduced correspondingly the value of the London Docks. Already the development of Tilbury has caused the closure of St Katharine Docks.

Aerofilms

The gradual spread of the container system will render more docks obsolete, with the result that the commercial part of the river will be moved to the estuary. Apart from giving large ships a far quicker turn-round, this will leave the dockland areas free for redevelopment. This pattern has already started. The GLC has just bought St Katharine Dock and plans to turn it into housing; an important part of this plan is the retention of the dock itself, which will be developed as a social amenity, as a yachting marina, for example.

The non-tidal river above Teddington is now used largely for pleasure. The dam/barrier will extend this area greatly. The Thames could once more become the main artery and social centre of London, as it was in the C17th. The redevelopment of the docks could turn the river into a pleasure area that stretches from Lechlade well into the Pool of London, if not further. Apart from pleasure, the river could provide a quick and convenient transport system linking the various Thamesside Estates, for example Pepys Estate, SE8, and Thamesmead. The hovercraft could be a suitable vehicle.

A feature of the Thames above Teddington is the relative cleanliness of the water. The Thames Conservancy maintains strict pollution control over the whole Thames Catchment Area. These controls include sewage and factory effluents, and the sanitation on vessels. This pollution control is necessary if the river is to give any pleasure, or if aquatic life is to survive.

The building of the dam/barrier would necessitate similar controls over the river through London. The Port of London Authority controls the pollution of this part of the river, and there are signs that the river is getting cleaner. Fresh water fish can now live well into London, while sea fish are moving slowly up the estuary. A curious side effect of the pollution is that the river is getting warmer. The discharge of cooling water from power stations has raised the temperature of the water at London Bridge $4\frac{1}{2}$°C over the last 40 years. A non-tidal river would also stop the huge daily deposit of drift wood.

Side effects of the dam/barrier may include silting of the river and tributaries, and changes in the water level in the Thames Catchment Area. To investigate these possibilities a working model of the tidal Thames has been built, at a cost of over £20,000.

The most important aspect of the dam/barrier is that it will end once and for all the threat of a devastating flood. There has never been such a disaster in London, but this is more by luck than judgement. London's history is punctuated by minor floods, and yet every year as the city sinks lower so the risk increases. Westminster Hall was flooded in 1762 and 1791. More recently, in 1881, 100 barges were sunk and Woolwich Pier was washed away. On 7 January 1928 a surge in the North Sea combining with a high tide caused the water to pour over the embankment. Fourteen were drowned, 4,350 families were homeless and the moat at the Tower was filled for the first time in centuries. In the flood disaster of 1953, 309 people lost their lives, 53 of them on Canvey Island. Since then little has been achieved except discussion. Because it has never happened, the risk of a major flood is not taken seriously. Yet what happened when the river Arno swept through Florence could easily happen here. In December 1965, a surge came within 4 inches of the top of the embankment. After the 1953 disaster the newspaper of the Metropolitan Police said: 'It is likely that sooner or later, unless something is done to remedy the situation, large areas of London will be devastated when the Thames bursts its banks'. Nothing has been done except the strengthening of the sea walls in Essex and Kent. This means that the river is now the only drain. In 1953 Canvey was swamped, and so saved London. Next time it can only be London.

The effects of the flood would be catastrophic. The centre of Government at Westminster and Whitehall would be disrupted, or put out of action. The tube would be flooded, the water reaching as far out as Camden Town, the Elephant and Castle and Shepherd's Bush. Apart from the death toll of people trapped in trains the break in effective communications could last for months. Most riverside industries would be out of operation. Electra House, the centre of the international telegraph network and Fleet Building, the telex centre and eleven telephone exchanges would all be affected. The backfiring of sewers would cause a serious health risk, and, combined with the lack of food and disrupted communications, epidemics could easily break out.

The only organisation who takes the flood risk seriously is Shell. The Shell Centre has a flood team on 24 hour call, all necessary equipment standing by and one annual rehearsal.

Warning of an impending flood could only be given a few hours before it occurs. Few precautions could be taken in the time available, particularly as few buildings have any precautions to take. The exceptionally high tides can be predicted each year, but since 1883 there have been only seventeen years when the river did not rise above the expected flood level.

The danger of this disaster alone justifies the building of the dam/barrier, regardless of cost. The decision, or rather the non-decision, to ignore the risk because it has not yet happened is simple ostrich thinking.

Various studies are under way with a view to improving the facilities of the river. The Thames-side Environmental Assessment, produced by the GLC Department of Architecture and Civic Design, is an intelligent study of the potential of the riverside in the London area. The Plan for the Development of the Thames between Lechlade and Cricklade, produced jointly by the Wiltshire and Gloucestershire County Councils, shows how this part of the river could become a great social amenity. While these are both suggestions rather than concrete proposals they are a move in the right direction.

However, any future development will be greatly influenced by the building of the dam or barrier, and so these plans can have little weight until the decision to build is taken. Preliminary studies are under way to decide the site of the structure, but there is still no final decision between a barrier and a dam. The type of structure is not vital, but the building of one or other in the immediate future is imperative.

The Geology of the Thames Valley

The wide, low marshes of the estuary, the soft chalk hill at Streatley, the clay vales below Oxford, in fact every feature, twist and turn of the river owes something to its geology. The tilt or warp of the rocks, their relative hardness, past changes in sea level and the drastic effects of the Ice Age have all combined to create the characteristic landscape of the Thames Valley.

As the river flows to the sea it meets formations which become progressively more recent in geological time, for such is the general tilt of these superimposed rocks, (clays, sands and limestones are all rocks to a geologist) that the older ones are brought to the surface towards the west. Several little brooks could make a fair claim that they were the source of the river but, in common with the one near Cirencester which is endowed with that honour, they all rise in the Jurassic rocks of the Cotswold Hills. Jurassic is the name given to the geological period of some 180 million years ago, when marine and flying reptiles inhabited the earth. The Cotswold limestones were deposited by ancient shallow seas bearing no relationship to the present shape of the continents. Once off the Cotswolds the river flows for the most part over Oxford Clay as far as Oxford itself: a clay easily eroded by the river, hence the wide, flat flood plains each side.

Below Oxford come the more recent rocks of the Jurassic period; first the sandy, shelly Corallian limestone which forms a distinct ridge, giving rise to the hills at Cumnor and Wheatley each side of the river, then the Kimmeridge Clay. The great loop of the river between Radley and Clifton Hampden is caused by some more resistant sands of the next geological period known as Cretaceous. 'Lazy waters' is an apt term for any river, for, powerful and destructive as they may be at times of flood or blockage, they will normally take the easiest course and cut their channels in the softer rocks. Below this great loop as far as Wallingford, there is a wide belt of clay, known as Gault Clay, which has been gently planed down to the wide flood plains around Dorchester.

At Moulsford the Thames meets the chalk, the soft, white, characteristic limestone of the Cretaceous period, laid down in seas some 100 million years ago, when the great reptiles were dying out and small mammals evolving. Fossil sea urchins of flint are quite common in the chalk and may often be picked up along the river where they have been washed out. Soft as it may be for limestones, the chalk is much more resistant to water than clay and sand, and, to get through it, the river has had to expend most of its energy in cutting downwards and not sideways, hence the narrow valley between the Chiltern Hills and Berkshire Downs known as the Goring Gap. Surprisingly, once nearly through the chalk at Reading, the Thames swings back into it and does not escape on to softer rocks until below Maidenhead, a fortunate phenomenon as it gives us the beautiful Henley Gorge and dramatic cliffs at Cliveden.

However, once below Maidenhead, the confined river spreads itself out into the London Basin, flowing over London Clay for the most part. Richmond Hill and the Isle of Sheppey are both of London Clay, the sediment of a tropical sea which covered what is now England 40 to 70 million years ago during the Eocene period. Many forms of extinct mammals lived at this time. Hills each side of London, such as Hampstead and Blackheath, are sandy remnants of the more recent Eocene rocks. Before reaching the sea the Thames just grazes against the chalk once more at Dartford and Purfleet.

The last major earth movement felt in Britain was probably about 25 million years ago, when the violent forces which produced the Alps and Himalayas sent ripples of pressure across southern England, lifting much of south east England out of the sea. From this time rain water in the west had to find its way to the sea, and, in doing so, the rocks were gradually worn away to something like the shape of Britain as it is, although no English Channel existed to make it an island. It is impossible to talk of a River Thames at this time but about 2 million years ago, at the beginning of the Pleistocne period, a sea stretched over the London Basin and lapped against the Chilterns and the North Downs. Into this great bay a river flowed which must have been the precursor of the Thames. This

The Geology of the Thames Valley

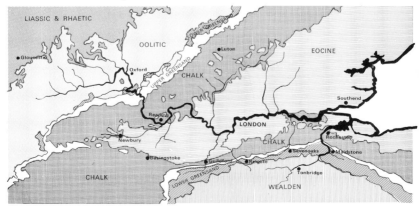

was 600 ft above the present sea, for since this time the sea level has gradually dropped. As the river has cut down it has left behind it remnants of its ancient flood plains, generally covered with flint gravel. The process of erosion still continues, and the occasional Thames Conservancy or Port of London dredger at work serves as a reminder.

The intensely cold phases of the Ice Age disrupted the normal drainage of the river; glacial ice never came further south than Upminster, but snow, melt-water and ice-dams had far-reaching effects. The Thames originally flowed through the vale of St Albans but an actual glacier blocked this vale some 500,000 years ago and diverted the river roughly to its present course. The sudden right-angled bend at Cookham has its origin in this impediment of the drainage.

During succeeding milder periods Stone Age man lived along the Thames, and his stone tools and sometimes the bones of the animals he hunted were swept into the old river gravels. At this time elephant, rhinoceros, horse, ox and deer roamed in the valley. It is only in more recent (geologically speaking) gravels that remains of Stone Age tools are found, that is, in gravels at about 100 ft or less above the present level of the river. Three main terraces are recognised in the Middle Thames Valley, best preserved around Maidenhead and Slough, which represent ancient gravel-covered flood plains left high and dry as the river has cut down its present level. These are at about 100, 75 and 40 ft above the river and are called the Boyn Hill, Lynch Hill and Taplow Terraces respectively. It is the Boyn and Lynch Hill terraces which produce the richest evidence of Stone Age Man: mammoth and woolly rhinoceros bones are typical of the lower, more recent terraces, suggesting that conditions were too icy most of the time for a pleasant life and Stone Age Man had moved south.

The last phase of the Ice Age finished about 10,000 BC and a very low sea level, probably as much as 300 ft below the present had caused the Thames in its lower reaches to cut a deep channel. This has since filled up with gravel, sand and silt and is concealed beneath the estuarine marshes. Since then, as the climate improved and the sea level rose, the English Channel was breached. Flood silt has accumulated a few feet or so in thickness along the river, and this can generally be seen on the river banks. It often contains bands of shells and, occasionally, Roman, Iron Age or even earlier pottery shards.

There is a special display on the geology of the Thames Valley in the Geological Survey Museum at Kensington.

The riverside at Grays, Essex

Places of interest

Buildings of England Series by Nikolaus
Pevsner. Penguin.
Pocket Guide to English Parish Churches by
John Betjeman. Collins.
Penguin Guide to London.
The Thames Highway by Fred S. Thacker.
2 vols. David & Charles.
The Shell Guides. Faber.
Thames-side Environment Assessment. GLC.
Visitors Guide to Country Workshops. Rural
Industries leaflet.
The Ordnance Survey 1 inch maps.

Eating, drinking & accommodation

Good Food Guide. Consumers Association.
Egon Ronay 1968 Guide. Four Square.
YHA Handbook. Youth Hostel Association.
Caravan Sites in Britain and Ireland.
National Federation of Site Operators.

Navigation

Stanford's Coloured Charts for Coastal
Navigators, Nos 6 and 7.
PLA River Byelaws.
PLA Guide to Users of Pleasure Craft.
Thames Conservancy Launch Digest.
Commercial Guide to the River Thames.
Pyramid Press.
Guide to the Waterways of the British Isles.
Canoe Union.
Thames Book. Link House Publications.
Stanford's Map of the Thames.

Natural history

The Observer Series. Frederick Warne.
Wayside and Woodland Series.
Frederick Warne.
Collins Pocket Guides.
Collins New Naturalist Series.
Flora of the British Isles by Clapham, Tutin
& Warburg. Cambridge.
Handbook on British Birds. H. S. and G.
Witherby.
Concise British Flora by Keble Martin.
Ebury Press and Michael Joseph.
Where to Watch Birds. John Gooders. Andre
Deusch.

Fishing

Angling Ways by Marshal Hardy. Jenkins.
English Reservoirs by Bill Howes. Benn.
Thames Fishery Byelaws. Thames
Conservancy.

Romney weir *W J Howes*

Shepperton Lock *R R Bolland*

Useful addresses

Thames Valley Tourist Association

Oxon. The White Hart, Dorchester on Thames. Tel Warborough 501. An association of individuals and companies who have links with tourism and are keen to promote its growth in this area. They will give information about accommodation, camping sites or holidays in the Thames Valley.

Local information offices

Abingdon, Berks

Town Clerk's Office, Abbey House. Tel 851. Mon-Fri *office hours.*

Cirencester, Glos

Public Library, Reference Section. Tel 2248. *Office hours.* Library staff willing to help with tourism enquiries.

London, SW1

British Travel Tourist Information Centre, 64 St James's Street. Tel (01) 629 9191. *Office hours and Apr-Sep Sat morning.* Information about London and all districts in England.

London, EC4

City of London Information Centre, St Paul's Churchyard. Tel (01) 606 3030. *Office hours and Sat morning.*

Oxford, Oxon

Oxford Information Centre, Carfax. Tel 48707. *Office hours and Sat; Sun Jun-Sep 10.30-12.30. 14.00-15.30.*

Reading, Berks

Reference Library, Blagrave Street. Tel 54382, ext. 484. *Office hours and Sat.*

Southend, Essex

Information Bureau, Pier Hill. Tel 44091. *Summer office hours daily, winter office hours.*

Wallingford, Berks

Town Clerk's Office, High Street. Tel 2561. *Office hours.*

Windsor, Berks

The Guildhall. Tel 60841. *Easter-Sep office hours.*

Overseas visitors

Country Houses and Castles, SW1

15 Pall Mall. Tel (01) 839 4289. Introductions arranged to country houses and castles of historic interest as a guest. $13 to $39 per night; includes dinner, drinks and breakfast. Overseas visitors only.

Boswell & Johnson, SW1

15 Pall Mall. Tel (01) 839 4108. Individually prepared itineraries for self-drive and chauffeur-driven tours. Accommodation at inns or manor houses. Overseas visitors only.

Accommodation

Hotels are noted in the map sections where they occur.

Youth Hostels Association

St Albans, Herts. Trevelyan House, 8 St Stephen's Hill. Tel 55215. The YHA provides cheap accommodation for people wishing to explore the countryside without a car. Subscription: 20s over 21, 12s6d over 16, 5s over 5. 5s per night exclusive of meals. Noted on map sections.

Camping

Sites are shown on the map sections. Camping craft and equipment may be hired from Salter Bros at Oxford (Tel 43421), Windsor (Tel 65832) and Kingston (Tel 7313). Approximately £10 per week for a two-berth boat.

Public transport: Airports

Gatwick Airport, Surrey

Tel (01) 283 8711. Terminal: Victoria Air Terminal, Victoria Station. Tel (01) 834 9411.

London Airport (Heathrow), Middx

Great West Road. Tel (01) 370 4224. Terminal: West London Air Terminal, Cromwell Road, SW7. Coach service from Reading Rail Station.

Public transport: Rail Terminals

Paddington Station, W2

Praed Street. Tel (01) 262 2767. Trains for Maidenhead, Henley, Reading, Pangbourne, Oxford and Cirencester.

Waterloo Station, SE1

York Road. Tel (01) 928 5100. Trains for Dartford, Gravesend, Staines, Twickenham and Reading.

Fenchurch Street Station, EC2

Fenchurch Street. Tel (01) 488 4868. Trains for Southend, Shoeburyness; Essex towns.

Victoria Station, SW1

Victoria Street. Tel (01) 730 3440. Trains to Chatham, Rochester and Sheerness.

Public transport: Bus Services

Bristol Omnibus Company, Wilts

Swindon. Fleming Way. Tel 22243. Area between Lechlade and Thames Head.

City of Oxford Motor Services, Oxon

Gloucester Green. Tel 41149. Area between Lechlade and Reading. Route 34 is particularly recommended; it passes through many Thames villages en route for Reading.

Thames Valley Traction Co, Berks

Bus Station, Reading. Tel 51438. From Reading to Oxford, and to London via Maidenhead.

Victoria Coach Station, SW1

164 Buckingham Palace Road. Tel (01) 730 0202. London terminal for provincial coach companies. Thames Valley towns served include Reading, Oxford, Cirencester and Southend. Book in advance.

London Transport Green Line Coaches, SW1

Eccleston Bridge. Tel (01) 222 1234. Route numbers 701, 702, 704, 705, 723 are the most convenient for the Thames.

Boat hire

Boat Enquiries

Oxford. 12 Western Road. Tel 48765/49097. Central agency for cruiser hire in England. Advisory service for the Thames. 24 hour recording service—Oxford 49097.

Thames Launches

Twickenham. York Villa, Church Street. Tel (01) 892 9041/2. Boat hire for day trips, cocktail parties, conferences, etc. Catering service.

Catamaran Cruisers
SE10. Greenwich Pier. Tel (01) 858 6566.
Motor catamaran can be hired for private
parties or business functions.

Car hire

Cricklade, Wilts
Blackwells Car Hire, 59 High Street.
Tel 225.
Gatwick Airport, Surrey
Hertz Rent-A-Car. Tel Crawley 28822.
London Airport (Heathrow), Middx
Godfrey Davis, Bath Road. Tel (01) 759
1189.
Kingston, Surrey
Lankester Eng Co, 39 Eden Street. Tel (01)
546 3151.
London, WC2
Autohall, 6 Upper St Martin's Lane.
Tel (01) 836 1525.
London, SW1
Godfrey Davis, 129 Wilton Road. Tel (01)
834 8484. 24 hour service.
Oxford, Oxon
Luxicars, St Aldates. Tel 41641.
Reading, Berks
Southern Car Services, 34 Carey Street.
Tel 55531.
Richmond, Surrey
Fox & Co, Sheen Road. Tel (01) 940 2944.
Southend, Essex
G. D. Hire Service, 589 London Road,
Westcliffe. Tel 41261.

Coach hire

Grays, Essex
Frank Harris Coaches, 8 Parker Road.
Tel 2212.
Henley, Oxon
A. G. Spiers, 4 Market Place. Tel 4312.
Kingston, Surrey
Blue & White Coaches, 4 Surbiton Crescent.
Tel 0161.
London, W1
Capital Coaches, 1 Hanover Street. Tel (01)
734 4987.
London, W12
White City Coaches, Bryony Road. Tel (01)
743 2275.
Northfleet, Kent
Moodys Coaches, Rose Street Garage.
Tel Gravesend 2467.
Reading, Berks
Smith's Luxury Coaches, 39 Mill Lane.
Tel 51241.
Richmond, Surrey
Conway Hunt, Castle Yard. Tel 5661.
Windsor, Berks
Windsorian Coaches, 17 Alma Road. Tel
63421.

Boat Trips

Oxford to Kingston
Salter Brothers, Folly Bridge, Oxford. Tel
43421/2. *Daily services mid-May until mid-
Sep between Oxford, Abingdon, Pang-
bourne, Reading, Marlow, Windsor and
Kingston.* Boats may be boarded at any of
these points. *Oxford-Kingston (from mid-
July) with overnight stops at Marlow and
Reading. Two-day inclusive tour Kingston-
Oxford (return by rail); cost approximately
£11.*

London and environs
Regular services operate in summer between
Westminster, Battersea, Greenwich, Tower
of London, Putney, Kew, Richmond, Kings-
ton and Hampton Court. Boats may be
boarded at any of these points at approxi-
mately 20 minute intervals.
Evening return cruise Westminster Pier to
Pool of London; *Whit to mid-Sep; 19.30-
21.30 daily.* Details from Westminster Pier,
Tel (01) 930 2074.
Port of London Authority cruise of London
Docks; *late May to mid-Sep.* Details from
PLA, Trinity Square, EC3. Tel (01) 481
2000, ext. 92/260.
Greenwich Pier and Tower Pier to Hampton
Court; *mid-Mar to mid-Oct;* day trips by
motor catamaran. Details from Catamaran
Cruisers Ltd, Greenwich Pier, SE10. Tel (01)
858 6566.
London to Southend and Margate
White Funnel Fleet. Details of occasional
Saturday trips from A. E. Martin & Co Ltd,
52/53 Crutched Friars, EC3. Tel (01) 709
0281, and from P. & A. Campbell Ltd,
Pier Hill, Southend. Tel 64906. Also
occasional day trips to France.

Coach Tours

From London:
A. Timpsons & Sons, Victoria Coach Station,
164 Buckingham Palace Road, SW1. Tel
(01) 730 0202. By coach along the Thames
to Benson, then by steamer to Reading.
Return by coach via Twyford and Kew.
Details and bookings from address above.
From Oxford:
South Midland Motor Services Ltd, 118
High Street, Oxford. Tel 44138/9. Wide
range of day and half day tours of the upper
Thames area.

Helicopter Trips

London Heliport
Lombard Road, SW11. Tel (01) 228 0181.
Piloted return trips by helicopter to Tower
Bridge. £2 each for 4 people.
Piloted charter flights £45 per air-hour;
summer as available.
British Executive Aircraft Service
Kidlington, near Oxford. Tel 4151. Piloted
charter flights £22 for 20 minutes (4
seater); £30 for 20 minutes (7 seater); as
available. Oxford and Blenheim Palace
could be seen in the time.

Self-drive Car Tour

Automobile Association, Leicester Square,
WC2. Tel (01) 930 1200. Leaflet maps a

route from Hyde Park Corner to Thames Head and back, mentioning places of interest, picnic places, boating and bathing.

Youth Training

Thames Youth Venture
71 Oxford Street, W1. Tel (01) 734 2272.
Courses in sailing, canoeing and rowing.
Central Council of Physical Recreation
26 Park Crescent, W1. Tel (01) 580 6822.
Mainly residential courses in sailing, rowing and canoeing. Bases are also available for youth leaders to hold their own courses.
See Marlow map.

Breakdown services

Garages listed here offer a 24 hour break-down service.

Cirencester, Glos
Cirencester Garages, Dyer Street. Tel 3314.
Dartford, Kent
Blue Star, Princes Road. Tel 24038.
Gravesend, Kent
Toll Gate Garages, Watling Street. Tel 2769.
Gillingham, Kent
Burtons, 31 Duncan Road. Tel 51294.

Kingston, Surrey
Willment's, 140a London Road. Tel (01) 546 7700.
London
In the event of breakdown in central London or in outlying areas as far as Richmond and Woolwich, contact the AA headquarters, Fanum House, Leicester Square, WC2.
Tel (01) 930 1200, who will put you in touch with the nearest breakdown garage.
Maidenhead, Berks
Maidenhead Autos, Taplow. Tel 29711.
Richmond, Surrey
Bells, 1 North Road. Tel (01) 876 6860.
Slough, Berks
Reeves, Windsor Road. Tel 28544.
Southend, Essex
SMAC, Elmer Approach. Tel 48222.
Swindon, Wilts
Green's, Marlborough Road. Tel 27251.
Staines, Middx
Crimble's, 10 Kingston Road. Tel 51143.
Walton-on-Thames, Surrey
Walton-on-Thames Motor Company, Bridge Street. Tel 23757.

W J Howes

First aid

Artificial respiration in case of drowning

Lay the patient on his back and tilt his head back as far as possible. See that his mouth and throat are clear of obstruction. Then open your own mouth and take a deep breath. Pinch the casualty's nostrils together and seal your own lips around his mouth. Blow into his lungs until his chest rises. Then remove your mouth until his chest deflates. Repeat the inflations as rapidly as possible at first. If the chest does not rise, check that his throat is free of obstruction and that the head is fully tilted. If air enters the patient's stomach, press the stomach gently, with the head of the patient turned to one side. After ten rapid inflations the pace can be slowed to twelve or fifteen a minute. In the case of babies and children do not blow too violently—20 inflations a minute is sufficient.

Bleeding and wounds

Firmly squeeze the sides of the wound together, or apply pressure with the thumbs at the sides of the wound. Cleanse around the wound. While maintaining pressure, apply dressing, cover with a pad, and bandage firmly. On no account should a tourniquet be used. If bleeding does not stop, treat the patient for shock and take him to the nearest hospital casualty department. Any bad cut should be seen by a doctor as it is often necessary to give an anti-tetanus injection.

Shock

Lay the patient down, raise the legs (except in the case of fracture), loosen clothing about neck, waist and chest, and ensure fresh air. Keep him warm.

Burns

Bathe with water or bicarbonate of soda solution. Do not apply ointments or oils or break the blister. Cover the burn with dry gauze and bandages. If burn is severe, treat for shock and take patient to hospital.

Broken bones

The patient should never be moved if a broken bone is suspected. Without moving, leave the casualty lying in as comfortable a position as possible and ring for an ambulance or doctor. Keep him warm.

Asphyxia

Treat with artificial respiration, as above.

First aid for birds

First aid hints have been compiled from information supplied by: Royal Society for the Protection of Birds, The Lodge, Sandy, Beds, and the Royal Society for the Prevention of Cruelty to Animals, 105 Jermyn Street, SW1.

Oiling

To remove slight oiling from birds, work into the feathers chalk or fuller's earth, then rinse well in cold water. If the oiling is heavy, the bird should be washed in detergent solution—$\frac{3}{4}$ oz washing powder to a gallon of water at 80°F. Rinse thoroughly, massage excess water from the feathers, and leave the bird to dry in a room at 80°F. It should not be released until it can fly after this treatment. If the bird is in an exhausted state it should be revived with food and warmth before treatment.

Broken wings and legs

Only a clean break of the leg in the mid-tarsus can be mended. Secure a splint with adhesive tape. In other cases the bird should be destroyed.

Injuries to the beak

If the beak is broken the bird should be destroyed.

Fish hooks swallowed

If the hook is well down the gullet do not attempt extraction but take the bird to the vet or RSPCA officer. If it is higher up it may be taken out with a disgorger, or the barbs of the hook gently released by hand. Do not pull the hook until the barbs are released.

Sickness

Birds suffering from cold or lack of food may be nursed back to health in time with care. They cannot live for more than a day on bread or canary food, and must be given 'Insectivorous Food'. If diseased, the bird will need anti-biotics from the vet.

Destruction

Pull the bird's head to break its neck.

Swans

They are strong enough to break an arm with a wing beat—expert advice should be sought.

The Thames Division of the Metropolitan Police

Founded in 1839, the river police used to carry out their duties in rowing boats and sailing craft. Now thirty-one diesel-powered duty boats maintain a 24 hour patrol of the river, and there are three large launches for supervisory and ceremonial duties.

Each duty boat carries a crew of three officers, all first class swimmers and skilled navigators, able to perform first aid to a very high standard. All duty boats are fully equipped to carry out rescue and resuscitation work, and if called (999) will usually arrive within fifteen minutes.

The Thames Division covers 54 miles of river, from Staines Bridge to a line between Dartford Creek and Havering Borough Boundary.

There are six police stations; the one at Waterloo Pier is the only floating police station in the world.

The division enforces river byelaws and the Merchant Shipping Acts, and also deals with vessels in collision, fires on ships, barges and wharves, and with salvage and securing barges adrift. They warn owners of riverside properties of abnormally high tides and flood dangers.

Death by drowning or suicide accounts for 70/80 people a year, and the bodies are recovered by the river police. The division has its own CID department to deal with crime; their success is evident in the low crime rate on the Thames.

There is an Underwater Search Unit at Wapping which can be used anywhere in the Metropolitan Police District.

Fire boats are stationed on the south bank by Lambeth Bridge, and are maintained by the Lambeth Fire Brigade.

Wallingford Bridge *W J Howes*

Millwall Docks *PLA.*

16 General Information

Useful addresses

Amateur Rowing Association
160 Great Portland Street, London W1.

Central Council of Physical Recreation
26 Park Crescent, London W1.

Inland Waterways Association
114 Regents Park Road, London NW1.

National Trust
42 Queen Anne's Gate, London SW1.

Ramblers Association
124 Finchley Road, London NW3.

British Trust for Ornithology
Beech Grove, Tring, Herts.

Natural history societies
The Council for Nature, Zoological Gardens, Regents Park, London NW1.
The national representative body of the voluntary natural history movement in Great Britain. They will provide details of the following societies:
Berkshire, Buckinghamshire and Oxfordshire Naturalists' Trust.
Cotswold Naturalists' Trust.
Essex Bird Watching and Preservation Society.
Essex Naturalists' Trust.
Essex Field Club.
Gloucestershire Trust for Nature Conservation.
Hertfordshire and Middlesex Trust for Nature Conservation.
Kent Field Club.
Kent Ornithological Society.
London Natural History Society.
Middle Thames Natural History Society.
North Gloucestershire Naturalists' Society.
Oxford Ornithological Society.
Reading Natural History Society.
Reading Ornithological Club.
South Essex Natural History Society.
Surrey Bird Club.
Surrey Naturalists' Trust.

Archaeological societies
Council for British Archaeology, 8 St Andrew's Place, London NW1.
The Council will provide details of the following societies:
Berkshire Archaeological Society.
Essex Archaeological Society.
Kent Archaeological Society.
London and Middlesex Archaeological Society.
Maidenhead and District Archaeological and History Society.
Middle Thames Archaeological Society.
Nonsuch and Ewell Antiquarian Society.
Surrey Archaeological Society.
Thames Basin Archaeological Society.
Wiltshire Archaeological and Natural History Society.

Nautical History
Cutty Sark Society, Cutty Sark, Church Street, London SE10.

Thames Barge Sailing Club
c/o Maritime Museum, Greenwich, London SE10.

Thames sailing associations

Association of Thames Yacht Clubs
The White House, Thorndon Approach, Herongate, Brentwood, Essex. Tel Herongate 231.

Royal Yachting Association
171 Victoria Street, SW1. Tel (01) 828 4197.
These will give details of the following clubs:
Abbey Sailing Club, Abingdon.
Alexandra Yacht Club, Southend
Aquarius Sailing Club.
Benfleet Yacht Club.
British Motor Yacht Club.
Catamaran Yacht Club (Sheppey).
Chapman Sands Sailing Club.
Cookham Reach Sailing Club.
Desborough Sailing Club.
Erith Yacht Club.

Essex Yacht Club.
Fort Halstead Yacht Club (Upnor).
Fulham Yacht Club.
Goring Thames Yacht Club.
Gravesend Sailing Club.
Greenwich Yacht Club.
Hampton Sailing Club.
Henley Sailing Club.
Hurlingham Yacht Club.
Hundred of Hoo Sailing Club.
Island Yacht Club, Canvey.
Lee & Stort Cruising Club.
Leigh-on-Sea Sailing Club.
Little Ship Club, London.
London Corinthian Sailing Club.
London River Yacht Club.
Marina Yacht Club (Hoo).
Medley Sailing Club, Oxford.
Medway Cruising Club, Gillingham.
Medway Yacht Club.
Middle Thames Yacht Club.
Minima Yacht Club, Kingston.
Oxford Ditch Cruising Club.
Penton Hook Yacht Club.
Ranelagh Sailing Club, London.
Reading Sailing Club.
Richmond Yacht Club.
St Pancras Cruising Club, London.
Sheppey Yacht Club.
Small Boat Club, Twickenham.
South Bank Sailing Club (Putney).
Sou'West Sailing Club.
Staines Sailing Club.
Strand-on-the-Green Sailing Club.
Strood Yacht Club.
Tamesis Club, Surbiton.
Tewkes Yacht Club, Canvey.
Thames Barge Sailing Club, London.
Thames Estuary Yacht Club.
Thames Motor Cruising Club (Hampton Court).
Thames Sailing Club, Surbiton.
Thames Valley Cruising Club, Reading.
Thorpe Bay Yacht Club.
Thurrock Yacht Club.
Twickenham Cruising Club.
Twickenham Yacht Club.
Upper Thames Motor Yacht Club.
Upper Thames Sailing Club (Bourne End).
Walton-on-Thames Sailing Club.
Wey Cruising Club.
Weybridge Mariners Club.
Weybridge Sailing Club.
The following clubs have sailing on gravel pits leased from the Ready Mixed Group:
Century Sailing Club (Shepperton).
Egham Lake Sailing Club (Chertsey).
Kingsmead Sailing Club.
Wraysbury Lake Sailing Club.

Navigation rules and hints

These basic rules and hints are largely compiled from the Thames Conservancy Byelaws. Copies from: Thames Conservancy, 15 Buckingham Street, WC2. Price 2s.

Registration
Your launch must be licensed by or registered with the Thames Conservancy.

Fire or explosion on a launch
The Thames Conservancy must be notified within 48 hours. Efficient fire extinguishing equipment should be carried on board.

Name of launch
Must be clearly marked on bow and stern.

Speed limit
Under no circumstances more than 7 knots.

Sound signals on launches
A whistle or horn is compulsory.
One short blast: 'I am going to starboard'.
Two short blasts: 'I am going to port'.
Three short blasts: 'I am going astern'.
Four short blasts: 'I am unable to manoeuvre'.
Four short blasts followed by one short blast: 'I am turning round to starboard'.
Four short blasts followed by two

short blasts: 'I am turning round to port.'
Note: starboard—right; port—left.

Sailing vessels
Power should *always* give way to sail. When it is impossible to manoeuvre, then sound four short blasts to indicate this.

Bridges and bends
A launch travelling upstream gives way to a vessel coming downstream when close to a bridge. It is unwise to cut bends—the water is often shallow on the inside.

Navigation

Locks
Follow lock keeper's instructions. You are responsible for controlling the boat, and making fast head and stern. Have enough mooring rope on board to pay out as the water in the lock rises or falls. The lock staff are only on duty from 9.00 until sunset.

Lock cut
Here launches must go in single file. No overtaking.

Weirs
Keep well away from weirs—red notice boards warn when they are particularly dangerous.

Dredgers
Slow down when passing dredgers. Navigate to the side where a white flag is shown.

Bathers
Watch out for and keep clear of bathers.

Electricity cables
Caution required. Cables normally 40 feet high. Lower your mast or aerial if necessary. Over backwaters and smaller channels they may be lower.

Lights
Four navigation lights must be shown if you are navigating at night:
Bright white light on the mast or staff at the bow not less than 4ft above the hull.
Green light on the starboard side.
Red light on the port side.
White light on the stern.

Anchor
An anchor is essential; rigged for immediate use.

Life jackets
All children should wear life-jackets. It is sensible for adults too!

Silencer
Exhausts must be silenced.

Petrol
Petrol must not be transferred while the launch is in or near a lock.

Sewage and rubbish
It is an offence for which you can be prosecuted to discharge sewage, oil, sink waste rubbish or any other matter into the water to cause pollution.

Insurance
Make sure that your insurance is valid and fully comprehensive.

Explanation of maps and text

Maps
These are all based on existing 2½ inches to the mile Ordnance Survey maps brought up to date where possible. All irrelevant information has been removed and much new useful information added.
All maps are positioned with north at the top, and the direction in which the Thames flows is shown on each map by a blue arrow. Towpaths (shown with a bright blue single line) are generally public rights of way.
On the *main* river the route *not* generally recommended for navigation is coloured solid blue. Ferries are still used as naming points although the actual ferry may now no longer exist.

Places of interest
Properties mentioned may not

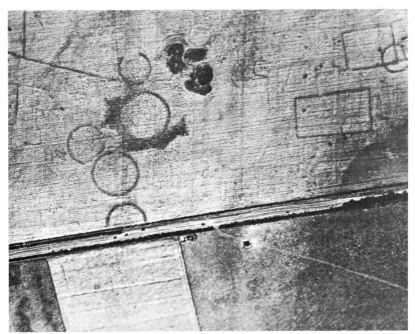

Cropmarks at Northfield Farm, Long Wittenham *Ashmolean Museum*

necessarily be open to the public. It is important to respect private property throughout the Thames area.

Places definitely open to the public have been indicated with times of entry.

Eating, drinking & accommodation
Prices given for bed and breakfast (BB) are the lowest available. Prices for meals are generally a fair average. Suitable symbols are given at the end of each entry for quick reference.

Boatyards
The symbol Ⓢ is used on the maps to indicate the various amenities of either one service point, or in some cases, several places grouped close together.

Mooring
This section is not a complete list of mooring sites. The ones given are either official (Thames Conservancy or Borough Council), or owned by boatyards, hotels or inns. The latter sites are generally for patrons only. Mooring elsewhere is possible, but permission from the various riparian owners should always be sought. Lock keepers and boatyards can always advise about mooring. Permanent or long-term moorings are generally available from boatyards, but customers should book well in advance.

Sewage and refuse disposal and public launching sites
These are given when they are for the use of the general public. Some boatyards have sewage and refuse facilities, but these are generally for the use of patrons only.
Likewise many boatyards have launching facilities which are for the use of patrons only. Some may be used by the public upon payment of a fee.

Public lavatories
Where given, these are fully equipped ladies and gentlemens lavatories. All locks have a gentlemen's lavatory, and so this is not mentioned.

Camping
This includes camping and caravan sites. Camping on the towpath is forbidden. Lock keepers should always be asked about camp sites in their area.

Navigation
This section is wholly concerned with navigational information. It includes the sizes of locks and the heights of bridges, the position of the main river channel (the channel not recommended appears as solid blue on the map), the location of ferries and islands of importance. All this information and more is contained in *The Launch Digest*, published by the Thames Conservancy. This booklet is essential reading for anyone thinking of taking a boat on the river.
In the tidal reaches Piermasters or Assistant Harbour Masters can always give information about navigation or mooring.

Archaeology
This section, presented in note form, outlines the main archaeological sites along the river. Our definition of archaeology in the Guide is pre-Norman. Where possible the sites are marked on the map, and, as a rule, sites have been chosen only where remains are visible or where finds are on display in a museum. Frequent mention will be found of crop marks, a term needing explanation.

Crop marks and aerial photography
The gravels flanking the Thames have been occupied and cultivated from the Neolithic period—that is for 5000 years and more—and many earthworks remain. An earthwork is a bank of earth in a fortification. When the bank is built, the earth with which it is formed is usually dug from round it, thereby creating a perimeter ditch. For example, barrows have ring ditches. Each successive generation in-

creasingly levels the earthwork, and during this process the top-soil gradually falls into the ditch and fills it. This creates a depth of rich soil providing abnormally fertile conditions and extra moisture for crops. Crops grown over ancient ditches grow darker and taller. The distinction is particularly noticeable when the area is photographed from the air, but can sometimes be recognised at ground level.
The visibility of the marks is greatly affected by the weather, the type of crop and the time of year. Grain crops in a very dry growing season give the best results.

Natural history
To avoid the destruction caused by nest robbing and excessive picking of wild flowers, locations of fauna and flora are not given. Use in conjunction with the bird identification drawings.

Fishing
This section identifies the banks along the river and gives the angler some idea of the various clubs that hold water. Use in conjunction with the fish identification drawings.
The *minimum* sizes for fish to be taken from the river are as follows:

Barbel	16 inches
Bleak	4 inches
Bream	12 inches
Carp	12 inches
Chub	12 inches
Dace	7 inches
Flounders	7 inches
Gudgeon	5 inches
Perch	9 inches
Pike or Jack	24 inches
Roach	7 inches
Rudd	8 inches
Tench	10 inches
Trout	14 inches

Night fishing is allowed above Staines, or from a boat below Staines.

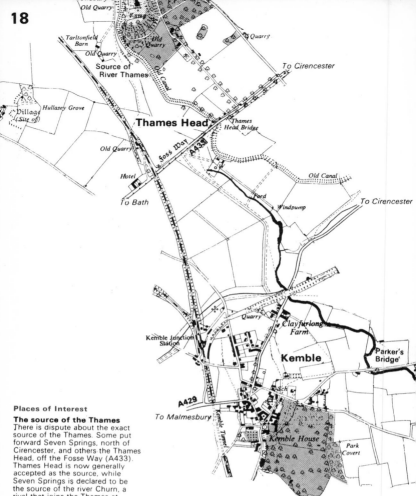

Places of Interest

The source of the Thames
There is dispute about the exact source of the Thames. Some put forward Seven Springs, north of Cirencester, and others the Thames Head, off the Fosse Way (A433). Thames Head is now generally accepted as the source, while Seven Springs is declared to be the source of the river Churn, a rival that joins the Thames at Cricklade. To clarify the confusion, the Thames Conservancy decided in 1958 to mark the Thames Head source with a reclining figure of Father Thames, rescued from the ruins of the Crystal Palace.
He now rules in solitary splendour over a source that is dry for most of the year. The statue is fairly inaccessible, there being no signposts, but a track starting by the Thames Head Inn will eventually lead you to it.

The Thames & Severn Canal
Opened in 1789. Once a valuable link between London and Bristol it was navigable by craft drawing up to four feet of water. Although closed in 1927 and now totally decayed, its course is generally traceable, often alongside or near the Thames. Beyond

the source of the river Thames the canal runs into Hailey Wood, along a deep cutting and then disappears into Sapperton Tunnel. The portals, in a rural Neo-Classical style, are still relatively intact; a marvellous C18th ruin very much in the romantic spirit.

Kemble
Glos. The first village on the Thames, dominated by a large council development. The church has a good Norman doorway. General shops, post office and public telephone.

Poole Keynes
Glos. A hamlet with a well situated church and rectory; the church contains Tudor carving and good C18th monuments. Public telephone.

Westonbirt Arboretum
Glos. Situated 3½ miles SW of Tetbury on the A433. The arboretum is maintained by the Forestry Commission, both for its scientific importance and its beauty. Founded in 1829, the arboretum comprises 160 acres devoted to the growing of broad-leaved trees and conifers from all countries in the temperate regions of the world. America is represented by cypresses and Californian redwoods, the Himalayas by rhododendrons which blossom in May, and Japan by maples that show vivid scarlet and gold colours in October. *Open all year. Free but a parking charge.*

Cirencester
Glos. EC Thur. MD Tue Fri. Not on the Thames, but the nearest large town with shops and hotels to answer all needs. A Roman town of great interest, especially

the church, one of the most beautiful Perpendicular buildings in England. The Corinium Museum, Park Street, has an excellent collection of Roman antiquities, all found locally. *Open Jul-Sep 10.00-13.00, 14.00-17.30 Oct-Jun 14.00-16.30. Closed Sun* Free.
Cinema: Lewis Lane. Films *Mon-Wed,* bingo *Thur-Sun.*

Country Crafts

Abbey Crafts
Malmesbury, Wilts. Market Cross. Tel 3129. Studio pottery, hand woven tweeds, willow furniture.

Archaeology

Trewsbury Camp
Iron Age hill fort enclosing about seventeen acres. Bivallate on south and east, disturbed by house gardens and canal on west and north.

Fosse Way
Roman road from Bath to Cirencester, Leicester and Lincoln. Causeway and bridge are not Roman and date from the construction of the canal.

Cirencester
Major Roman town – Corinium Dobunnorum, capital of the Dobunni. Corinium Museum contains a fine collection of Roman sculpture, mosaics and small objects such as glass, bronze and pottery. Notable, and in this case topical, is a head of a river god carved in the local oolite, a provincial contrast to the marble river god from the Walbrook, London. The ramparts are well preserved on the east side of the town, and a stretch of the town wall is in course of being exposed and consolidated.

Kemble
Site of a pagan Saxon cemetery of the C6th and C7th. Notable for being one of the most westerly pagan cemeteries known. (Finds dispersed; a few are in Liverpool Museum.)

Poole Keynes
Palaeolithic flint handaxe of Acheulian type was found in gravel pit. This is the earliest type of stone tool to be used in Britain, and the nearest to the source of the Thames that has been found. (In Bristol Museum)

Eating, drinking & accommodation

Abbey Crafts   X
Malmesbury. Market Cross. Tel 3129. C13th building. Coffee Tea Homemade cakes.   X ⲩ BB

Thames Head Inn
On A429. Tel Kemble 259. 6 rooms BB 25s. L 12s6d. Hot snacks. Coffee. Parking.

Tunnel House Inn   ⲩ
Coates. Tel Kemble 280. 100 yards from entrance to canal tunnel. Hot snacks. Coffee. Skittle alley. Quoits.

Wild Duck Inn   X ⲩ
Ewen. Tel Kemble 310. Established 1568; open fires and traditional comfort. A la carte only. International menu with duck specialities. Also snacks. LD daily. *Closes 21.30.* Parking. Garden. Public tel.

YHA
Duntisbourne Abbotts, Cirencester, Glos. Tel Miserden 346. 5 miles NW of Cirencester. *Closed Sun.*

Natural history
Near Somerford Keynes there are large flocks of wintering pochard. Near Thames Head the water is covered in spring with white flowers of *Ranunculus pseudofluitans* (water crowfoot), with floating leaves and finely cut submerged leaves. *Ranunculus sceleratus* (celery-leaved crowfoot), a waterside buttercup with small yellow flowers, is as common in America and on the banks of the Ganges as it is by the Thames.

Fishing
As the river often dries out near the source there is no fishing until the Kemble and Ewen area. The river runs fast and shallow through private land and the fishing is strictly preserved for trout. Dace, small chub and gudgeon can also be found.

Emergency
Police: The Forum, Cirencester. Tel 2121
Hospital: Memorial Hospital, Sheep Street, Cirencester. Tel 2375

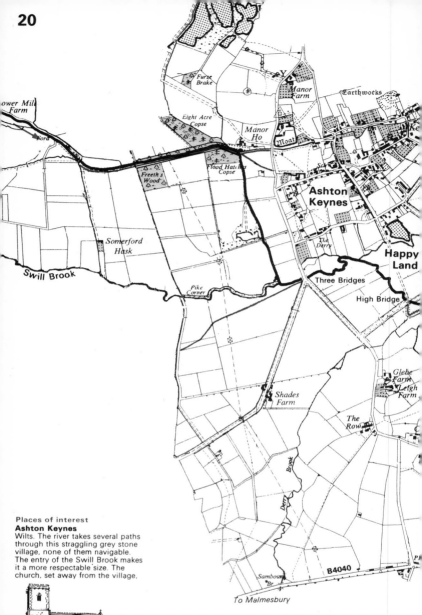

Places of interest
Ashton Keynes

Wilts. The river takes several paths through this straggling grey stone village, none of them navigable. The entry of the Swill Brook makes it a more respectable size. The church, set away from the village,

is partly Norman, with C13th and Perpendicular additions; it was restored by Butterfield in 1876-7. There are many enjoyable walks near the village; a particularly pretty one leads upstream along the south bank of the river, passing through woodland. The Manor House can be seen on the north bank, a fine C17th building with a river garden, and farm attached. General shops and post office. Public telephone outside Ellison's Garage.

Sport

Water ski-ing, yachting, hydro-plane racing and swimming on lakes at South Cerney. Foxhounds and beagles meet at Wild Duck Inn Ewen.

Archaeology
Ashton Keynes

Roughly rectangular earthwork known as Hell's Claws; date uncertain, probably medieval or later.

Purton

Bury Hill, Iron Age hillfort enclosing about six and a half acres; univallate, considerably reduced by ploughing. Ringsbury Camp, Iron Age hillfort enclosing about eight and a half acres; bivallate, entrance on east side, interior cultivated.

From Waterhay Bridge

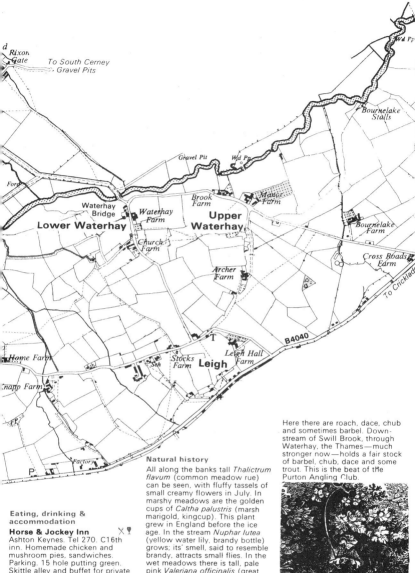

Natural history

All along the banks tall *Thalictrum flavum* (common meadow rue) can be seen, with fluffy tassels of small creamy flowers in July. In marshy meadows are the golden cups of *Caltha palustris* (marsh marigold, kingcup). This plant grew in England before the ice age. In the stream *Nuphar lutea* (yellow water lily, brandy bottle) grows; its' smell, said to resemble brandy, attracts small flies. In the wet meadows there is tall, pale pink *Valeriana officinalis* (great valerian). A tea made from this plant is sometimes used to calm the head and prevent hysteria Coot and moorhen breed in this area. At South Cerney gravel pits, 1 mile north of Ashton Keynes, there are kingfishers and great crested grebe; in winter, pochard tufted duck and wigeon.

Fishing

From Somerford Keynes to Ashton Keynes the fishing is mostly private, but the Ashton Keynes Angling Club have a stretch for members, where mainly trout, dace, chub, gudgeon and the occasional barbel are caught. The Club also holds the fishing on Swill Brook which joins the Thames just below Ashton Keynes.

Here there are roach, dace, chub and sometimes barbel. Downstream of Swill Brook, through Waterhay, the Thames—much stronger now—holds a fair stock of barbel, chub, dace and some trout. This is the beat of the Purton Angling Club.

Ashton Keynes Angling Club
Secretary: John Parker, 1 Morston Road, Wootton Bassett, Wilts.
Purton Angling Club
Secretary: Mr. Godwin, 26 Davis Street, Swindon, Wilts.

Tackle shops

Frank Woodward
Havelock Street, Swindon, Wilts. Tel 3879.

Emergency : see map 19

Eating, drinking & accommodation

Horse & Jockey Inn
Ashton Keynes. Tel 270. C16th inn. Homemade chicken and mushroom pies, sandwiches. Parking. 15 hole putting green. Skittle alley and buffet for private parties.
Old Manor Farm   BB
Ashton Keynes. Tel 267. 4 rooms BB 21s. Parking. Fishing permits obtainable

Navigation

The following remarks apply also to the previous map. Quite apart from the lack of water, there is no right of navigation over this section. The river and the banks belong to various riparian owners whose permission must always be sought before using the river. Also there are many barbed wire barriers and fences at water level. Canoeing is possible according to the state of the water: but much portaging will be necessary. Launches are not allowed.

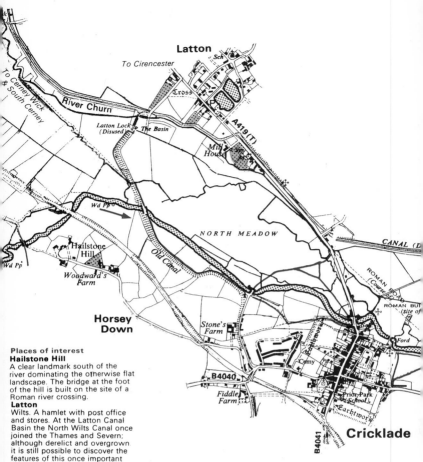

Latton

To Cirencester

River Churn

To Cerney Wick
& South Cerney

Cross

A419 (T)

Latton Lock
(Disused)   The Basin

Mill House

Wd Pp

NORTH MEADOW

Hailstone Hill

CANAL (D

Old Canal

ROMAN RO
(Course)

ROMAN BUI
(site of

Ford

Wd Pp

Woodward's Farm

Horsey Down

Stone's Farm

Cemy

B4040

Fiddle Farm

Prior Park School

Earthwork

B4041

Cricklade

Places of interest

Hailstone Hill
A clear landmark south of the river dominating the otherwise flat landscape. The bridge at the foot of the hill is built on the site of a Roman river crossing.

Latton
Wilts. A hamlet with post office and stores. At the Latton Canal Basin the North Wilts Canal once joined the Thames and Severn; although derelict and overgrown, it is still possible to discover the features of this once important junction.

Cricklade
Wilts. EC Wed. The proud Tudor tower of St Sampson's church dominates this quiet town. Apart from the tower, the church exhibits details from C12-C16th.

The heraldic display in the tower vault is fine, showing a curious Spanish influence. In the church-yard of St Mary in the High Street, there is a complete C14th cross. Behind the predominantly C18th High street are several buildings of interest: the remains of the priory, founded in 1231, can just be seen, while in Bath Road are the C17th buildings of Robert Jenner's School, founded in 1651. The Museum is in the old weigh-house. Locally orientated, it includes silver pennies made at the Cricklade mint, which was in operation from Ethelred to Rufus. *Open Sat 15.00-16.00 or by arrangement.* The Cricklade Town Band, formed in 1872, still thrives with over twenty members. General shops, banks, post office, public tele-phone and public lavatories.

Marston Meysey
Wilts. An attractive village with one long stone street. Half a mile from the river there is a derelict Round House by the canal. Post office and stores.

Sport

Marlborough College Beagles
Meet within a radius of about ten miles from Marlborough. Hounds meet at *14.10 on Tue, Sat and some Thur.* Secretary: J. S. Savage The College, Marlborough, Wilts. Cap 2s6d.

Country workshops

The Cricklade Pottery
Founded 1951 by Ivan Martin. Traditional slipware and stoneware influenced by Bernard Leach. *Open 09.00-18.00 Mon-Sat, Sun during the summer.*

John Battye
The Old Post Office, No. 4 Latton. Tweeds and woollen goods. *Open 09.00-18.00.*

Eating, drinking & accommodation

Gregs Cafe   X BB
Cricklade. 102 High Street. Tel 235 3 double rooms BB 19s. LD from 5s daily *08.00-20.30.* No licence. Parking. Mooring.

The King's Head   Y BB
Cricklade. Tel 439. 4 double rooms 22s6d. Snacks. Parking.

The Red Lion Inn   Y BB
Cricklade. High Street. Tel 398. Old coaching inn. 3 rooms BB 21s. Parking. Darts. Skittles. Snacks.

The Vale Hotel   X Y BB
Cricklade. High Street. Tel 223. 8 rooms BB 37s6d. C19th hotel. International menu, with coq au vin a speciality. LD from 15s daily. Parking.

The White Hart Hotel   X Y BB
Cricklade. High Street. Tel 206. Traditional coaching inn. 15 rooms BB winter 38s, summer 40s. L 13s6d. D 14s6d daily *until 20.15.* Parking. Bar billiards.

Navigation

The right of navigation begins at Cricklade, but the river is still small despite the confluence with the river Churn. Launches are not recommended.

Bridges
There are five footbridges over this section. All can be used but a certain amount of scrambling through bushes is necessary to get to the ones above Cricklade.

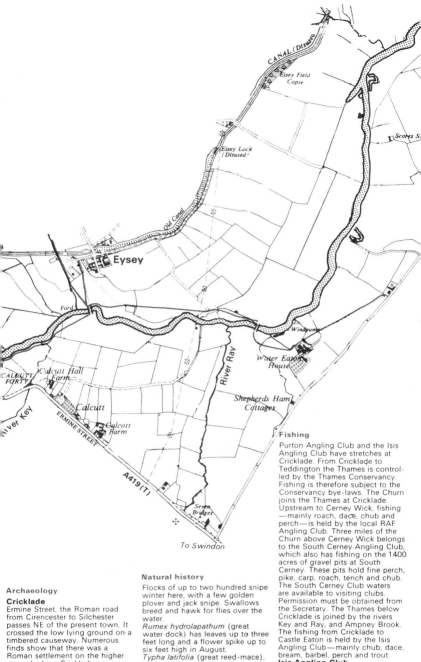

Archaeology

Cricklade

Ermine Street, the Roman road from Cirencester to Silchester passes NE of the present town. It crossed the low lying ground on a timbered causeway. Numerous finds show that there was a Roman settlement on the higher ground where Cricklade now stands. Cricklade has the remains of late Saxon defences, probably C9th. The rampart is visible as a denuded mound around the south and east sides. At Kingsmill Farm, site of a Roman building, excavated in 1952. The finds are in Cricklade Museum.

Latton

In the parish of Latton are a number of small rectangular enclosures showing only as cropmarks. Two have proved to be Roman. They may have been signal stations or small camps for gangs working on Ermine Street.

Natural history

Flocks of up to two hundred snipe winter here, with a few golden plover and jack snipe. Swallows breed and hawk for flies over the water.

Rumex hydrolapathum (great water dock) has leaves up to three feet long and a flower spike up to six feet high in August.

Typha latifolia (great reed-mace), often wrongly called bulrush, grows in wet places or in ponds. The true bulrush, *Scirpus lacustris* (a large rush) is also found along the Thames, but is less common.

Fishing

Purton Angling Club and the Isis Angling Club have stretches at Cricklade. From Cricklade to Teddington the Thames is controlled by the Thames Conservancy. Fishing is therefore subject to the Conservancy bye-laws. The Churn joins the Thames at Cricklade. Upstream to Cerney Wick, fishing —mainly roach, dace, chub and perch—is held by the local RAF Angling Club. Three miles of the Churn above Cerney Wick belongs to the South Cerney Angling Club, which also has fishing on the 1400 acres of gravel pits at South Cerney. These pits hold fine perch, pike, carp, roach, tench and chub. The South Cerney Club waters are available to visiting clubs. Permission must be obtained from the Secretary. The Thames below Cricklade is joined by the rivers Key and Ray, and Ampney Brook. The fishing from Cricklade to Castle Eaton is held by the Isis Angling Club—mainly chub, dace, bream, barbel, perch and trout.

Isis Angling Club
Secretary: D. Horsman,
9 Noredown Way, Wootton Bassett, Wiltshire. Tel. Wootton Bassett 718.

RAF Angling Club
Apply RAF Camp, Lyneham, Wilts.

South Cerney Angling Club
Secretary: Mr Franklin,
Sisters Farm, South Cerney. Tel 362.

Emergency
Police: Princes Street, Swindon Tel 28111
Hospital: Princess Margaret Hospital, Okus Road, Swindon Tel 6231

Places of interest

Castle Eaton
Wilts. A small village attractively placed by the river. The church was restored by Butterfield in

1862, who added the pretty bell-turret with a spire. A few general shops and a public telephone.

Fairford
Glos. EC Thur. Joined to the Thames by the river Coln (not navigable at the junction with the Thames). A gracious Cotswold town built around the church of St Mary the Virgin, a complete and perfect Perpendicular building. The tower was probably the inspiration for St Sampson's, Cricklade. The church contains what is generally considered to be the best C15-C16th stained glass in England, sufficiently intact to be judged as a whole. The glass was buried during the civil war, and so escaped Cromwell's vandals. However it is now threatened again, this time by the testing of the Concorde nearby.

Hannington Hall
Berks. Built in 1653, the hall has a pleasant pastoral setting, with views over the Thames valley. Private.

Kempsford
Glos. Kempsford was once the home of the Plantagenet family. Its grandeur has faded, and so has its importance, after the closing of the Thames and Severn Canal. It is now quiet and peaceful, especially when seen from the river. The church has a splendid Perpendicu-

lar tower built by John of Gaunt in 1390. The tower vaulting has heraldic painting, and there are good examples of Victorian stained glass, some by Kempe. It is the only English church that can claim the honour of having an Irish peer buried under the organ. General shops and post office.

The Railway Museum
Swindon. Faringdon Road. A few miles from the river. Concerned largely with the Great Western Railway, the exhibits include locomotives and the Brunel room. *Mon-Sat 10.00-17.00, Sun 14.00-17.00.* 1s. Children 6d.

Archaeology

Blunsdon
Castle Hill, 3 miles south of Castle Eaton. Iron Age fort enclosing $7\frac{1}{2}$ acres; univallate defences, bivallate on the south side. Romano-British pot found about 1880.

Hannington Bridge
Oak planks and piles found in dredging, indicating a former Roman bridge at this point. Complete Roman pot found on North bank. (In Ashmolean Museum)

Hannington
1 mile SE of Hannington Bridge lie four enormous circles, low earthworks with a broad low bank surrounding a wide shallow ditch. They vary in diameter from 80 to 100 yards and are far larger than any Bronze Age barrow circles. Slight evidence suggests they are Roman. They are a local phenomena occuring elsewhere in the neighbourhood, and so are known as circles of the Highworth type. SE of the bridge, site of Roman villa. Finds in Devizes Museum.

Castle Eaton
Ancient British Gallo-Belgic gold stater found $\frac{1}{4}$ mile SW of village in 1965. Probably C1st BC.

Kempsford
In the fields between the river and Manor Ham Barn, extensive crop-marks of ring ditches, enclosures and ditched droveways.

Eating, drinking & accommodation

The George
Kempsford. Tel 236. Snacks. Parking. Darts and shove halfpenny. Attractive garden, ideal for children.

The Red Lion
Castle Eaton. Tel 280. A fine Georgian building overlooking the river. Snacks. L *Mon-Sat.* Parking. Mooring. Fishing rights. Canoe club activities.

Camping

The Red Lion. Castle Eaton. Camping at water's edge.

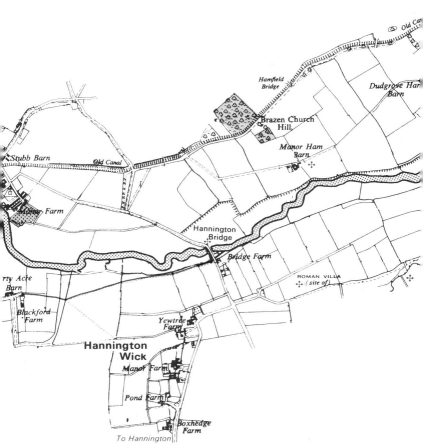

Natural history

Many beautiful waterside plants of late summer grow here. *Alisma plantago-aquatica* (water plantain) with large sprays of palest lilac flowers; the acrid juice from the very large leaves was once used to cure dropsy. *Lysimachia vulgaris* (yellow loosestrife). *Butomus umbellatus* (flowering rush) has heads of deep pink flowers on a tall leafless stem; a local name is pride of the Thames. Growing in the water is *Sagittaria sagittifolia* (arrowhead). This plant has three kinds of leaves, long, translucent submerged ones, oval floating ones, and the characteristic arrowshaped ones standing up out of the water; the three white petals have a purple spot at the base. In his C17th herbal, Gerard called it water archer. *Hottonia palustris* (water violet), an uncommon water plant, has whorls of delicate lilac flowers and submerged leaves. In the woods around Fairford *Campanula trachelium* (nettle-leaved bellflower, bats-in-the-belfry, and the rare *Tulipa sylvestris* (wild tulip), introduced in the C16th, can be found. The *Iris foetidissima* (gladdon, stinking iris) grows in open woods; the attractive seed pods open to disclose bright orange-red seeds.

Fishing

As far as Castle Eaton the fishing belongs to the Isis Angling Club. The fishing on the Old Canal, parallel with the Thames' north bank, is privately owned. From about Hannington to Inglesham rights belong to the Haydon Street Working Men's Club. The river, still rather shallow, holds bream, chub, roach, dace, barbel, pike and some trout.

Isis Angling Club
See Cricklade map page 23

Emergency: see map 23

Navigation

This section has little to offer. There are no amenities for river users and most of the bank is private property. There are few footpaths, the walk up to Hannington being the most rewarding.
Boats must pay attention to the state of the water, and launches are not recommended.

Boatyards
Bagshawe Cruisers
Whelford, Near Fairford, Glos. Tel 564. Cruisers for hire.

Hannington Bridge

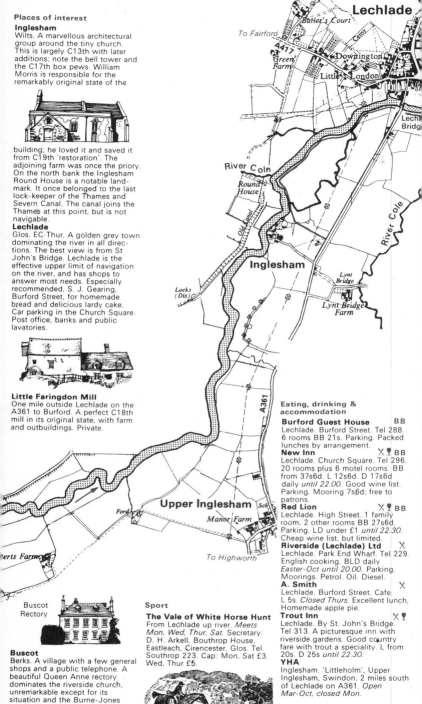

Places of interest

Inglesham

Wilts. A marvellous architectural group around the tiny church. This is largely C13th with later additions; note the bell tower and the C17th box pews. William Morris is responsible for the remarkably original state of the building; he loved it and saved it from C19th 'restoration'. The adjoining farm was once the priory. On the north bank the Inglesham Round House is a notable landmark. It once belonged to the last lock-keeper of the Thames and Severn Canal. The canal joins the Thames at this point, but is not navigable.

Lechlade

Glos. EC-Thur. A golden grey town dominating the river in all directions. The best view is from St John's Bridge. Lechlade is the effective upper limit of navigation on the river, and has shops to answer most needs. Especially recommended, S. J. Gearing, Burford Street, for homemade bread and delicious lardy cake. Car parking in the Church Square. Post office, banks and public lavatories.

Little Faringdon Mill

One mile outside Lechlade on the A361 to Burford. A perfect C18th mill in its original state, with farm and outbuildings. Private.

Buscot

Berks. A village with a few general shops and a public telephone. A beautiful Queen Anne rectory, dominates the riverside church, unremarkable except for its situation and the Burne-Jones windows.

Buscot Park

Built about 1780 in the Adam style, with park and gardens laid out by Harold Peto. Fine furniture, and paintings by Rembrandt, Reynolds, Murillo and Burne-Jones. National Trust. *Open Apr-Sep Wed, first Sat and Sun in month. Oct-Mar 14.00-18.00 2s6d.*

Sport

The Vale of White Horse Hunt

From Lechlade up river. *Meets Mon, Wed, Thur, Sat.* Secretary: D. H. Arkell, Bouthrop House, Eastleach, Cirencester, Glos. Tel Southrop 223. Cap: Mon, Sat £3. Wed, Thur £5.

Country workshops

R. Trinder & Son

Lechlade. The Forge, Filkins. Tel Filkins 244. All kinds of ornamental ironwork. *Mon-Sat 08.00-17.00, Sun by appointment.*

Eating, drinking & accommodation

Burford Guest House   B B

Lechlade. Burford Street. Tel 288. 6 rooms BB 21s. Parking. Packed lunches by arrangement.

New Inn   X ! B B

Lechlade. Church Square. Tel 296. 20 rooms plus 6 motel rooms. BB from 37s6d. L 12s6d. D 17s6d daily *until 22.00*. Good wine list. Parking. Mooring 7s6d; free to patrons.

Red Lion   X ! B B

Lechlade. High Street. 1 family room, 2 other rooms BB 27s6d. Parking. LD under £1 *until 22.30*. Cheap wine list, but limited.

Riverside (Lechlade) Ltd   X

Lechlade. Park End Wharf. Tel 229. English cooking. BLD daily *Easter-Oct until 20.00*. Parking. Moorings. Petrol. Oil. Diesel.

A. Smith   X

Lechlade. Burford Street. Cafe. L 5s. *Closed Thurs*. Excellent lunch. Homemade apple pie.

Trout Inn   X !

Lechlade. By St. John's Bridge. Tel 313. A picturesque inn with riverside gardens. Good country fare with trout a speciality. L from 20s. D 25s *until 22.30*.

YHA

Inglesham. 'Littleholm', Upper Inglesham, Swindon. 2 miles south of Lechlade on A361. *Open Mar-Oct, closed Mon.*

Camping

Bridge House

Lechlade. Half a mile beyond Halfpenny Bridge. Tents and dormobiles.

St. John's Priory Caravans

Lechlade. By St. John's Lock. Tel 360. *Open Mar-Sep*. No tents.

J. W. Lee

Lechlade. High Street. Camping equipment for sale and hire.

Buscot Rectory

Boatyards
Riverside (Lechlade) Ltd.
Lechlade. Park End Wharf. Tel 299.
Petrol, oil, water, gas, hire launches,
small and large punts and skiffs,
Canadian canoes, camping punts
and skiffs. Moorings, launching
sites, storage. *Open Apr-Sept.*

Mooring
New Inn
Lechlade. 7s6d per night.
Riverside (Lechlade) Ltd
Lechlade.

Navigation
Maximum draught: Lechlade to
Oxford 3ft.

Bridges
Lechlade Bridge (or Halfpenny
Bridge, so named because it was
once a toll bridge). A361. 15ft6.
St John's Bridge. A417. 13ft10.
Locks
St John's Lock. The first on the
river. 110ft3 x 14ft10.
Buscot Lock. 109ft10 x 14ft8.

Natural history
Flocks of yellow wagtails and
redpolls winter here. Kingfishers
breed in this area and there are
many pochard.
Bright blue *Cichorium intybus*
(chicory) grows on road-sides;
roasted and ground roots are added
to coffee, while the leaves are
used in salads and for producing a
blue dye. *Menyanthes trifoliata*
(bog bean) is one of our most

beautiful marsh plants, though not
very common; 'A bush of feather-
like flowers of a white colour,
dasht over slightly with a wash of
light carnation.' Gerard. The leaves
were used to flavour beer in the
north country.

Fishing
The Trout Inn at Lechlade has 3½
miles of fishing, mainly on the
south bank. The water is rather
shallow at Inglesham, but fishing
is good for chub, roach, bream and
the occasional trout, particularly

around the mouth of the Coln
tributary. Downstream of Halfpenny Bridge is equally rewarding
Permits for coarse fishing, 3s6d
per day (for trout £1), from the
Trout Inn. The trout permit
includes the weir pool by St John's
Bridge (trout 4-5 lbs) and
adjacent to the Inn garden. The
London Angler's Association have
fishing rights downstream from St
John's Bridge. Most of this fishery
is reached via the A417 and is
reserved for members only. Day
tickets for fishing the Gloucestershire bank can be obtained from
the bailiff: 3s. for seniors, 1s. for
juniors. Good for chub, bream,
dace and the occasional big trout.
There is a car park by St. John's
Bridge.
London Angler's Association
Secretary: R. S. Davison, MBE,
50 Elfindale Road, Herne Hill,
SE 24.

Tackle shops
The Black Cat
Lechlade. High Street.

Emergency: see map 29

St John's Bridge, Lechlade

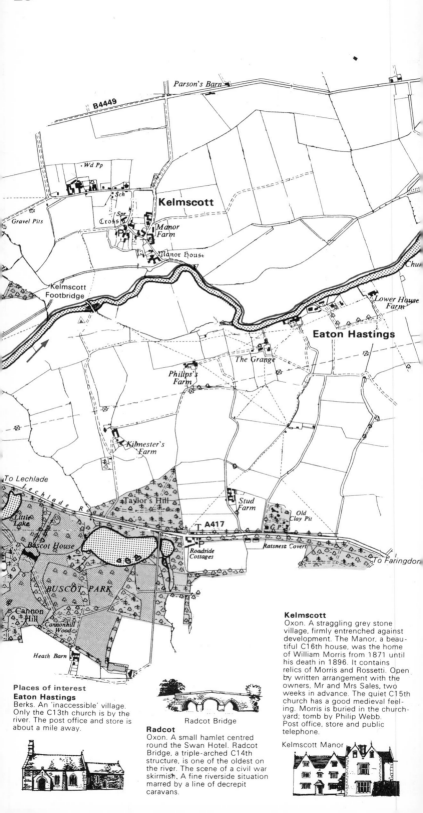

Parson's Barn

B4449

Wd Pp

Sch

Gravel Pits

Spr

Cross

Kelmscott

Manor Farm

Manor House

Chu

Kelmscott Footbridge

Lower House Farm

Eaton Hastings

The Grange

Philips's Farm

Kilmester's Farm

To Lechlade

Lechlade Road

Taylor's Hill

Stud Farm

A417

Old Clay Pit

Little Lake

Buscot House

Roadside Cottages

Ratsnest Covert

To Faringdon

BUSCOT PARK

Cannon Hill

Cannonhill Wood

Heath Barn

Places of interest
Eaton Hastings
Berks. An 'inaccessible' village.
Only the C13th church is by the
river. The post office and store is
about a mile away.

Radcot Bridge

Radcot
Oxon. A small hamlet centred
round the Swan Hotel. Radcot
Bridge, a triple-arched C14th
structure, is one of the oldest on
the river. The scene of a civil war
skirmish. A fine riverside situation
marred by a line of decrepit
caravans.

Kelmscott
Oxon. A straggling grey stone
village, firmly entrenched against
development. The Manor, a beautiful C16th house, was the home
of William Morris from 1871 until
his death in 1896. It contains
relics of Morris and Rossetti. Open
by written arrangement with the
owners, Mr and Mrs Sales, two
weeks in advance. The quiet C15th
church has a good medieval feeling. Morris is buried in the churchyard; tomb by Philip Webb.
Post office, store and public
telephone.

Kelmscott Manor

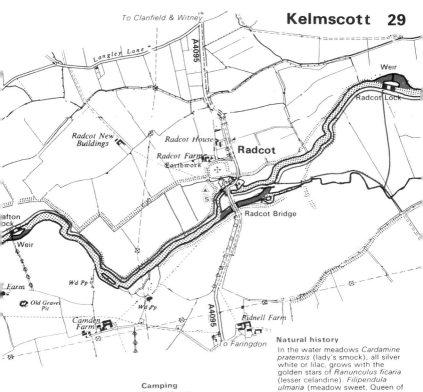

Faringdon House
A mansion well situated in parkland. A stone building of five bays About 1780-90. Some elegant stucco work inside.

Country workshops
Crowdys Wood Products
Clanfield, Oxon. The Old Bakery. Home-made wooden items and a selection of other crafts. *09.00-18.00 daily.*

Archaeology
Radcot
Rectangular bank and ditch enclosure with outwork to E and W, known as 'The Garrison'; almost certainly of the civil war period. Waterlogged hollows along the river bank may represent wharves and docks; this was a loading point for the dispatch of Taynton stone used in the building of the crypt of St Paul's cathedral.
Great Coxwell
3 miles south of Eaton Hastings, Badbury Hill, Iron Age hillfort. Originally bivallate, but the banks were levelled during C19th, and now survive as little more than a scarp round the edges.

Eating, drinking & accommodation
Anchor Inn   ✕ ♟
Eaton Hastings. Tel Faringdon 3230. Originally an C18th weir keeper's house. Caravan accommodation 4/5 berth. LD from 5s6d daily *until 22.00.* Parking. Fishing.
Swan Hotel   ♟
Radcot Bridge. Near Clanfield. Tel Clanfield 220. 3 rooms 21s. Snacks. Parking. Mooring. Fishing.

Camping
Swan Hotel
Radcot Bridge.

Boatyards
Swan Hotel
Radcot Bridge. Tel Clanfield 220. Petrol, oil, moorings, hire punts and rowing boats, camping, caravanning, lavatories.
Anchor Inn
Eaton Hastings. Gas, water, provisions. Free overnight moorings.

Mooring
Swan Hotel
Radcot Bridge. Short periods south bank.
Anchor Inn
Kelmscott.

Sewage and refuse disposal
Radcot Lock.

Navigation
Maximum draught: Lechlade to Oxford 3ft.
Bridges
Kelmscott Foot Bridge by Anchor Inn. 9ft9. Radcot Bridge. A4095. Awkward current under bridge, take northern channel under the single arch. 11ft7.
Locks
Grafton Lock. 113ft6 x 15ft1. Radcot Lock. 113ft6 x 15ft.

Natural history
In the water meadows *Cardamine pratensis* (lady's smock), all silver white or lilac, grows with the golden stars of *Ranunculus ficaria* (lesser celandine). *Filipendula ulmaria* (meadow sweet, Queen of the meadows) flowers in summer; it was used to flavour mead, and to add sweetness to the rushes that formerly were strewn on floors. Masses of *Epilobium hirsutum* (hoary willow herb, codlins and cream) grow by the waterside, tall stems with bright pink or white flowers. In July the deep pink, lightly-striped flowers of *Onobrychis viciifolia* (sainfoin) can be found. It is much cultivated for fodder, and its name, borrowed from French, means 'wholesome hay'. In June the intense violet-blue flowers of *Geranium pratense* (meadow cranesbill) border the lanes for miles; the plant is also attractive in autumn when the leaves turn red and tawny.

Fishing
Fishing rights at Eaton Hastings are controlled by the Eaton Fisheries. Day tickets cost 3s, season tickets 30s, obtainable at the Anchor Inn. Good for bream, chub, barbel, roach, dace, perch and pike. Grafton Lock and Weir are included in the Thames Conservancy Weir Permit. Fishing continues to be good through to Radcot and is largely owned by the Radcot Angling Association. Day tickets for 2¼ mile stretch cost 2s6d. from the Swan Hotel, near Radcot Bridge. Radcot Weir pool (a Thames Conservancy Permit is needed) is noted for big trout, up to 8lbs14oz.

Eaton Fisheries
Anchor Inn, Eaton Hastings.
Radcot Angling Association
B. Neville, Coronation Cottage, Clanfield, Oxon.
Thames Conservancy
15 Buckingham Street, WC2. Tel (01) 839 2441.

Emergency
Police: Coach Lane, Faringdon Tel 2122.
Hospital: Cottage Hospital, Cotswold Road. Tel 2119.

Bampton

Weald

To Witney

Works

Drane's Farm

Lady Well

Castle

Hall Court

A4095

To Faringdon

Wright's Hill

Fisher's Bridge

Weir

Old Man's Footbridge

Radcot Lock

Sharney Brook

Burroway Brook

Rushy Weir

Places of interest

Bampton

Oxon. A very attractive grey stone town one and a half miles from the river, easily approached by a selection of footpaths. It has a timeless appearance in that all new development is built from the same materials and often in a style similar to the old. The result is both unusual and pleasing without being consciously archaic. The church, largely C13th and C14th, is dominated by a slightly uneasy octagonal spire. Inside, the C14th reredos is cut from a single piece of stone, while the Horde chapel contains excellent Baroque monuments. Beside the church is the Grammar School, founded in 1653. There are an unusual number of pubs in Bampton, many featuring well-painted signs in the traditional style. Perhaps the many fairs associated with the town explain so varied a selection of beers. Morris Dancing is reputed to have originated here, a tradition celebrated each year at the Bampton Horse Fair. General shops, post office, banks and public lavatories.

Tadpole Bridge
A handsome C18th arch.

Buckland
Berks. One mile south of Tadpole Bridge. A village intimately connected with Buckland House. The walk up from the river is the best approach as there is an excellent view over the Thames valley. The church has an unusually wide C12th nave; the south transept is splendidly decorated in rich late Victorian mosaic, about 1890.

Buckland House
Built in 1757 by Wood of Bath, it is one of the most imposing C18th houses in Berkshire. The wings were added in 1910, but are still convincing. There is a Gothic stable in the park. The house is now owned by Oxford University.

Sport

Tadpole Bridge Canoe Centre
The Youth Service, Berkshire Education Committee, Reading.

Archaeology

Bampton
On the island formed by the main river and the Burroway Brook, a roughly circular bank and ditch enclosing five acres. The bank has been eroded and the ditch silted up, and so the feature shows up best under conditions of flooding. The ditch has been excavated and Iron Age pottery shards were found.

Eating, drinking & accommodation

Bampton Restaurant ✕ BB
Bampton. A Georgian building with a snack bar and cafe. Fruit machines, pin tables etc. BB and full board.

The New Inn ✕ ✙ BB
Bampton. Tel Bampton Castle 217. C12th coaching inn with darts and shove halfpenny. 3 rooms BB 25s. English cooking. L 15s Mon-Fri. Snacks. Coffee. Parking. Garden.

The Talbot Hotel ✙ BB
Bampton. Tel Bampton Castle 326. 4 rooms BB 27s. Snacks. Parking and garage. Morris Dancing.

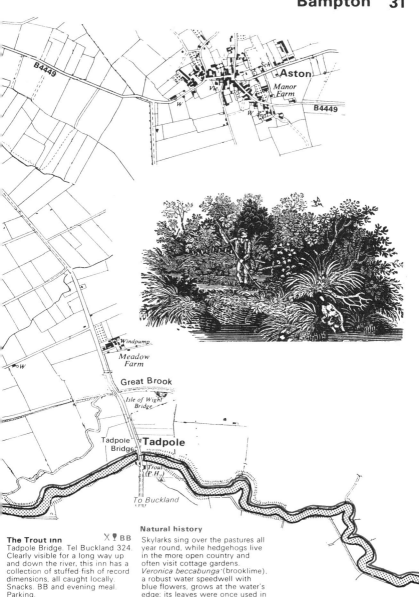

The Trout Inn ✗ 🍷 BB
Tadpole Bridge. Tel Buckland 324. Clearly visible for a long way up and down the river, this inn has a collection of stuffed fish of record dimensions, all caught locally. Snacks. BB and evening meal. Parking.

Camping
The Trout Inn
Tadpole Bridge.

Navigation
Maximum draught; Lechlade to Oxford 3 ft.

Bridges
Old Man's Bridge. Footpath to Bampton. 14ft.
Tadpole Bridge 14ft10.

Locks
Rushey Lock. A path crosses the weir. 113ft6 x 15ft1.

Natural history
Skylarks sing over the pastures all year round, while hedgehogs live in the more open country and often visit cottage gardens. *Veronica beccabunga* (brooklime), a robust water speedwell with blue flowers, grows at the water's edge; its leaves were once used in salads. *Lythrum salicaria* (purple loosestrife) grows by the banks in clumps of tall red-purple spikes, as in Millais' painting of Ophelia.

Old Man's Bridge

Fishing
Below Radcot Lock, the constant twisting and turning of the river creates a variety of swims with barbel, chub, bream, roach, dace and perch. The stretch is controlled by Coventry and District Angling Association down to Rushy Weir and is reserved for members only. Rushy Weir Pool, stocked with good trout, chub and barbel, is available to Thames Conservancy Weir permit holders. From Rushey Weir to Tadpole Bridge, the fishing belongs to the Trout Inn, Buckland, who also hold rights for 2 miles downstream to Tenfoot Bridge. Day tickets are obtainable at the Trout Inn for 3s6d. Part of the Great Brook, between the Isle of Wight Bridge and Shifford, is held by the Oxford Angling and Preservation Society.

Coventry and District Angling Association
Secretary: H. Twynham, 81 Woodway Lane, Coventry. Tel Walsgrove 5078.

Oxford Angling and Preservation Society
Secretary: G. Wilkinson, 54 Evans Road, Eynsham. Tel 441.

Thames Conservancy
See Kelmscott map page 29

Emergency: see map 29

Places of interest

Shifford Cut
The island formed by the Shifford lock cut, a tree-lined canal, is

pleasantly wooded. A footpath across it leads to Duxford via a ford which is passable in boots; attention must be paid to the state of the river as the current is sometimes very strong.

Shifford
Oxon. A church and a small hamlet surrounded by lush pasture land are all that remains of a once important town. Alfred held a meeting of the English Parliament here in 890. The church is romantically situated in the middle of a field about a quarter of a mile from the river; for some reason it is surrounded by barbed wire and securely locked and barred.

Standlake
Oxon. On the river Windrush. An untidy town with much recent development hiding the older parts. General shops, post office and public telephone.

Hinton Waldrist & Longworth
Berks. Two pleasant straggling villages up on the ridge overlooking the valley. Longworth church

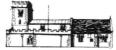

contains a good example of Arts and Crafts stained glass by Heywood Sumner, 1906. General shops, post office and public telephones.

Harrowdown Hill
Very dominant breast-shaped hill on the south bank, easily approached from the river.

Newbridge
Berks. A fine C13th stone bridge, one of the oldest on the river. The site of a civil war battle when the Parliamentarians tried, and failed, to approach Faringdon. The river Windrush joins the Thames here.

Archaeology
Standlake
Extensive traces of Bronze and Iron Age settlement and burial on the gravels N and S of the village. These show as crop marks or may be seen on the sides of the numerous gravel quarries. Malthouse Farm. Site of a pagan Saxon cemetery of late C5-C6th, excavated in c. 1850. Finds in Ashmolean Museum. Iron Age sword with decorated bronze scabbard fittings in fine late Celtic style dredged from the river just above Langley's Weir. Now in Ashmolean Museum.

Newbridge

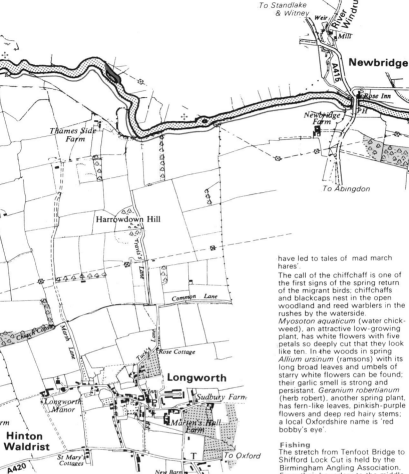

To Standlake & Witney

River Windrush

Weir

Mill

Newbridge

A415

Rose Inn

Thames Side Farm

Newbridge Farm

PH

To Abingdon

Harrowdown Hill

Travis's Lane

Common Lane

Church Copse

Marsh Lane

Tuck's Lane

Rose Cottage

Longworth

Sudbury Farm

Longworth Manor

Marten's Hall Farm

Hinton Waldrist

St Mary's Cottages

A420

New Barn

T

To Oxford

Longworth Manor

have led to tales of mad march hares'.

The call of the chiffchaff is one of the first signs of the spring return of the migrant birds; chiffchaffs and blackcaps nest in the open woodland and reed warblers in the rushes by the waterside. *Myosoton aquaticum* (water chickweed), an attractive low-growing plant, has white flowers with five petals so deeply cut that they look like ten. In the woods in spring *Allium ursinum* (ramsons) with its long broad leaves and umbels of starry white flowers can be found; their garlic smell is strong and persistant. *Geranium robertianum* (herb robert), another spring plant, has fern-like leaves, pinkish-purple flowers and deep red hairy stems; a local Oxfordshire name is 'red bobby's eye'.

Fishing
The stretch from Tenfoot Bridge to Shifford Lock Cut is held by the Birmingham Angling Association. From their boundary to the middle of the loop at Duxford the fishing is private. Then a club affiliated with the Oxford Anglers Alliance owns the beat between Duxford and Shifford Weir. This Weir is included on a Thames Conservancy permit, and is noted for trout. Below the ferry at Shifford the Birmingham Angling Club have another stretch. Fishing is mainly for chub, roach and bream. At Newbridge the Maybush Inn issues day tickets at 3s. for ½ mile of fishing on the south bank upstream of the bridge. The Rose Revived, also at Newbridge, have 5s. tickets for a stretch of the Thames and the Windrush. Fish are mainly barbel, chub, roach, dace, grayling.

Birmingham Angling Association
Secretary: W. Coyne, 31 Nayland Croft, Shirley, Solihull.

Oxford Angler's Alliance
Secretary: G. Wilkinson, 54 Evans Road, Eynsham. Tel 441.

Shifford
Quantity of late Saxon iron weapons dredged from the river. Now in Ashmolean Museum.

Hinton Waldrist
Rectangular earthwork in Achester Wood. Bank and ditch about 6ft high. Date uncertain.

Eating, drinking & accommodation
Maybush Inn ⓨ B B
Newbridge, Oxon. Tel Longworth 249. 3 rooms 21s. Snacks. Parking Free moorings to patrons. Fishing.

Rose Revived ✕ ⓨ B B
Newbridge. Standlake 221. Inn and restaurant. 6 rooms, 45s. A la carte English and French cooking. *LD until 21.00.* Parking. Fishing.

Boatyards
Rose Revived
Newbridge. Petrol, water.

Mooring
At the Maybush Inn and Rose Revived, Newbridge.

Navigation
Maximum draught: Lechlade to Oxford 3ft. The Duxford backwaters are not navigable.

Bridges
Tenfoot Bridge. Footbridge. 12ft2.
Shifford Cut Footbridge. Footpath to Chimney. 12ft.
Newbridge. A415. 12ft.

Locks
Shifford Lock. 113ft8 x 15ft1.

Natural history
Brown hares live in the open drier pastures. At mating time this usually solitary animal gathers in numbers, and the 'boxing', leaping and chasing of its courtship ritual

Tackle shops
Bridgeman's
Witney. 76 The High Street. Tel 2587.

Emergency: see map 29

To Eynsham
Sutton

B4449

Moat

Sch

(P)

Stanton Harcourt

Works

Church & Pope's Tower

B4449

To Bampton

Places of interest

Appleton
Berks. A meandering thatch and stone village, with new development to the west. The Manor, situated beside a splendid weatherboarded barn and gateway, was built at the end of the C12th. An amazing amount remains, note especially the doorway.
General shops, post office and public telephone.
It is worth walking along the river bank here, particularly through the wooded Appleton Lower Common.

Cumnor
Berks. The walk up to Cumnor, one mile from Bablock Hythe, is recommended for those with energy to spare. It was the scene of the tragedy of Amy Robsart, but nothing remains but the memory. The church, built from the C12th onwards, contains much Jacobean and Georgian woodwork; note the splendid spiral staircase in the tower, dated 1685, the choir stalls and the two-decker pulpit. Hidden away in the vestry is a lifelike statue of Queen Elizabeth I, reputedly erected by the Earl of Leicester. General shops and post office.

Bablock Hythe
Until two years ago there had been a ferry on this site for over 1000 years. The river here is ruined by a caravan sprawl, thoughtless and untidy as usual.

Northmoor
Oxon. A remote village. The C13th cruxiform church contains a restored bell-loft, dated 1701; note the dedication poem. Behind the church is a Tudor rectory. Post office and stores, the public telephone is by the church.

West End

Lower Farm

Moat Manor Farm

Gaunt House

Moat

Gaunthouse Mill

Ford

FB

Northmoor

Brook Farm

Vic

Sch

Watkins Farm

Pencots

Ford

River Windrush

Northmoor Lock

Newbridge

se Inn

M o r e t o n

Moreton Farm

Harts Weir Footbridge

Appleton Lower Common

Stanton Harcourt

Oxon. A superb grey village between the Windrush and the Thames, the waters reflecting the quiet glory of the buildings. The grand cruxiform church, still predominantly Early English and Perpendicular, has fine monuments in the Harcourt chapel. The Harcourts built the C15th manor. Only Pope's Tower, the scene of his translation of the *Iliad*, and the unique Great Kitchen survive. General shops and post office.

Archaeology

Stanton Harcourt

SW of the village the whole area was heavily settled from late Neolithic times onwards. Much has been dug away for gravel, and another part destroyed by the airfield runways. Occupation attested for Neolithic/Bronze age henge monuments. Also ring ditches of barrows, and Iron Age and Roman enclosures and farms. The 'Devil's Quoits' are three Megalithic orthostats from a larger number that stood in a ring in a henge monument. They were moved during the wartime construction of the airfield, and have subsequently been lost.

Bablock Hythe

Roman stone altar dredged from the river at the ferry. On the front a Genius standing in a niche. Now in Ashmolean Museum.

Tubney Wood

Half a mile south of Appleton a tumulus, presumably a barrow. Levelled at the end of C19th, but still visible.

Eating, drinking & accommodation

The Chequers ✗ ♈ BB
Stanton Harcourt. Bablock Hythe Ferry. Tel Cumnor 2433. Snacks. LD under 20s *daily until 22.00.* Parking. Chalets. Entertainments in dance hall.

The Harcourt Arms ♈
Stanton Harcourt. Tel Standlake 322. C15th inn. Snacks. Bar billiards, darts. Parking.

The Red Lion ✗ ♈
Northmoor. Tel Standlake 301. Was originally part of C13th ecclesiastical buildings. Snacks. LD to order. Village store in conjunction with off licence. Parking. Garden.

The Vine ♈
Cumnor. Tel 2567. Snacks. Morning coffee. Parking. Garden. Games room with juke box, pin table, fruit machines.

Boatyards

The Chequers
Stanton Harcourt. Bablock Hythe Ferry. Tel Cumnor 2433. Petrol, oil, gas, water, launching, moorings, lavatories, refuse and sewage disposal and chandlery.

Camping

The Chequers
Stanton Harcourt. Bablock Hythe Ferry. Caravans.

Elms Farm
Stanton Harcourt. West End. Tel Standlake 210.

Mooring

The Chequers.

Sewage and refuse disposal

The Chequers.

Public lavatories

The Chequers.

Navigation

Maximum draught: Lechlade to Oxford 3ft.

Bridges
Hart's Weir Footbridge. Footpath to Northmoor 10ft9½.

Locks
Northmoor Lock. Footpath from Appleton to Northmoor crosses the weir. 113ft6 x 15ft1.

Natural history

In July open banks are bright with short spikes of yellow flowers; this is *Genista tinctoria* (dyers' greenweed), a flower that produced a yellow dye. When mixed with the blue extracted from woad it made a green dye, hence the name. Early in spring come the green spathes of *Arum maculatum* (wild arum), each containing a green or purple spadix. The curious appearance of this flower has given rise to many local names including parson-in-the-pulpit, lords and ladies, snake's meat and cuckoo-pint. In autumn its fruit is a spike of bright red berries.
The reed bunting breeds by the river, and another bunting, the yellow hammer, in the open country.

Fishing

Below Newbridge the Witney Angling Society have the rights as far as Hart's Weir footbridge. Downstream of this an Oxford Alliance club own the north bank up to Northmoor Lock. The local Appleton and Tubney Angling Club, members of Oxford Alliance control the next reach to Bablock Hythe. At Bablock Hythe the Chequers Inn issues day tickets at 5s. for a 1½ mile stretch. From the Chequers Inn the Oxford Alliance controls the fishing through to Pinkhill Lock and Weir. The reaches are noted for bream, as well as fair-sized chub, barbel, roach, dace, perch and pike.

Oxford Anglers Alliance
See Shifford map page 33
Witney Angling Society
Secretary: W. Ward,
17 Perretts Close, Witney, Oxon

Emergency: see map 39

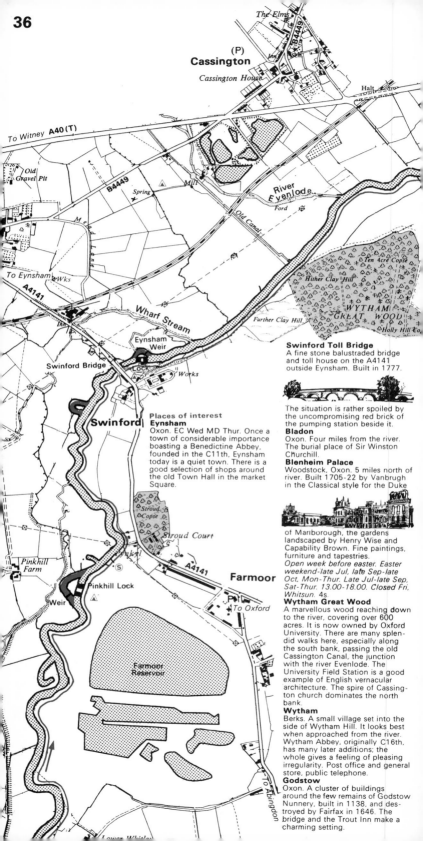

(P)
Cassington
Cassington House
The Elms
Halt

To Witney **A40(T)**

Old Gravel Pit

B4449
Spring
Mill
Old Canal
River Evenlode
Ford

To Eynsham
Wks

A4141

Wharf Stream

Further Clay Hill
Hither Clay Hill
WYTHAM GREAT WOOD
Ten Acre Copse
Holly Hill Co

Eynsham Weir
Swinford Bridge
Lock
Works

Swinford
Eynsham

Stroud Copse
Stroud Court

Pinkhill Farm
Pinkhill Lock
Weir

A4141

Farmoor
To Oxford

Farmoor Reservoir

To Abingdon

Places of interest

Eynsham
Oxon. EC Wed MD Thur. Once a town of considerable importance boasting a Benedictine Abbey, founded in the C11th, Eynsham today is a quiet town. There is a good selection of shops around the old Town Hall in the market Square.

Swinford Toll Bridge
A fine stone balustraded bridge and toll house on the A4141 outside Eynsham. Built in 1777.

The situation is rather spoiled by the uncompromising red brick of the pumping station beside it.

Bladon
Oxon. Four miles from the river. The burial place of Sir Winston Churchill.

Blenheim Palace
Woodstock, Oxon. 5 miles north of river. Built 1705-22 by Vanbrugh in the Classical style for the Duke

of Marlborough, the gardens landscaped by Henry Wise and Capability Brown. Fine paintings, furniture and tapestries.
Open week before easter. Easter weekend-late Jul, late Sep-late Oct, Mon-Thur. Late Jul-late Sep, Sat-Thur. 13.00-18.00. Closed Fri, Whitsun. 4s.

Wytham Great Wood
A marvellous wood reaching down to the river, covering over 600 acres. It is now owned by Oxford University. There are many splendid walks here, especially along the south bank, passing the old Cassington Canal, the junction with the river Evenlode. The University Field Station is a good example of English vernacular architecture. The spire of Cassington church dominates the north bank.

Wytham
Berks. A small village set into the side of Wytham Hill. It looks best when approached from the river. Wytham Abbey, originally C16th, has many later additions; the whole gives a feeling of pleasing irregularity. Post office and general store, public telephone.

Godstow
Oxon. A cluster of buildings around the few remains of Godstow Nunnery, built in 1138, and destroyed by Fairfax in 1646. The bridge and the Trout Inn make a charming setting.

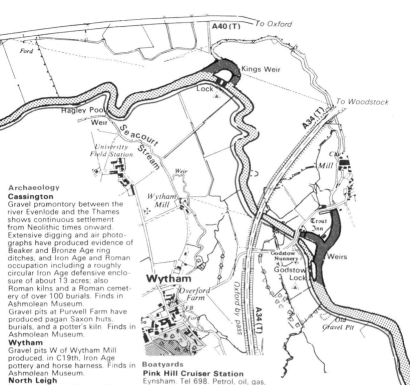

To Oxford — A40 (T)

Kings Weir

Lock

To Woodstock — A34 (T)

Hagley Pool

Weir

Seacourt Stream

University Field Station

Weir

Wytham Mill

Cl Mill

Trout Inn

Godstow Nunnery

Weirs

Godstow Lock

Wytham

Overford Farm

FB

Oxford by pass

A34 (T)

Old Gravel Pit

Ford

Archaeology

Cassington

Gravel promontory between the river Evenlode and the Thames shows continuous settlement from Neolithic times onward. Extensive digging and air photographs have produced evidence of Beaker and Bronze Age ring ditches, and Iron Age and Roman occupation including a roughly circular Iron Age defensive enclosure of about 13 acres; also Roman kilns and a Roman cemetery of over 100 burials. Finds in Ashmolean Museum.

Gravel pits at Purwell Farm have produced pagan Saxon huts, burials, and a potter's kiln Finds in Ashmolean Museum.

Wytham

Gravel pits W of Wytham Mill produced, in C19th, Iron Age pottery and horse harness. Finds in Ashmolean Museum.

North Leigh

Four miles north. Roman villa of courtyard type, foundations exposed and consolidated, and freely accessible. One room with mosaic covered by small hut.

Port Meadow

The 'Round Hill' is presumably a Bronze Age barrow. It has been suggested that it was retained, if not actually built, by farmers to serve as a look out point for guarding sheep.

Eating, drinking & accommodation

Swan Hotel ✗ ♟ BB

Eynsham. Tel 225. 6 rooms BB 30s. Traditional English cooking in C17th inn. LD from 12s6d. Snacks. Book for Sun L. Parking.

The Talbot ♟ BB

Eynsham. Tel 348. A4141. Old coaching inn. 3 rooms BB 25s. Snacks. Parking Fishing permits arranged.

The Trout Inn ✗ ♟

Godstow. Tel Oxford 54485. Built in 1138 as a hospice for Godstow Nunnery. 30 peacocks and large fish. Grills in winter. LD 16s6d. Salads May-Aug. *Daily until 22.00.* Parking. Mooring for short periods.

Camping

At Pinkhill, Eynsham, King's and Godstow Locks. Apply to the lock-keeper. 2s per night, own tent. On B4449 from Cassington to Eynsham.

Boatyards

Pink Hill Cruiser Station

Eynsham. Tel 698. Petrol, oil, gas, water, diesel fuel. Hire 2-6 berth cruisers, repairs, Evinrude dealer, new and secondhand boats for sale, launching slipway, moorings, chandlery. *Open Mon-Sat 08.30-18.00.*

Mooring

The Trout Inn

Godstow. For short periods.

Sewage and refuse disposal

Eynsham Lock

Navigation

Maximum draught: Lechlade to Oxford 3 ft.

Bridges

Swinford Toll Bridge. Eynsham. A4141. Cars 5d. 14ft9.
Oxford by-pass Bridge. A34. 13ft6.
Godstow Bridge. 8ft8.

Godstow Bridge

Locks

Pinkhill Lock. 113ft6 x 16ft1.
Eynsham Lock. 113ft3 x 16ft4.
King's Lock. 113ft1 x 16ft4.
Godstow Lock. 110ft x 16ft3.

Natural history

At Eynsham Bridge there are nearly 100 house martins' nests, and there has been a heronry at Wytham for more than 80 years. In Wytham woods the hobby has nested where nightingales and warblers sing; teal visit in winter and may breed. At Stanton Harcourt there is a colony of 350 sand martins. Hawfinches live in the woods near the town and feed on hornbeam seeds. At Bablock Hythe moorhen, sedge warbler and whitethroat nest. Known only in the Thames Valley is a species of ram's horn or trumpet snail, *Planorbis acronicus,*
which has a flat spiral shell; it is unusual among snails in having red blood.

Riverside plants include *Bidens tripartita* (bur-marigold) whose barbed seeds catch in the fur of passing animals and are thus widely distributed; and *Scutellaria galericulata* (skullcap), its blue flowers shaped like the galerum or helmet worn by Roman soldiers.

Fishing

Farmoor's newly constructed reservoir is well stocked with brown and rainbow trout. Fishing rights are held by the Farmoor Fly Fishing Club. Most of the fishing between Pinkhill Lock and Godstow Lock is held by the Oxford Anglers Alliance, who also have fishing on both banks of the Old Canal as far as the railway bridge and on the Evenlode. The Seacourt Stream as far as Botley also belongs to the Alliance. A record bream, 10lb13½oz, was caught on these reaches at Eynsham. Eynsham Weir is included in the Thames Conservancy permit. The pool holds barbel, chub, dace and some trout, but the area is also good for pike, perch and bream. From Godstow, the Oxford and District Angling Association has fishing through to Port Meadow. Bream can be caught.

Farmoor Fly Fishing Club

Secretary: Fred Taylor, James Street, Oxford.

Oxford Anglers Alliance

See Shifford map page 33

Oxford and District Angling Association

Secretary: F. Jones, 20 Merlin Road, Oxford.

Emergency: see map 39

Godstow Nunnery

Places of interest

Binsey

Oxon. A tiny hamlet surrounds the green. The church has Saxon foundations. Close by is a Holy Well to St Margaret. On the opposite bank of the river lies Port Meadow, a wide expanse of Common Land presented to the town of Oxford by William the Conqueror. The ponies grazing on it are rounded up annually.

Iffley

Oxon. Of particular interest is the Norman church with its especially fine west front, rich in beakhead and zigzag carving. The yew in the churchyard is several hundred years old.

Littlemore

Oxon. Cardinal Newman held a living here in 1845 and built the Church of St Mary's. The nave is an example of the Gothic revival. The College where Newman lived a quasi-monastic life with some men studying for Orders can also be visited. It is now owned by the Fathers of the Birmingham Oratory.

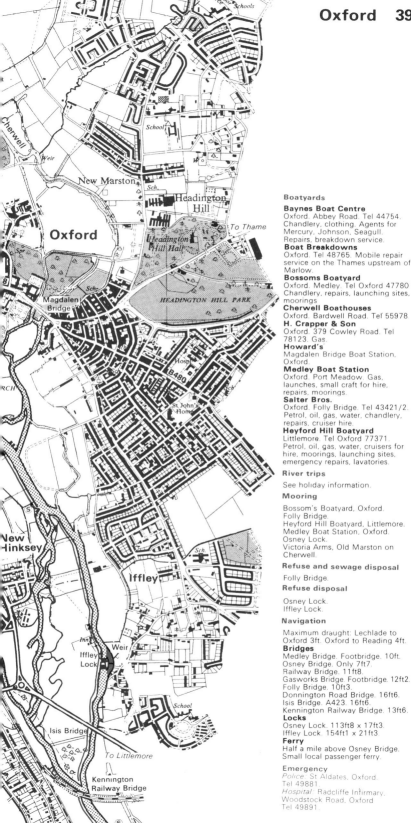

Boatyards

Baynes Boat Centre
Oxford. Abbey Road. Tel 44754.
Chandlery, clothing. Agents for
Mercury, Johnson, Seagull.
Repairs, breakdown service.
Boat Breakdowns
Oxford. Tel 48765. Mobile repair
service on the Thames upstream of
Marlow.
Bossoms Boatyard
Oxford. Medley. Tel Oxford 47780
Chandlery, repairs, launching sites,
moorings
Cherwell Boathouses
Oxford. Bardwell Road. Tel 55978
H. Crapper & Son
Oxford. 379 Cowley Road. Tel
78123. Gas.
Howard's
Magdalen Bridge Boat Station,
Oxford.
Medley Boat Station
Oxford. Port Meadow. Gas,
launches, small craft for hire,
repairs, moorings.
Salter Bros.
Oxford. Folly Bridge. Tel 43421/2.
Petrol, oil, gas, water, chandlery,
repairs, cruiser hire.
Heyford Hill Boatyard
Littlemore. Tel Oxford 77371.
Petrol, oil, gas, water, cruisers for
hire, moorings, launching sites,
emergency repairs, lavatories.

River trips

See holiday information.

Mooring

Bossom's Boatyard, Oxford.
Folly Bridge.
Heyford Hill Boatyard, Littlemore.
Medley Boat Station, Oxford.
Osney Lock.
Victoria Arms, Old Marston on
Cherwell.

Refuse and sewage disposal

Folly Bridge.

Refuse disposal

Osney Lock.
Iffley Lock.

Navigation

Maximum draught: Lechlade to
Oxford 3ft. Oxford to Reading 4ft.
Bridges
Medley Bridge. Footbridge. 10ft.
Osney Bridge. Only 7ft7.
Railway Bridge. 11ft8.
Gasworks Bridge. Footbridge. 12ft2.
Folly Bridge. 10ft3.
Donnington Road Bridge. 16ft6.
Isis Bridge. A423. 16ft6.
Kennington Railway Bridge. 13ft6.
Locks
Osney Lock. 113ft8 x 17ft3.
Iffley Lock. 154ft1 x 21ft3.
Ferry
Half a mile above Osney Bridge.
Small local passenger ferry.

Emergency
Police: St Aldates, Oxford.
Tel 49881.
Hospital: Radcliffe Infirmary,
Woodstock Road, Oxford.
Tel 49891.

The City of Oxford
Oxon. EC Thur. MD Wed. The town was founded in the C10th and has been a university city since the C13th. Today it is also a thriving industrial centre—the headquarters of the British Leyland Corporation. The thirty-nine colleges can all be visited, but those noted here have been selected as particularly representative of their periods. City maps and guide books may be obtained from the City Information Centre, Carfax, *Open 09.00-17.30 on weekdays and from 11.00-14.00 on Sundays from Spring Bank Holiday until the first Sunday in September.*
2-hour walking tours start from the Information Centre daily during the summer at *10.45 and 14.15.* The charge is 4s. It is also possible to hire a private guide.

Merton College
One of the earliest collegiate foundations, dating from 1264, the buildings, which are almost unrestored, are especially typical of the Perpendicular and Decorative periods. The Chapel was begun in 1294 and Mob Quad was the first of the Oxford quadrangles. The library, mainly C14th, has a famous collection of rare books and mss. During the Victorian era, the College was enlarged and the Grove Buildings with alterations in 1929 by T. Harold Hughes. *Open 10.00-16.30.*

New College
The College was founded by William of Wykeham, Bishop of Winchester, in 1379. The chapel, a noble example of early Perpendicular, has been greatly restored by Sir George Gilbert Scott in the C19th. The great west window, after a cartoon by Reynolds, and Epstein's 'Lazarus' are noteworthy. The C14th cloister and the workmanship of the wrought iron screen, 1684, between the Garden Quad and the Garden, are outstanding memorials of their times. *Open 14.00-17.00 weekdays; Sat and Sun 12.00-18.00.*

Keble College
Built by William Butterfield in 1870, Keble is the only Oxford College entirely in the Victorian Gothic style. The frontage of red and grey patterned brickwork and the tracery windows have a godlike self-confidence. The chapel, with its glass and mosaics, bricks, tiles and brass, contains Holman Hunt's 'Light of the World'. *Open 10.00-16.45 daily.*

St Catherine's College
An important and interesting example of the new University by the Danish architect, Arne Jacobsen, 1964. The entrance to the College is reached through an unprepossessing car park area, but in the main quadrangle the effect is one of stark impact. The mass of glass windows with their bands of ribbed concrete stretch like concertinas on either side of the quadrangle. All is bleak but full of atmosphere. The furniture and college plate were also designed by Jacobsen. *Open 14.00-19.00 daily.*

St Anne's College
This women's college reflects some of the most exciting new building in Oxford. The Wolfson block in the main quadrangle was designed by Howell, Killick and Partridge, 1964. With its two curving wings and square jutting windows, all of precast concrete, this building is impressive and original. Facing the block is the Dining Hall by Gerald Banks, 1964, and to one side is Hartland House, mainly 1930s' but with 1951 additions by Sir Giles Gilbert Scott

Radcliffe Camera
Radcliffe Square. Dr Radcliffe left £40,000 for the building of this

library by James Gibbs, 1739, to house his 'physic' library. It is a vast domed Italianate rotunda, now a Bodleian reading room, and not open to the public. The staircase and skylight can be admired through the doorway.

Sheldonian Theatre
Broad Street. Built by Christopher Wren in the mid-C17th under the auspices of Gilbert Sheldon, Archbishop of Canterbury, who disapproved of the annual irreverant performances of plays taking place in St Mary's. The theatre was also designed to be used for University ceremonies. Degrees are awarded here. For many years it also housed the workshops of the University Press. The interior with its ceiling by Robert Streeter is delightful. *Open 10.00-13.00, 14.00-16.00 weekdays.*

The Old Bodleian
Schools Quadrangle. Named after Thomas Bodley, who died in 1613 leaving a fine collection of rare mss, the old Bodleian buildings, mainly C16th and early C17th, also incorporate Duke Humphrey's library, C15th. Bodley extended Duke Humphrey's library and also financed the entire rebuilding of the Schools Quadrangle, completed seven years after his death. The Bodleian obtains a copy of every book published and has over 60,000 mss. *Open 09.30-17.00 weekdays.*

St Cross Building
St Cross Road. The new Bodleian English and Law Library by Sir Leslie Martin, 1965, is a striking composite structure of some originality. A long flight of steps, a central feature of the building, leads between graded massive blocks. The structural frame is of reinforced concrete clad externally with brickwork. The building won a Civic Trust award in 1966 and is a refreshing contrast to the uninspiring Science buildings off South Parks Road.

Christ Church Cathedral
Christ Church. The Cathedral with its inconspicuous entrance in Tom Quad was originally part of the priory of St Frideswide. It is mainly C12th with later additions and is typically Romanesque. The most splendid feature is the C16th

stone-vaulted fan roof of the choir. There is medieval glass and also glass by Burne Jones, C19th. The Chapter House is a C13th masterpiece.

St Mary the Virgin
The High Street. The fine C14th spire is a landmark. The church is typical of the Perpendicular style apart from the magnificent Baroque porch with its twisted columns by Nicholas Stone, 1637. The iron-work gates are C18th. Before the building of the Sheldonian Theatre the church was also used as a theatre.

St Philip & St James
Woodstock Road. This church by G. E. Street, 1860-6, with its bands of pink sandstone in the brickwork, has an originality of its own, particularly revealed in the West front. The interior, built on the Tractarian plan, is rather dark.

Ashmolean Museum
Beaumont Street. One of the most rewarding museums outside London, it has an outstanding

collection of Near Eastern and European archaeology, as well as the Farrer collection of C17th and C18th silver. The Heberden Coin Room has a vast display of early coins, whilst in the Department of Fine Art, the Michelangelo and Raphael drawings are to be admired. The Museum also has the bulk of the archaeological material from the Upper Thames. Much of this is exhibited and there is a permanent display of air photographs of sites in the Thames Valley. *Open 10.00-16.00. Sun 14.00-16.00.*

Christ Church Gallery
Christ Church. Built by Powell and Moya, 1967, the Gallery displays Christ Church's private collection. Exceptional Renaissance drawings by Michelangelo, Veronese, Tintoretto are to be seen, as well as C14-C18th paintings, mainly Italian. *Open 10.00-16.00 daily except Sun.*

Museum of Modern Art
Pembroke Street. Although there is a small standing exhibition of painters of the 1960's including Paolozzi, Hilton, Hitchens, Frost, this gallery specialises in 'way out' exhibitions—anything from environment to architecture, graphics, photography. *Open 10.00-18.00 daily except Mon. Sun 15.00-18.00.*

Museum of Dolls
Grove House, Iffley Turn. The museum is intended for collectors and no children under 16 are allowed. There is an exceptional collection of early dolls houses, 1700-1885, displayed with their furniture and silver. They are thus illustrative of social history. From the centre of Oxford take a 3 or 4 bus. *Open Sun only May-Sept. 14.15-17.00.*

University Museum
Parks Road. The building by Deane and Woodward, 1855-60, in high Victorian Gothic was much admired by Ruskin. Built to house a collection of the Natural Sciences, the interior is a forest of columns and skeletons covered by a glass roof. One great rarity is the head and claw of a Dodo. *Open 10.00-13.00, 14.00-16.00 daily.*

Christ Church Meadows
The meadows lie behind Christ Church and Merton and have fine views and a path leading down to the river. The path is lined with college barges, not many remaining, and boathouses. In the afternoon one can watch the rowing Eights. Enter the Meadows from St Aldate's.

Magdalen Water Walks
Access to the Water Walks is through Magdalen College, *open*

Oxford County Hall

Old Tom Tower

St Peter's Hall

Worcester College

Clarendon Building

Carfax Tower

St John's

Magdalen Tower

Magdalen Bridge

St Michael's Church

Trinity

Botanic Gardens Gateway

Martyrs' Memorial

14.00-17.00 weekdays. Sun 10.00-17.00. Close to the Walks lies the Deer Park. The fifty fallow deer can sometimes be seen over the railings. The Walks pass beside the streams from the Cherwell and thick shoes are advised in the winter.

University Botanic Garden

High Street. Oldest botanic garden in Britain founded by Henry Lord Danvers. In the C17th the. Garden was intended for the culture of medical plants, but today it fosters an extensive collection of rare plants for research and teaching. The gateway is by Inigo Jones. *Open 08.00-17.00 (Sun 10.00-12.00). Free.*

University celebrations

Commemoration Balls

The Balls are held in the College quadrangles at the end of the summer term. They are lavish, all-night affairs with marquees and champagne. Tickets are expensive.

Eights Week

Late in May the College boat races take place on the Isis close to Folly Bridge. Saturday, the finals day, is a social occasion with tea-parties and champagne in the boathouses and barges. The Races are followed by the Eights Week Dances.

May Day

At 06.00 on May morning a Latin hymn is sung from Magdalen

Tower in the medieval tradition. Then Morris dancers dance through the streets.

Feast of St Giles

On the Monday after the first Sunday in September, there is a Fair in the middle of St Giles. Roundabouts and side-shows block the road.

Galleries, book & antique shops

Bear Lane Gallery

Bear Lane. Exhibitions of modern painting, sculpture and graphics in a tiny gallery. *Open 10.00-17.00. Thur 10.00-13.00.*

Oxford Gallery

The High. Has the largest collection of modern original prints outside London. It also sells old

Oxford

42 Oxford

prints, and jewellery and pottery by leading craftsmen. *Open 10.00-17.00 Mon-Fri.*

Bonfiglioli Gallery
104 The High. A good selection of prints and rare books. *Open 10.00-17.00 Mon-Fri.*

Basil Blackwell
Broad Street. One of the best stocked bookshops in the country. There is also a rare books department. *Open 09.30-17.00 Mon-Fri.*

Reginald Davis
34 The High. Some fine pieces of Georgian and Victorian silver can be found here. There are several antique shops in the High, specialising in a variety of pieces. For junk, there are two shops at the bottom of St Clement's Street near the Plane.

Country workshops
Osborne & Son
5 Hurst Street. Tel 43374. Table lamps hand-carved from Cotswold stone. They can be made to order.

Concerts
All enquiries about concerts should be made at C. Taphouse and Son, 3 Magdalen Street where information and tickets can be obtained.

Cinemas
ABC, George Street. Tel 44607. Regal, Cowley Road. Tel 44234. Super, Magdalen Street. Tel 43067. Scala, Walton Street. Tel 54909. Mainly foreign films. Cine Moulin Rouge, New High Street, Headington. Tel 62718. Mainly classics.

Theatres
New Theatre, George Street. Tel 44544. Visiting productions. Oxford Playhouse, Beaumont Street. Tel 47133. Performances by the resident company or university dramatic societies.

Sport
Bathing
Iffley. Long Bridges, near Donnington Bridge. Oxford. Parson's Pleasure and Dame's Delight, University Parks. Osney. Tumbling Bay Bathing Place. Wolvercote. Wolvercote Bathing Place, Port Meadow.

Beagling
The Christ Church and New College Beagles meet in the winter terms and this can be an exhilarating way of spending an afternoon in the countryside. A bus departs most Saturdays from Oriel Square at 01.30, but this should be checked with the porter at Christ Church or New College.

Golf
The City Golf Club, Southfields, Hill Top Road. Tel 42158. North Oxford Golf Club, Banbury Road. Tel 54415.

Riding
The Old Manor House Riding School, North Hinksey Lane. Tel 42274.

Archaeology
Oxford
The gravel terrace on which Oxford stands probably enjoyed settlement in Prehistoric times in much the same way as Cassington or Standlake. Finds from all periods have been made at various times though they are naturally scrappy, and of little interest as individual finds.

East Oxford
The hills to the east of the city were extensively occupied during the Roman period by people engaged in making pottery. Workshops have been found at Headington, Cowley Centre, Rose Hill, Cowley, the Churchill Hospital, Littlemore, Blackbird Leys and Sandford. The industry began in the late C1st and maintained a local production till the middle of C3rd. In the late C3rd and C4th the production and distribution increased to cover the whole of southern England and much of Wales. Finds in Ashmolean Museum.

Eating, drinking & accommodation
Cherwell Boat House X ✚
Oxford. Bardwell Road. Tel 55978. A restaurant in an old boat house. Good food well cooked and snacks in the summer. Wine licence. Closes 21.30. *Closed Mon.*

Clarendon Restaurant X ✚
Oxford. 6-16 George Street. Tel 42511. Excellent self service with a wide selection of freshly cooked meals. Closes 20.00. Licensed.

Eastgate Hotel X ✚ BB
Oxford. Merton Street. Tel 44416 & 42363. 52 rooms BB 50s. English cooking. L 13s6d D 15s6d daily until 22.00. Parking.

Golden Lantern X ✚
Oxford. 129 High Street. Tel 42883. Chinese food. L 5s6d D a la carte. *Daily until 23.30.* Licensed.

Health Food Store X
Oxford. 3 King Edward Street. Tel 43407. Vegetarian. L 5s. No smoking.

Luna Caprese Restaurant X
Oxford. 4 North Parade. Tel 5412. Speciality Italian fish dishes. Cheerful decor. LD 27s6d *daily until 23.30.* Parking.

Newman Bookshop X
Oxford. 87 St Aldates. Tel 44654. C17th building, once a bishop's palace. Hot snacks, salads, home-made cakes. Coffee. Afternoon teas. L from 5s6d.

The Old Parsonage BB
Oxford. 3 Banbury Road. Tel 54843. 42 rooms BB 30s. Parking.

The Perch Inn X
Binsey. Tel Oxford 42984. Good hot and cold snacks. LD 25s *until 21.00.* Book only. Parking. Mooring for patrons.

Randolph Hotel X ✚ BB
Oxford. Beaumont Street. Tel 47481. 114 rooms from 60s. English and Continental cooking. B 7s L 18s6d D 21s *until 20.45* In Ox-in-the-Cellar grill-room *until 23.45.* Closed Sun night and Mon. Parking and garage. Petrol nearby. No dogs in dining room or lounges.

Restaurant Elizabeth X ✚
Oxford. 84 St. Aldates. Tel 42230. French and Spanish cooking. D from 25s L Sun only. Licensed. Parking nearby.

La Sorbonne X ✚
Oxford. 130a High Street. Tel 41320. Built 1637. French cooking. LD 30s *daily until 23.00.* Licensed.

The Tree Hotel X BB
Iffley. Tel Oxford 79116. 10 rooms BB 30s. L *Mon-Fri* 13s6d. Parking.

Turf Tavern X
Oxford. 10 Bath Place, Holywell. Tel Oxford 43235. C13th inn. LD from 4s6d daily. Garden.

Victoria Arms X
Old Marston. Marston Ferry. Tel Oxford 48386. LD under 35s. daily until 22.00. Punting on the Cherwell. Parking.

Vintage Car Restaurant X ✚
Oxford. Boswell House, Broad Street. Tel 43459. All meals from 5s6d daily until 23.30. Dinner dance Fri, Sat. Licensed.

YHA
Oxford. Jack Straw's Lane. Tel 62997. *Closed Mon.*

Natural history
The spires of Oxford make ideal nesting sites for kestrels, while swifts nest in the museum tower. The little ringed plover nests on newly disturbed gravel in suitable pits. *Fritillaria meleagris* (fritillary or snake's head) grows in riverside meadows. It has drooping chequered bells of reddish-purple or greenish-white. This flower was common: in 1872 there were 120 acres of it in meadows near Oaksey. It is now extremely rare owing to excessive picking. By Magdalen Bridge is the biggest silver pendant lime tree, *Tilia petiolaris*, in the country.

Fishing
Most of the fishing on this stretch of the river is divided between the Oxford Alliance and the Oxford and District Angling Association. The Oxford Alliance holds rights to the Oxford Canal from Green Lock through Wolvercote and into Oxford. It also has a stretch between Pixey Mead, Godstow, past the Trout Inn, and down to Godstow Lock. The Alliance also controls fishing on the River Cherwell from the Northern bypass to Kenham Corner, as well as water on the River Ray from Oddington to Islip. The Oxford and District hold fishing on Port Meadow and through to Osney Bridge, and this is a noted stretch for bream and barbel. Non-members must apply to the Secretary for permission to fish. Citizens of Oxford fish free. The stretch from Folly Bridge to Iffley, also held by the Oxford and District, is good for roach. Two record fish were caught at Oxford—a pike of 29lb from Hinksey Backwater and a perch of 4lb11oz. The fishing on the Potts Stream, connecting with the Seacourt Stream, belongs to the White Horse Angling Club, and the entrance to the fishery is near the Oxford Railway Station. The tributary is particularly noted for chub, bream, barbel, perch and roach.

Oxford Anglers Alliance
See Shifford map page 33
Oxford and District Angling Association
See page 33
White Horse Angling Club
Secretary: N. Kimbrey, 19 Franklin Road, Headington, Oxford. Tel 61517.

Tackle shop
Venables & Son
Oxford. 99 St Aldates. Tel 44257.

Oxford from the air *Aerofilms*

Quarry

Heyford Hill

To Oxford

Vic.

Sta.

Hospital

Clinic

Hospital

Works

Allotment Gardens

Preceptory

Site of

Little London

Quarry

School

Temple Farm

Rock Farm

Weirs

P.H.

Sandford Pool

Sandford on Thames

Cranbrook House

Lock

Mill

Lower Farm

Radley Little Wood

W

Park Farm

Works

Gravel Pit

Upper Farm

Spring

School

Church Farm

Ditch Course

Radley Station

New Boat House

Spr.

Rectory

To Barrow Hills

Tumulus

Radley

Eney

Spring

The Lake

Goose Acre Farm

Gravel Pit

Spring

Home Farm

Gravel Pit

The Mansion

NUNEHAM PARK

Pumney Farm

Levery

Gravel Pit

Gravel Pit

°*Mon*

Lock Cottages

Lock Wood

Mast

Places of interest
Sandford
Oxon. The river leaves Oxford through a curious mixture of woodland, suburbia and light industry. Sandford is essentially a picturesque group of lock and mill. The north bank is marred by a caravan shanty town. General shops, post office and public telephone.
Radley
Berks. A straggling commuter suburb on the main London-Oxford railway, with much indiscriminate new development. The church is predominantly Perpendicular, with unusual wooden pillars in the aisle. Note the C15th pulpit canopy, reputedly from the House of Commons, and the C17th choir stalls. General shops and post office.
Radley College
Founded in 1847. The college is based on Radley Hall, 1721-7, with many later additions. It is famed as a rowing school.
Nuneham Courtenay
Oxon. C18th model village separated, deliberately, from Nuneham Park. The C18th mansion is splendidly situated; the wooded grounds rise steeply from the river bank, with fine views over the valley. It is now owned by Oxford University and the grounds are closed to the public.

Sport
Radley College Beagles
Area: Oxford-Wallingford, Faringdon-Bampton. Secretary, The Radley College Beagles, Radley College, Near Abingdon. Tel Kennels, Abingdon 1621. Meets Tues 14.00, Sat 13.30. Cap 5s.

Archaeology
Sandford
Three bronze daggers, a bronze sword and a bronze spearhead were dredged from the river by Sandford lock. Now in the British Museum.
Radley
In the field called Barrow Hills ¼ mile west of Radley village, air photography has revealed a number of ring ditches, including thirteen in a straight line. Presumably the field, though now flat, takes its name from these features. A part has been quarried away and excavation has produced Beaker culture burials.

Eating, drinking & accommodation
King's Arms
Sandford. Tel Oxford 77095. High quality buffet. Snacks. Bar billiards etc. Garden.

Camping
Temple Farm Country Club
Sandford. Tel Oxford 79359. Camping and caravans.

Public launching slip
North bank, upstream of Donnington Road.

Navigation
Maximum draught: Oxford to Reading 4ft.
Locks
Sandford Lock. 127ft x 18ft9. Footpath across lock.

Natural history
Redstarts and tree sparrows nest in pollarded willows and there is a heronry in the woods at Radley. In the meadows by the river you can find flowering grasses, *Chrysanthemum leucanthemum* (moon daisies), and *Ranunculus acris* (meadow buttercups). In the woods in spring are *Anemone nemorosa* (wood anemone, windflower) with white flowers sometimes tinged with purple, and *Oxalis acetosella* (wood-sorrel), called Alleluiah because it flowers at Easter. Its three leaflets fold back at night giving it another name—sleeping beauty.

Fishing
From Littlemore the Oxford and District continue to control the water down to Sandford, but there is some free fishing in this area. Sandford Weir is included on the Thames Conservancy permit. Below Sandford Lock the fishing on the south bank is held by an Oxford Alliance Club. The north bank is part of a private estate. The Alliance also holds the fishing rights to two gravel pits: Thrupp and Radley lakes.
Oxford A.A.
See Shifford map page 33
Oxford and District A.A.
See Wytham map page 37

Emergency: see map 47

Nuneham Courtenay

A423 (T)

Knowle Plantations

Windmill Hill

To Wallingford

Sandford Lock *R R Bolland*

To Oxford

Barton Court

Abingdon

Mills

Weir

Abbey Stream

Lock

To Witney

River Ock

Rye Farm

Weir

Playing Fields

Andersey Island

St. Andrew's Church (site of)

Back Water

Culham Brake

The Warren

Spurious Abbey ruins

Hill Farm

A415

Culham College

Culham House

P.H.

Manor House

Culham

School

Works

Lock

Sutton Bridge

Culham Cut

Weir

Otney

Sutton Pools

Weir

Manor House

Drop Short

B4016

Sutton Courtenay

St Helen's Church

Places of interest

Abingdon

Berks. EC Thur MD Mon. An attractive C18th market town which grew up around the abbey, founded in 675.

Little of it now remains, except the Gateway and the Long Gallery. The abbey ruins are *open: Mon-Sat*

11.00-13.00, 14.00-18.00 or dusk. Sun 14.30-17.30. 1s. The Abbey Meadow, by the river, is now a public park with swimming pool, car park, lavatories, café and putting green.
The best view of the town is from the bridge, medieval in origin, but rebuilt in 1927. The river is dominated by the gaol, an impressive stone bastille, built 1805-11, and

by St Helen's church. Set among C17th and C18th almshouses, the church has five aisles, making it broader than it is long. Perpendicular in style with a C17th painted roof. Note the pulpit, dated 1636, and the reredos by Bodley, 1897.

In the market square is the Town Hall, built 1678-82 by Christopher

Kempster, one of Wren's city masons; high and monumental with an open ground floor, it has been called the finest town hall in England. Originally the ground floor was used as a market, the upper as a court room. Now there is a coffee bar in the basement. St Michael's church, Park Road, is a quiet and dignified design by Gilbert Scott, 1864-7.
A good shopping centre, with banks and post office.
The Mayor of Ock Street, Abingdon. Each year on the nearest

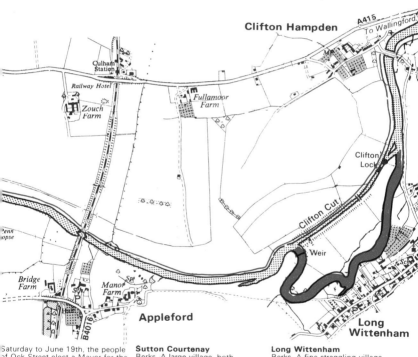

Public lavatories
Abbey Meadow, Abingdon.
Closed winter.
Culham Lock.

Public launching site
Abingdon. St Helen's Wharf.

Navigation
Maximum draught: Oxford to
Reading 4ft.
Bridges
Nuneham Rail Bridge, 15ft9.
Abingdon Bridge, A 415, 13ft11.
Culham Cut Foot Bridge, 12ft5.
Culham Bridge, 14ft9.
Appleford Rail Bridge, 13ft.
Clifton Cut Foot Bridge, 13ft4.
Clifton Hampden Bridge, 13ft5.
Locks
Abingdon Lock, 120ft x 18ft9.
Culham Lock, 130ft10 x 17ft6.
Clifton Lock, 129ft10 x 19ft.

Emergency
Police: Henley Road, Abingdon.
Tel 303.
Hospital: Marcham Road,
Abingdon. Tel 1005.

Boatyards
Abingdon Boat Centre
Nags Head Island. Tel Abingdon
125. Petrol, oil, gas, water, boat
hire, brokerage and sales, repairs,
launching, moorings, chandlery.
Red Lion Cruisers
Abingdon. Wilsham Road. Tel
562, 1760. Evinrude distributors.
Petrol, oil, gas, water, 4-5 berth
cruisers and canal cruiser for hire,
24 hour repair service, launching,
moorings, chandlery.

Mooring
Abingdon
Abingdon Boat Centre, Nags Head
Island.
Red Lion Cruisers, Wilsham Road.
Long Wittenham
The Plough.
Official overnight mooring. Along
tow path above Abingdon Lock.

Sewage & refuse disposal
Abingdon Lock.

Refuse disposal
Clifton Lock.

Saturday to June 19th, the people
of Ock Street elect a Mayor for the
day. Morris Dancers dance the
length of the street, performing
outside each inn. This custom has
been carried on for hundreds of
years. Its origins are lost, but it
may have grown from a pagan
fertility ritual.
Abingdon Museum
County Hall. Tel 3703. *Open
14.00-17.30 daily.*
Culham
Oxon. The cooling towers of Didcot
power station dominate the flat
landscape for several miles. Culham
Manor, built in calm grey stone in
the C17th, overlooks Culham Cut.
The old river course is not
navigable, owing to weirs, but is
good walks along the river, or
through woodland to Sutton
Courtenay. Post office and general
store.

Sutton Courtenay
Berks. A large village, both
wealthy and rewarding, built round
a green. The well-kept church has

late Norman work, a fine Jacobean
pulpit and pleasantly naive C17th
inscriptions. Eric Blair (George
Orwell) is buried in the churchyard. Opposite the church is
Norman Hall, a remarkably original
late C12th manor house. The
C14th abbey was never used as
such, but as a grange. It is now a
school. General shops and post
office.
Appleford
Berks. An agricultural village with
much new development. The post
office and stores also sells railway
tickets.

Long Wittenham
Berks. A fine straggling village
along the old course of the river.
The C13th church contains choir
stalls from Exeter College, Oxford,
and a late Norman font. General
shops and a post office.
Pendon Museum
A museum of miniature landscape
and transport. *Open Sat, Sun,
Bank holidays.* 3s6d children 2s.
Clifton Hampden
Oxon. An excellent, if self-
conscious riverside situation dominated by the brick bridge, a

Norman folly built in 1864. The
church, well placed on a mound
overlooking the river, is a small
light building. It was delicately
remade by Gilbert Scott. Post

office and stores, and a public telephone.

Sport

Swimming
Abbey Meadow. *Open summer only.*

South Oxfordshire Hunt
Area: Oxon & Bucks. Jt. Hon. Secretary, J. Shuter, Monkery Farm, Great Milton, Oxon. Tel 364. *Meets 10.45 Tues, Thur and Sat.* Cap £3.10.0.

Cinemas
Abingdon. The Regal, The Square. Tel 322. Films 3 days, bingo 4 days.

Abingdon Bridge

Archaeology

Abingdon
Neolithic causewayed camp producing round-bottomed pottery of Windmill Hill type. Situated ¼ mile SW of Barrow Hills field, but now largely built over. Finds in Ashmolean Museum.

Abingdon
Finds of the Roman period dating back to the mid C1st from several places in the centre of the town, but the nature of the settlement is uncertain.

Abingdon
Saxton Road. Site of pagan Saxon cemetery discovered during road construction about 1930. Finds of C5th and C6th with inhumation and cremation in large numbers. Finds divided between Abingdon and Ashmolean Museums.

Sutton Courtenay
Drop Short. Site of a Roman villa; recent excavations not yet published. Finds in Reading Museum.

Sutton Courtenay
Site of a pagan Saxon village. Well known because it was the first to be recognised. The site, a disused gravel pit, is now a public works depot. It also produced remains of a Neolithic occupation and of a Cursus—two parallel ditches of unknown use running ½ mile or so.

Appleford
Recent gravel extraction in Appleford Field has produced the following: a hoard of iron age currency bars (iron bars about three feet long thought to have been used as currency), a hoard of over 5000 Roman coins of the first half of the C4th, buried in two pots, and a hoard of 22 Roman pewter plates and iron tools. All now in Ashmolean Museum.

Long Wittenham
Site of pagan Saxon cemetery of about 190 burials, mostly of the C6th. One important find, 'Long Wittenham Stoup', a small wooden bucket covered in bronze sheets decorated with a Christian monogram and scriptural scenes—a Christian object in a pagan grave. Now in the British Museum. Also

a small Saxon cemetery of the C6th and C7th, presumably Christian. Finds in the British Museum. Northfield Farm and surrounding fields are heavily patterned by cropmarks of ring ditches and droveways, a site recognised and planned in 1893, before the advent of air photography.

Clifton Hampden
Site of a small Roman building excavated around 1876. No plan survives.

Eating, drinking & accommodation

The Barley Mow Inn   X ¶ BB
Clifton Hampden. Tel 215. C14th inn. 6 rooms 35s. LD 21s. English cooking. *Weekdays until 21.30, Sat 22.30.* Snacks. Parking.

Circle Cafe   X
Abingdon. County Hall. Tel 3805. Snacks. Discotheque. *Fri-Sun until 23.30.* Juke box, pin tables, fruit machines, football machines.

Crown & Thistles   X ¶ BB
Abingdon. Bridge Street. Tel 87. 23 rooms BB 45s. LD from 15s. *Daily until 21.00, Sat 21.30.* English cooking. Snacks.

The George & Dragon   X ¶ BB
Sutton Courtenay. Church Street. Tel 252. C12th inn with later additions. 2 rooms BB 30s. LD from 11s6d *until 22.00.* English cooking. Snacks. Aunt Sally. Parking.

Oriel Hotel & Restaurant   X BB
Abingdon. Ock Street. Tel 400. 26 rooms BB 25s. D 8s6d *daily until 20.00.* Parking. No licence.

Plough Inn   X ¶ BB
Long Wittenham. Tel Clifton Hampden 238. C16th inn. 6 rooms 35s. LD 14s6d. *Open until 21.00 (Sat 21.30).* Parking. Mooring. Fishing, patrons only.

Restaurant of the Upper Reaches   X ¶ BB
Abingdon. Thames Street. Tel 4585/6. 10 rooms. Coffee, tea. LD from 10s6d. *Daily until 22.00.* Parking. Mooring.

Camping
Abingdon. Abbey Meadow. Apply Town Clerk, The Abbey House, Abingdon. Tel 851.

Natural history
In this area there is a large colony of breeding house martins; nests can be seen under Clifton Hampden Bridge. There are flocks of brambling in early spring. Pied wagtails and yellow wagtails breed in low lying meadows

Sweet scented *Galium odoratum* (sweet woodruff) has tiny white flowers in the shape of a cross. When dried it smells like new mown hay and was used to stuff pillows and to strew on floors. According to Gerard, it was put into wine "to make a man merry" Other woodland plants: *Adoxa moschatellina* (moschatel or town hall clock): four small, green, five-petalled flowers are arranged back to back like the faces of a clock on a tower, and a fifth flower with only four petals tops them like a roof; *Galeobdolon luteum* (yellow archangel or weasel snout) has glossy leaves and yellow flowers marked with brown.
Many mute swans in the river near Abingdon. A favourite place for Oxfordshire bird watchers where there are many inland waders in autumn—redshank, greenshank, sandpiper, ruff and little ringed plover.

Fishing
Above the Lock Wood (or Nuneham) railway bridge, the Pumney Farm stretch, on the south bank, is Oxford Alliance water. Below the railway bridge, on the north bank, the North Berkshire Federation of Anglers holds fishing as far as the Swift Ditch backwater. The Corporate Fishery, owned by the Borough of Abingdon, extends from the backwater on the north bank and the railway bridge on the south bank downstream to Culham. The fishery also includes the Abbey Stream and the Abingdon Weir Pool.
A wide variety of species can be caught on these reaches: chub, barbel, roach, dace, gudgeon, bleak, perch, pike and occasionally trout. Day tickets for the fishery cost 2s for the first day and 1s for each subsequent day. Local residents may fish free.
From Culham to Appleford Railway Bridge on the north bank, including Culham Reach, most of the fishing belongs to the Culham Estate Fishery. The Berkshire bank is held by the Anchor A.A. and by the Sutton Courtenay A.C. who have fishing above and below Sutton Courtenay Weir. Fishing on the Weir is included in the Thames Conservancy Permit. A perch of 4lb 1oz was caught here in 1961.
On the north bank, the Abingdon and District A.R.A. have a stretch from Sutton Road Bridge to the railway bridge. The stock in these reaches is mainly chub, bream, roach and dace.

Abingdon & District Angling and Restocking Association
Secretary: R. Pitson, 11 Finmore Close, Abingdon, Berks.

Abingdon Corporate Fishery
Apply: Town Clerk, The Abbey House, Abingdon. Tel 851.

Culham Estate Fishery
Secretary: R. Pitson, 11 Finmore Close, Abingdon.

Clifton & District Preservation Society
Secretary: G. King, 9 Sinodun Close, Wittenham, Near Abingdon.

London Anglers Association
See Lechlade map page 27

Oxford Alliance
See Shifford map page 33

Sutton Courtenay Angling Club
Secretary: K. Stevens, 12 Church Lane, Drayton, Near Abingdon. Tel Drayton 423.

Tackle shops

Didcot Tackle
Didcot, The Broadway.

R. C. Winter
Drayton, Gravel Lane.

Abingdon

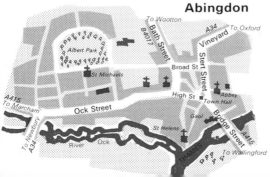

Places of interest

Burcot
Oxon. A small village with no public right of landing. Post office and stores on A415.

Sinodun Hills/Wittenham Clumps
A large mound dominating the otherwise flat landscape. It is well worth the walk up from Day's Lock, as there are splendid views over the valley.

Little Wittenham
Berks. A village climbing up the hill away from Day's Lock. The

wooded church situation is pretty. There are good walks in Little Wittenham Wood, which descends to the river bank. Post office and stores.

Dorchester on Thames
Oxon. EC Wed. A large main road village more on the Thame than the Thames, Dorchester is one of the oldest English cities. Today only the abbey shows that it was

once the centre of the largest diocese in England. Approached through a Butterfield lynch gate, the abbey gives little clue to the splendid size and proportion of the interior. Mostly Decorated in style. The most important feature is the Jesse window, its stone work imitating trees. The figures seem to grow organically from the body of Jesse. Note the tomb of Sir John Holcombe; the surprising realism and fluidity of the effigy has inspired many modern sculptors. The Old Monastery Guest House is a museum, but most Roman finds are in the Ashmolean Museum. A few general shops and post office. The main street is taken up largely by antique shops and hotels.

Warborough
Oxon. ¼ mile north of Shillingford. A traditional English village built round a green. Buildings of all periods. Post office and stores.

Shillingford
Oxon. A discreet residential area, built around the three-arched

stone bridge, one of the best situated on the river.

Archaeology

Little Wittenham
Castle Hill Camp, Sinodun Hills. An Iron Age hill fort, univallate, the interior part cultivated. The fort commands a fine view of Dorchester and the Thames.

Brightwell cum Sotwell
Brightwell Barrow. ½ mile SE of Sinodun Hills. A circular mound on top of Brightwell Hill about 60 feet in diameter. Opened in 1923 and Iron Age pottery found. Finds in British Museum.

Dorchester
A small rectangular Roman town. The walls have been quarried away, but the rampart is faintly visible on the south side. It was important as the junction of three Roman roads.
The gravels north of the town were well populated in Prehistoric times. Air photographs show Neolithic and Bronze Age henge and cursus monuments, ring ditches, and Iron Age and Roman field and enclosure ditches. Many have been excavated, including Roman pottery kilns found during quarrying. Finds in Ashmolean Museum. A considerable number of middle and late Bronze Age weapons have been found near Dorchester. A bronze spear tip buried in a human pelvis came from Queensford Mill, while a bronze sword chape was dredged from the river at Day's Lock. Most finds are in the Ashmolean Museum.

Dyke Hills
South of Dorchester a promontory at the junction of the Thames with the Thame is closed on the north side by a massive earthwork known as Dyke Hills. It encloses about 114 acres, and air photographs show it to be patterned with Iron Age hut circles and enclosures. The Hills consist of a double bank with ditches between and on the north side. The ditches are now somewhat silted up, and the eastern end of the banks has been levelled. From inside the height of the banks is about 8 feet, but from the bottom of the ditches it is 12-15 feet.

Warborough
A stone coffin with skeleton found in 1780, but could not be dated. Air photographs show an extensive cemetery here; probably late Roman or early medieval.

Eating, drinking & accommodation

The Chequers Inn ✕ ❢
Burcot. Tel Clifton Hampden 271. L 7s6d Mon-Fri. Curry supper Wed until 22.00. Snacks. Parking. Bar games.

The George Hotel ✕ ❢ BB
Dorchester on Thames. The High Street. Tel Warborough 404. Built 1450 as part of abbey, galleried. 14 rooms BB 50s LD a la carte 25s *daily until 22.00 (Sat until 22.30). (Closed Sun)*. Parking. Garage.

Riverside Hotel ✕ ❢ BB
Burcot. Tel Clifton Hampden 382/232. 15 rooms BB 50s. LD from 17s6d *daily until 21.15. (Sat until 22.00)*. Boats for hire, baths and showers for boat users, fishing, tennis, croquet lawn, putting green. Parking. Garage.

Six Bells ❢
Warborough. Tel 265. Built 1516, thatched. Sandwiches. Bar billiards. Parking.

Shillingford Bridge Hotel ✕ ❢ BB
Warborough. Tel 567. 18 rooms. C16th inn by river. BB 45s. L 16s6d D 19s6d. Coffee, tea daily. *Open to 21.30.* Fishing for patrons. Parking.

White Hart Hotel ✕ ❢ BB
Dorchester on Thames. High Street. Tel Warborough 501. C16th coaching inn. 14 rooms BB 42s. LD 18s. *Daily until 22.30.* English cooking, snacks. Bar billiards. Parking.

Floods at Clifton Hampden

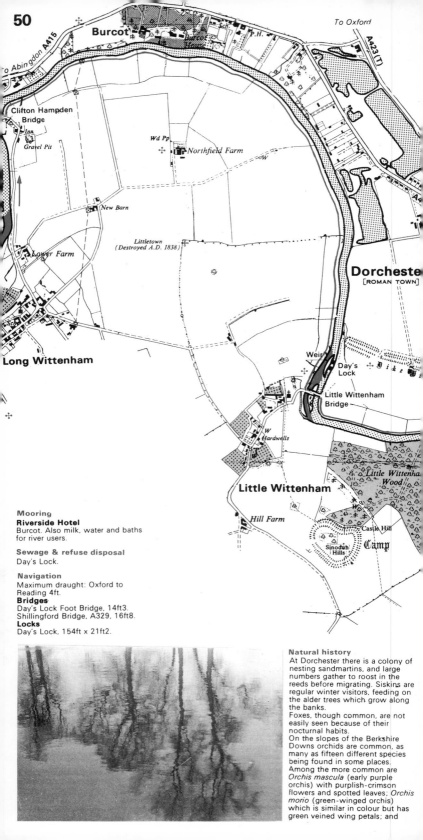

Burcot

To Oxford

To Abingdon A415

A423(T)

Clifton Hampden Bridge

Inn

Gravel Pit

Wd Pp

Northfield Farm

W

New Barn

Littletown (Destroyed A.D. 1838)

Lower Farm

Dorcheste

[ROMAN TOWN]

Long Wittenham

Weir

Day's Lock

Little Wittenham Bridge

W Hardwells

Little Wittenha Wood

Little Wittenham

Hill Farm

Castle Hill

Sinodun Hills

Camp

Mooring
Riverside Hotel
Burcot. Also milk, water and baths for river users.

Sewage & refuse disposal
Day's Lock.

Navigation
Maximum draught: Oxford to Reading 4ft.
Bridges
Day's Lock Foot Bridge, 14ft3.
Shillingford Bridge, A329, 16ft8.
Locks
Day's Lock, 154ft x 21ft2.

Natural history
At Dorchester there is a colony of nesting sandmartins, and large numbers gather to roost in the reeds before migrating. Siskins are regular winter visitors, feeding on the alder trees which grow along the banks.
Foxes, though common, are not easily seen because of their nocturnal habits.
On the slopes of the Berkshire Downs orchids are common, as many as fifteen different species being found in some places. Among the more common are *Orchis mascula* (early purple orchis) with purplish-crimson flowers and spotted leaves; *Orchis morio* (green-winged orchis) which is similar in colour but has green veined wing petals; and

Gymnadenia conopsea (fragrant orchis) with sweetly scented lilac flowers.

Fishing

On the Oxfordshire bank to Clifton Hampden Bridge, and then on both banks to Burcot, the water belongs to the Clifton & District Preservation Society.
Carp, as well as the usual species, are taken in the Clifton area. The water is private from the bridge to the Chequers Hotel. From upstream of Day's Lock the Dorchester A.C. have fishing on the Oxfordshire bank almost to Meadside. They also have a beat on the Thame up to Dorchester road bridge.

From Day's Lock to the far edge of Little Wittenham Wood on the south bank, the fishing belongs exclusively to the London A.A. The best of the fishing is for chub, but roach, bream, dace, perch and the occasional barbel can be caught.
From Measiqe to Shillingford boat house, the Warborough and Shillingford A.C. hold a stretch, but there is a small free section between the boat houses.
Upstream of Shillingford Bridge, on the south bank, the fishing is privately shared between the High Wycombe Thames A.C. and the Shillingford Hotel. Downstream of the bridge, the south bank fishing is private and the north bank is held by Benson & District A.C.
Benson & District Angling Club
Secretary: W. Aldridge, Orchid Crown Square, Benson, Oxon. Tel 317.

Clifton & District preservation Society
See Abingdon map page 47
Dorchester Angling Club
Secretary: K. Barber, 93 Fane Road, Berrinsfield, Near Oxford.
High Wycombe Thames Angling Club
Secretary: N. Charik, 46 Disraeli Gardens, Park Estate, High Wycombe. Tel 21886.
Warborough & Shillingford Angling Club
Secretary: P. G. Andrews, 6 Henfield View, Warborough, Oxon.

Emergency: see map 53

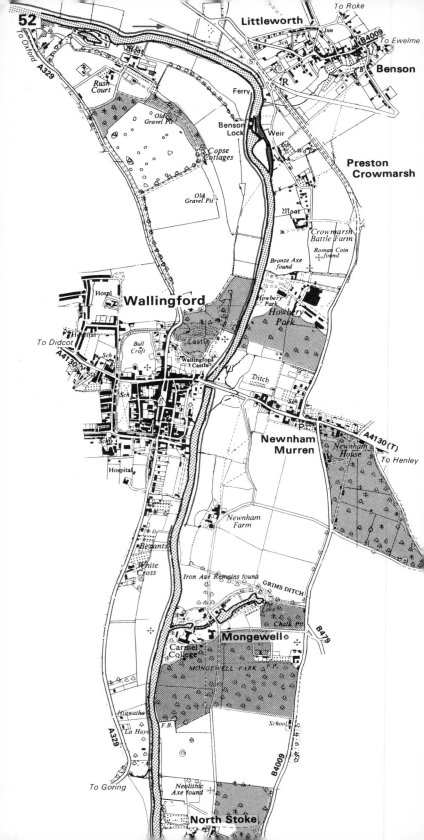

Places of interest

Benson
Oxon. An airforce town. The old

coaching inns are surrounded by married quarters and supermarkets. There is a huge car breakers yard overlooking the north end. Good for shopping however.

Ewelme
Oxon. Three miles from the Thames; up in the hills behind Benson. Ewelme is a picture-book brick and flint village, rising up from the watercress beds in the Chiltern foothills. It is an amazing C15th survival. The late Perpendicular castellated church stands over the thirteen almshouses, founded in 1437. In the church the font cover and St John's Chapel are of interest; note the tombs of Alice, Duchess of Suffolk and of Thomas Chaucer, son of the poet. Below the church is the school also founded in 1437. The whole has far more in common with Suffolk than Oxfordshire. Post office and stores.

Wallingford
Berks. EC Wed MD Fri. One of the oldest Royal Boroughs, the town received its charter in 1155. From the river the town is dominated by the surprising openwork spire of St Peter's church, built by

Sir Robert Taylor in 1777. A walk along the south bank towards Benson will reveal the remains of Wallingford Castle. It was destroyed by Fairfax in 1646. Howbery Park, now the home of the Institute of Hydrology, is on the north bank. Surrounded by a good selection of period shops is the Town Hall. Built in 1670, it

has a typical open ground floor. General shops, post office and banks. The Regal Cinema.

Wallingford Bridge
Altogether seventeen arches of

medieval origins. It was largely rebuilt in 1809 when the balustrade was added.

Sport

Swimming
Riverside Park, Wallingford. Enquiries to The Borough Council. Tel 2561. *May-Sep.*

Archaeology

Wallingford
Well-preserved banks and ditches of the Saxon defences which enclosed town on three sides. In the NE corner the defences are covered by the motte and bailey of the Norman castle. Recent excavations have uncovered some of the late Saxon streets and buildings beneath the castle earthworks. Many Bronze Age tools and weapons dredged from the river just below Wallingford Bridge. Finds in Ashmolean and Reading Museums.

Crowmarsh
Grim's Ditch. Part of the long Saxon bank and ditch which ran from here to near Henley. Well seen where the road from Crowmarsh to North Stoke cuts it opposite Mongewell Park.

Cholsey
Three bag-shaped Neolithic bowls found in river bank opposite Mongewell. Two in Reading Museum, one in British Museum.

Eating, drinking & accommodation

Bull Hotel   X ⵏ BB
Streatley. Tel Goring 2507. A friendly inn with cobbled courtyard and antique furniture. 5 rooms BB 35s. English cooking, homemade paté speciality. LD 14s6d (closed Sun D) *until 21.00.*

Castle Inn   X ⵏ BB
Benson. 6 rooms BB 30s. LD from 12s6d daily *until 21.00.* Parking.

Chicken in the Basket   X ⵏ
Benson. Tel 331. Swedish style building. LD from 15s a la carte only. High quality buffet, snacks daily. *Open until 23.15.* Licensed. Parking. Dancing except Mon, band Fri, Sat; cabaret Tues, Wed, Thur, Sun.

Fleur de Lys   X
Wallingford. 4 High Street. Tel 2249.
L Mon-Fri 7s Sat 7s6d Sun 8s6d. *Closed Wed.* Coffee. Devonshire Cream Teas. No licence.

The George Hotel   X ⵏ BB
Wallingford. High Street. Tel 3136. Tudor with inglenook fireplace. 8 rooms BB 36s6d. L weekdays 9s D a la carte daily *until 22.00.* Parking.

Home Sweet Home Inn   X ⵏ
Roke. 1 mile NE of Benson. Tel Benson 249. C16th inn. L 25s D 35s. *Closed Sun evening and Mon. Open until 21.30.* Parking.

Nautical Wheel Restaurant   X
Wallingford. Tel 2507. International cooking. L 8s D a la carte. *Closed Sun evening and Mon. Open until 20.50.* Mooring.

Swan Inn   X ⵏ BB
Streatley. Tel Goring 2498. Built about 1700. Overlooking the Thames. 28 rooms BB 40s. L 14s6d D 17s6d daily *until 20.45.* Mooring. Fishing.

Camping

Wallingford Municipal Camping & Caravan Site. Tel 2561/2266. *May-Sept.*

Gilletts
Wallingford. Tel 2005/3065. Camping, caravans.

Benson Cruiser Station
Tel 304. Camping, caravans.

Boatyards

Benson Cruiser Station
Benson. Tel 304. Petrol, oil, gas, water, hire, 8 cabin cruisers, repairs, launching, mooring, chandlery, lavatories, refuse-disposal, snacks.

Gilletts
Wallingford. The Bridge Boat House. Tel 2205/3065. Petrol, oil, gas, water, 60 boats for hire, repairs, agents for Dolphin Cruisers, Evinrude, Seagull Crescent. Launching, moorings, chandlery, lavatories. Restaurant.

Maid Boats
Wallingford. Yacht Station, Chalmore Meadow. Tel 2163. Petrol, oil, gas, water, cabin cruisers for hire, repairs, launching, moorings, chandlery, parking.

Mooring

Benson Cruiser Station

Wallingford
Gilletts Boatyard. Maid Boats. The Nautical Wheel Restaurant.

Navigation

Maximum draught: Oxford to Reading 4ft.

Bridges
Wallingford Bridge. *Use centre arch.* 16ft5.

Locks
Benson Lock. 133ft1 x 17ft11.

Natural history

Cuckoos breed here, laying their eggs in the nests of reed warblers by the water, meadow pipits on the downs, and dunnocks and pied wagtails in the hedges. The cuckoo's egg resembles that of its host.

Ulex europaeus (gorse or furze) flowers on the hills all through the year and the scent on a hot June day is like peaches.

Fishing

From Shillingford Bridge down to the Benson Cruiser Station, the fishing belongs to the Benson & District A.A. Below this there is free fishing along the Parish Council recreation ground. The opposite Berkshire Bank is private up to Benson Lock and Weir. Below Benson the Oxfordshire bank down to Wallingford is mainly Government property and is inaccessible.
On the Berkshire bank the Jolly Anglers hold rights at Wallingford Bridge and also on the Oxfordshire bank downstream to Mongewell Park. Day tickets 4s, weekly 10s.
From Wallingford Bridge the Berkshire bank is private as far as White Cross. Here the London A.A. have the Bow Bridge Fishery and a short stretch of the Mongewell Park bank. These reaches hold mainly bream, roach, dace, pike and perch.

Benson & District Angling Association
See Dorchester map page 51

Jolly Angler Angling Club
Secretary: A. G. Brown, 12 Hambleden Drive, Wallingford, Berks.

London Anglers Association
See Lechlade map page 27

Tackle shops

Shepherds Tackle
Wallingford. 23 High Street. Tel 3262.

Benson Cruiser Station
Benson. Tel 304. Tackle and bait.

Emergency

Police: Reading Road, Wallingford Tel 2242.

Hospital: Cottage Hospital, Reading Road, Wallingford. Tel 3133.

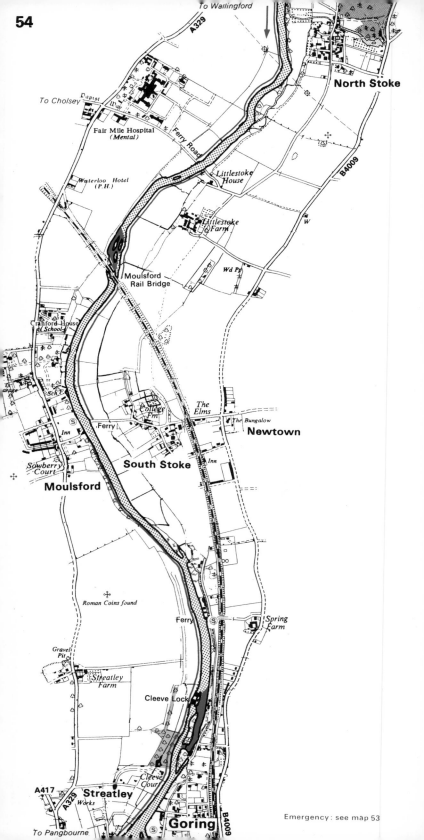

To Wallingford

A329

North Stoke

To Cholsey

Baptist Way

Fair Mile Hospital
(Mental)

Ferry Road

B4009

Waterloo Hotel
(P.H.)

Littlestoke
House

Littlestoke
Farm

W

Wd Pt

Moulsford
Rail Bridge

Cranford House
School

Sch

arage

College
Fm

The
Elms

The Bungalow

Newtown

Ferry

Inn

Inn

South Stoke

Sowberry
Court

Moulsford

Roman Coins found

Ferry

Spring
Farm

Gravel
Pit

Streatley
Farm

Cleeve Lock

Cleeve
Court

A417

A329

Streatley

Works

B4009

Goring

To Pangbourne

Emergency: see map 53

Places of interest

North Stoke
Oxon. Throughout this section the valley gradually becomes hillier until it reaches the steep wooded banks by Goring. North Stoke, an attractive red brick village, is buried among trees. The church is pleasingly original and unrestored; note the wall paintings and the canopied pulpit. Post office and general stores.

Moulsford Rail Bridge
Four beautiful brick arches by Brunel. Built on a slant so that the brick work causes an interesting visual distortion when seen from the north side.

South Stoke
Oxon. A residential village set back from the river, hidden by trees. Best approached along the towing path from North Stoke.

Moulsford
Berks. A roadside village with large houses by the river. The church, small and secluded, was rebuilt by Gilbert Scott in 1846; his fee was reputedly £64. Post office and stores.

Cholsey
Berks. Away from the river but worth visiting for the largely Norman cruciform church. Good selection of shops and post office. Between Cholsey and the river is the Fairmile Psychiatric Hospital, built 1867-70.

Goring
Oxon. EC Wed. Set in a splendid deep wooded valley by one of the most spectacular reaches on the river. Goring makes little use of its situation, however. A holiday paradise of indeterminate age, it has now been taken over by the commuter. The over-preserved

church contains a large bell, dated 1290, one of the oldest in England. General shops, post office and banks.
Between Goring and Henley the Thames passes through the Chilterns Area of Outstanding Natural Beauty. It comprises 309 square miles of the most beautiful scenery in Bucks, Beds, Herts and Oxon. Maintained by the National Parks Commission.

Goring Mill

Streatley
Berks. EC Thur. An extension of Goring on the other side of the river, and in a similarly spectacular setting. The town has a quiet, late C18th feeling. Note the old malthouses well converted into a village hall by W. Ravenscroft in 1898. A few shops and post office.

Archaeology

North Stoke
Many Prehistoric features including a Neolithic cursus and Bronze Age ring ditches which are well shown in crop marks.

Moulsford
A spectacular middle Bronze Age gold torque, perhaps a chieftain's neck ornament, was ploughed up in 1960 in a field west of the village. Now in Reading Museum.

Goring
Site of the most important Prehistoric ford across the river, linking the Icknield Way and the Ridgeway, the natural route along the Chilterns and the Berkshire Downs from the Wash to Stonehenge.

Streatley
Grim's Ditch, a late Bronze Age boundary work crossing the Downs, meets the river E of Streatley. Not to be confused with the earthwork at Crowmarsh. Grim, the devil, was commonly thought in the medieval period, to be responsible for such earthworks.

Eating, drinking & accommodation

Beetle & Wedge Hotel ✗ ¶ B B
Moulsford. Tel Cholsey 381. The beetle in the name is a woodcutter's hammer. 13 rooms BB 35s LD a la carte *daily until 21.00.* Snacks. Mooring, fishing. Parking.

Bull Hotel ✗ ¶ B B
Streatley. Tel Goring 2507. Old whitewashed inn with cobbled courtyard. 5 rooms BB 35s. Ld 14s6d *until 21.00. Closed Sun D.* Parking.

Miller of Mansfield ✗ ¶ B B
Goring. Tel 2829. C16th inn. 10 rooms BB 27s. L 12s6d D 15s weekdays (more at weekends). *Daily until 20.25.* Snacks. Parking.

Ye Olde Leatherne Bottel ✗ ¶ B B
Goring. Tel 2667. There was a well here in Roman times which produced medicinal water. 7 rooms 35s. LD 12s6d. *Daily until 21.30. (Closed Sun).* Mooring. Parking.

YHA
Streatley. Hill House, Reading Road. Tel Goring 2278.

Boatyards

Beetle & Wedge Hotel
Moulsford. Petrol, oil, gas, water, repairs, launching, mooring, chandlery, lavatories, refuse disposal, provisions, baths.

Ye Olde Leatherne Bottel
Goring. Petrol, oil, water, diesel, mooring.

Hobbs & Son
Goring. Tel 2106. Launch and boat hire, mooring, storage.

Cleeve Lock
Water.

Swan Inn
Streatley. Water: Baths for river users.

Mooring

Moulsford
Beetle & Wedge Hotel

Goring
Ye Olde Leatherne Bottel.
Hobbs & Son.
Official overnight mooring along towpath below Goring Lock.

Streatley
Swan Inn. Patrons only 2s6d.

Refuse disposal
Beetle & Wedge Hotel, Moulsford. Goring Lock.

Public launching slip
Papists' Lane, South Stoke.

Public lavatories
Cleeve Lock.

Navigation
Maximum draught: Oxford to Reading 4ft.

Bridges
Moulsford Rail Bridge, 21ft8.
Goring Bridge, B4526, 16ft11.

Locks
Cleeve Lock, 133ft7 x 18ft2.
Goring Lock, 179ft5 x 21ft.

Natural history
Lapwing, sometimes in tens of thousands, congregate in the autumn with many golden plover and snipe. Migrating sandpipers are often heard calling and corn buntings are plentiful. Many villages here have colonies of breeding housemartins.
There are many flowers characteristic of chalk hills. Among them some of our native *Gentianaceae, Centaurium erythraea* (centaury); *Gentianella amarella* (felwort) and *Blackstonia perfoliata* (yellowwort). *Clematis vitalba* (travellers' joy) straggles over bushes. Its small greenish flowers are succeeded by long silky plumed seeds which earn it the name of old man's beard, or tuzzy-wuzzy.

Fishing
The Fairmile Hospital Angling Club have private fishing on the Berkshire bank down to Ferry Road. On the Berkshire bank. Ye Olde Leatherne Bottel Inn at Goring has a mile of fishing at 5s per day.
Downstream of Ferry Road the London Anglers Association have a beat to the Moulsford Railway Bridge. The fishery is reached via the A329 Wallingford to Pangbourne Road. At Moulsford the Beetle & Wedge Hotel issue permits for a short stretch. Day tickets with parking 5s.
The Thames record crucian carp of 3lb 1oz was caught here in 1966. Further downstream the London Anglers hold another stretch down to Cleeve Lock. TC permit operates on the upper Weir at Cleeve Lock. Downstream of Goring the fishing is free on the Oxfordshire bank. Bream, chub, barbel, roach, dace, perch and pike can be caught.

Fair Mile Hospital Angling Club
Fair Mile Hospital, Cholsey, Berks.

London Anglers Association
See Lechlade map page 27

The Weir at Streatley *W J Howes*

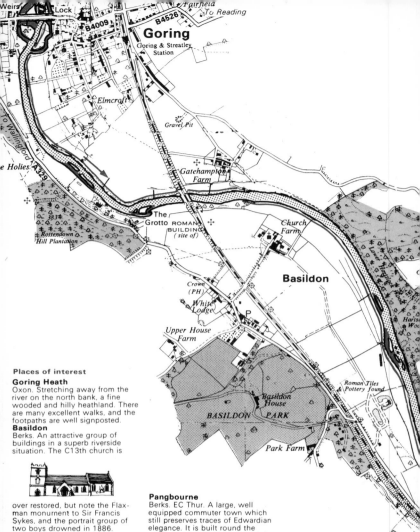

Places of interest

Goring Heath
Oxon. Stretching away from the river on the north bank, a fine wooded and hilly heathland. There are many excellent walks, and the footpaths are well signposted.

Basildon
Berks. An attractive group of buildings in a superb riverside situation. The C13th church is

over restored, but note the Flaxman monument to Sir Francis Sykes, and the portrait group of two boys drowned in 1886.
To the east of Basildon is the collection of statuary built up by Gilbert Beale. View by appointment.

Basildon Park
Berks. Built by John Carr for Sir

Francis Sykes in 1776. It is the most splendid Georgian mansion in Berkshire. Private.

Pangbourne
Berks. EC Thur. A large, well equipped commuter town which still preserves traces of Edwardian elegance. It is built round the confluence of the Thames and the river Pang, a famous trout stream. The Nautical College, an imposing William and Mary style mansion, is by Sir John Belcher. Built 1897-8. All shops, banks, post office.

Whitchurch
Oxon. A quieter, more attractive development of Pangbourne approached via the Whitchurch Toll Bridge. There is a good group of mill buildings, overlooked by the rather inaccessible church. Very few shops, as Pangbourne answers most needs.

Country crafts

Mrs A. G. Rhodes
Whitchurch. Hill House. Tel Pangbourne 2827 for appointment to view a collection of crafts from workshops in Britain. Proceeds to Medical Research.

Archaeology

Gatehampton
Crop marks reveal ring ditches on the north bank on either side of the railway. Probably Bronze Age. One low mound visible near Gatehampton Farm.

Whitchurch
Bozedown Camp. Remains of an Iron Age hill fort strategically placed at the confluence of the river Pang and the Thames. Largely destroyed by ploughing. On private land.

Whitchurch Toll Bridge

Boatyards

Hobbs & Son
Pangbourne. Tel 2907. Mooring, launching, launch and boat hire. Storage.

Swan Hotel
Pangbourne. Water 1s, meals delivered to boats.

Mooring

Pangbourne
Hobbs & Son.
Swan Hotel, for patrons only.

Sewage & refuse disposal

Whitchurch Lock.

Navigation

Maximum draught: Oxford to Reading 4ft.

Bridges
Gatehampton Rail Bridge, 22ft10.
Whitchurch Bridge, B471, Toll 6d, 13ft7.

Locks
Whitchurch Lock, 135ft3 x 18ft.

Natural history

Tree-creepers, like small brown mice, run up the tree-trunks looking for insects. Long-tailed tits, with striking black, white and pink plumage build almost spherical nests of moss, wool and feathers. These are usually in a thick bush, and are protected from the weather by a covering of lichen and spiders' webs.
Barn owls breed here.
Viburnum opulus (guelder rose) is one of our most beautiful shrubs and is found here. It has large flat umbels of creamy flowers in May and bunches of glossy, scarlet berries and brilliant red leaves in autumn.

Fishing

The Weir pool at Goring is excellent for barbel and chub and can be fished on a Thames Conservancy permit.
From the bridge a free stretch of fishing extends on the Oxfordshire bank to the gate by the railway bridge, where there is another London Anglers fishery. The London Anglers have another stretch near Gatehampton Farm, where there is a car park, and a further mile near Hartslock Wood. From Basildon to Pangbourne on the south bank, above Pangbourne Weir, is free fishing. The Thames record dace of 1lb 3½oz was caught at Pangbourne in 1924. Downstream of Whitchurch bridge there is free fishing for individuals but clubs must make bookings through the local council.
The Speedbird Club has 2-3 meadows downstream. Good bream, roach, dace, pike and perch can be caught on these reaches.
London Anglers Association
See Lechlade map page 27

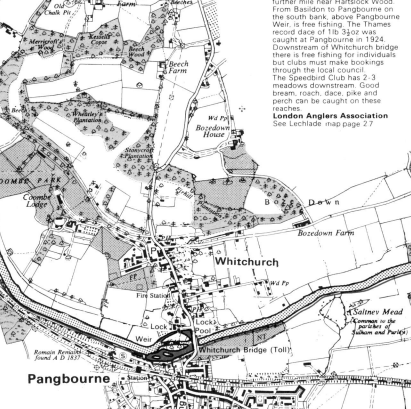

Pangbourne

A large Neolithic pottery bowl and accompanying burial found on Courtlands Hill. Both now in Reading Museum.

Eating, drinking & accommodation

The Copper Inn X ! BB
Pangbourne. Tel 2244. Old coaching inn. 11 rooms BB 65s. English food. L 15s6d D a la carte (average 25s) *daily until 22.00 (21.00 Sun)*. Parking.

Swan Hotel X ! BB
Pangbourne. Tel 3199. The hotel is beside the river. 6 rooms BB 40s. English and French cooking. LD 17s6d *daily until 21.15, except Sun until 20.45*. Snacks. Mooring, fishing. Parking.

Emergency: see map 59

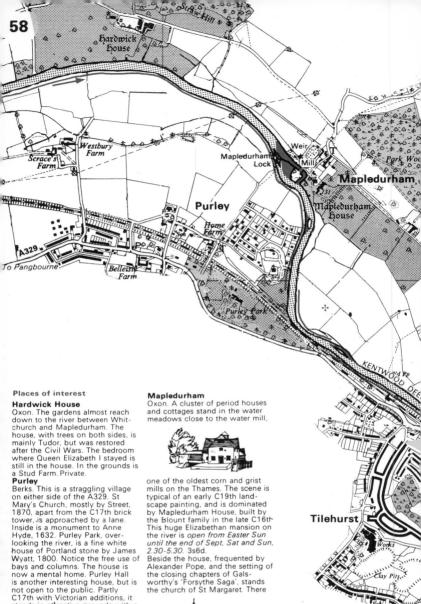

Places of interest

Hardwick House

Oxon. The gardens almost reach down to the river between Whit-church and Mapledurham. The house, with trees on both sides, is mainly Tudor, but was restored after the Civil Wars. The bedroom where Queen Elizabeth I stayed is still in the house. In the grounds is a Stud Farm. Private.

Purley

Berks. This is a straggling village on either side of the A329. St Mary's Church, mostly by Street, 1870, apart from the C17th brick tower, is approached by a lane. Inside is a monument to Anne Hyde, 1632. Purley Park, over-looking the river, is a fine white house of Portland stone by James Wyatt, 1800. Notice the free use of bays and columns. The house is now a mental home. Purley Hall is another interesting house, but is not open to the public. Partly C17th with Victorian additions, it stands in attractive grounds with a lake and Georgian summer house. The entrance lodges, late Georgian and very pretty with bands of rough flint decorating the brick and small portholes, can be admired from the road.

Tilehurst

Berks. The station, rather an ugly building, is on the river, but the main part of this sprawling suburb lies further inland. In the Church of St Michael by Street, 1856, there is an exquisite east window in the south aisle by William Morris, 1869. Angels with musical instruments surround a Virgin and Child, all on a blue background with yellow flowers. There is an interesting alabaster monument to Sir Peter Vanlore, his wife and children, 1627, beside the window. The chancel windows by Wailes are gay splashes of pattern. Outside the porch are some finely carved C18th gravestones. A note-worthy monument of the early 1930's is the tall white reservoir tower in Park Lane.

Mapledurham

Oxon. A cluster of period houses and cottages stand in the water meadows close to the water mill,

one of the oldest corn and grist mills on the Thames. The scene is typical of an early C19th land-scape painting, and is dominated by Mapledurham House, built by the Blount family in the late C16th. This huge Elizabethan mansion on the river is *open from Easter Sun until the end of Sept, Sat and Sun, 2.30-5.30.* 3s6d.

Beside the house, frequented by Alexander Pope, and the setting of the closing chapters of Gals-worthy's 'Forsythe Saga', stands the church of St Margaret. There

are many fine memorials, in particular the tomb to Sir Richard Blount and his wife, early C17th.

Reading

Berks. The town seems to lack a cohesive centre and is an amalgam of university and industry— Huntley & Palmers and Sutton Seeds have factories here. But historically and architecturally it has interest. The new university buildings are disappointing, but there are numerous Victorian buildings and the museum boasts one of the most interesting archaeological collections in the country.

Abbey Ruins

Fragmentary remains of the C12th Abbey, built by Henry I, lie on the edge of Forbury Park. The Abbey, one of the largest in England, was comparable with Bury St Edmunds. The Gatehouse, C13th, still stands, although it was greatly altered by Gilbert Scott in 1869, and the Church of St Lawrence near the Market Place was originally attached to the Abbey outer gate. Fragments from the Abbey can be seen in the Reading Museum and the Victoria and Albert Museum.

The Gaol

Forbury Road. Designed by Scott & Moffat, 1842-4, in Scottish

Boatyards

Bridge Boats
Reading. Fry's Island. Tel 50346.
Moorings.
Caversham Bridge Hotel
Reading. Tel 53793. Moorings.
Conch Cruisers
Reading. Piper's Island. Tel 72256
Hire cruisers, day boats.
Concoform Marine
Reading. 121 Castle Hill. Tel
50362. Moorings, repairs, boat
hire, chandlery.
Kennet Mouth Boathouse
Reading. Kennet Side. Tel 64186
Hire. Moorings, launching.
Popular Boats
Reading. Caversham Bridge. Tel
75777. Moorings, hire cruisers.
Chandlery.
Reading Marine Company
Reading. Crane Wharf. Tel 53917.
Water, repairs, moorings, launch-
ing, chandlery, lavatories.
Reading Marine Services
Reading. Tel 27155. Petrol, oil,
gas, water, moorings, launching,
repairs, chandlery, lavatories, hire
2/8 berth.

Mooring

Reading
Bridge Boats, Fry's Island.
Caversham Bridge. Hotel, Caver-
sham Bridge.
Concoform Marine.
Kennet Mouth Boathouse.
Popular Boats, Caversham Bridge.
Reading Marine Company.
Reading Marine Services.
Public Mooring Site, Recreation
Ground. North bank above
Reading Bridge.

Sewage & refuse disposal

Caversham. Wolsey Road, Caversham Bridge.

Public lavatories
Caversham Bridge

Public launching site
Caversham Bridge.

Navigation

Maximum draught: Oxford to
Reading 4ft. Reading to Windsor
4ft6.
Locks
Mapledurham Lock, 202ft5 x
21ft1.
Emergency
Police. Calpy Street, Reading.
Tel 53211
Hospital. Royal Berkshire Hospital.
London Road, Reading. Tel 85111

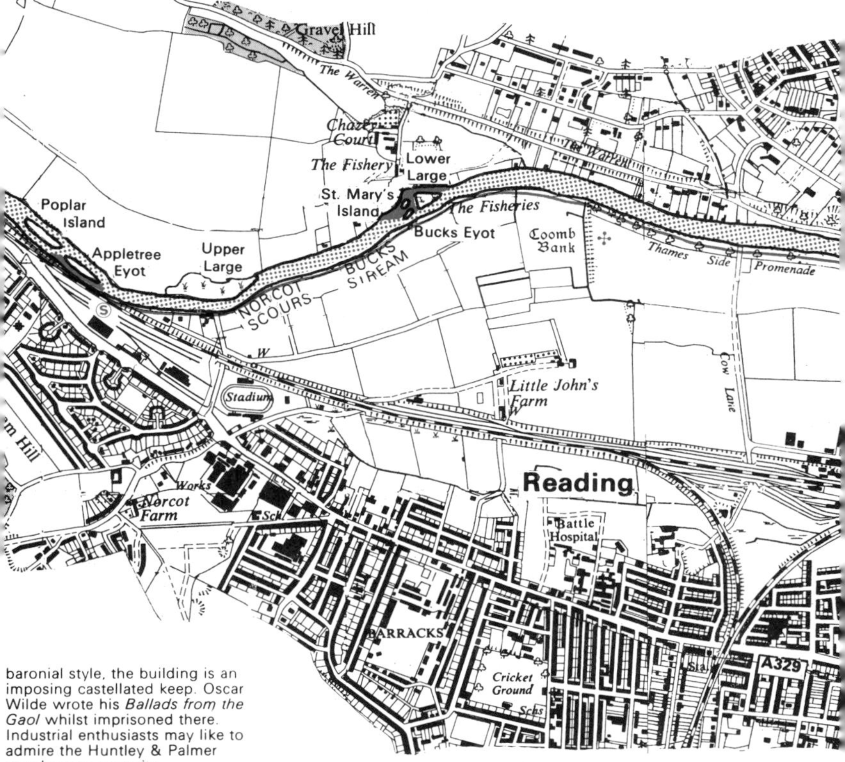

baronial style, the building is an
imposing castellated keep. Oscar
Wilde wrote his *Ballads from the
Gaol* whilst imprisoned there.
Industrial enthusiasts may like to
admire the Huntley & Palmer
warehouses opposite.
Royal Berkshire Hospital
London Road. This magnificent
facade of Bath stone with its

grand classical portico would be
worthy of a Royal residence. Built
by Henry Briant, 1837-9, the

wings were added in 1861, and
further additions were made by
Morris & Smallwood in 1881.
Seven Bridges House
Bridge Street. The main interest of
this small Georgian house is that it
was built by Sir John Soane, 1790.
Red brick with a porch, it has a
traceried fan glass over the door.
There is also an obelisk by Soane
in the Market Place. It has been
much degraded and is now standing with the public lavatories on
either side.

Nos 7-25, Station Road
All of yellow and red brick, steep
gables and varied decoration, these
interesting buildings by Joseph
Morris & Son are fantastic late
Victorian folly.
St James
Forbury Road. Entirely in the
Norman style and untypical of his
later work, this church by Pugin,
1837-40, has been enlarged by the
addition of north and south aisles,
1925 and 1962. Pugin may have
opted for the Norman style

because of the proximity to the Abbey ruins. The church looks its best when viewed from Forbury Gardens in the middle of which stands a huge cast iron lion, a memorial to those who died in the Afghan Wars.

St Bartholomew
London Road. The church is mainly by Waterhouse, 1879, but with a chancel by Bodley, 1881. Red brick with blue pattern work. The decoration of the sanctuaries, Lady chapel and high altar are by Sir Ninian Comper.

Multi-storey car park
Chatham Street. Designed by Jan Bobrowski and Partners from Poland, this is a gleaming white concrete building of originality, 1968.

Museum of English Rural Life
Whiteknights Park. The museum is devoted to material relating to all aspects of rural life in England. *Open May-Oct 10.30-17.00. Sun 14.30-17.00. Nov-Apr 14.30-17.00 Wed and Sat only.*

Museum of Greek Archaeology
Whiteknights Park. This teaching collection consisting mainly of Greek pottery and Egyptian antiquities is not generally open to the public except on special application (Reading 82481).

Reading Museum and Art Gallery
Friar Street. The museum has an exceptional natural history and local archaeological collection. The Silchester collection, on loan from his Grace the Duke of Wellington, is displayed so that the visitor can obtain a vivid picture of everyday life in the Romano-British town of Calleva Atrebatum (Silchester). The Thames Conservancy Collection includes Prehistoric metalwork, Palaeolithic hand axes from Caversham Heights, Iron Age and Roman pottery as well as Saxon grave goods. *Open 10.00-17.30 except Sun.*

Cinemas
ABC Central Cinema, 25A Friars Street. Tel 53931
Odeon, Cheapside. Tel 52707.

Caversham
Berks. The town is now a residential continuation of Reading. The most attractive part is by the river where Caversham Court Gardens stretch alongside. There are two typical brick pattern buildings by Waterhouse: the Baptist Free Church, 1875-7 on the corner of South Street, and the West Memorial Institute, 1865-6, almost opposite. The Public Library in Church Street is an amusing Edwardian building, 1907, with a central green copper clock supported by an angel.

Caversham Park House
Berks. This large white stuccoed mansion with columns in the Palladian tradition was built in 1850 on the site of four earlier houses. Of the Elizabethan house, built for Sir Francis Knollys, 1568, only the ice house remains. In the C18th the house was owned by the Earl of Cadogan and rebuilt in 1718 and 1776. The Gardens were by Capability Brown. William Crawshay, a Welsh iron master, owned the house in the C19th and rebuilt it in the present form after a fire. It is now owned by the BBC Monitoring Service.

Sport

Swimming
Central Swimming Pool, Reading. Battle Street: Tel 40905.
Outdoor Swimming Bath, Reading. Kings Meadow Road. Tel 51737. *Summer only.*

Garth & South Berks Hunt Club
Area along the Thames from Wallingford to Henley. Sec. Brig. D. C. Barbour, Shortheath House, Sulhamstead, Reading. Tel Burghfield Common 2057. *Meets Wed and Sat.* Cap: £3 plus 10s Field Money.

Archaeology

Mapledurham
Dredging has produced large numbers of flint blades and chipped axes of Mesolithic type from this stretch of the river. This is partly explained by a rich outcrop of flint in the chalk of the Berkshire bank at this point.

Sulham
A late Bronze Age cemetery, excavated in a gravel pit, produced seven crude cremation pots. Now in Reading Museum.

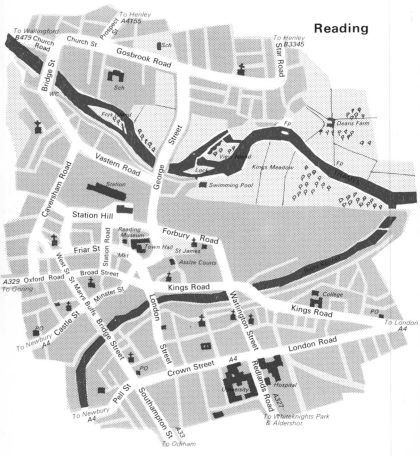

Reading

Reading

Coomb Bank, the low remains of a bank and ditch, may be a defensive earthwork connected with the Danish raids of 871 or 1006. Many iron spearheads have been dredged from the river at this point. A visit to Silchester, 9 miles south of Reading, site of the Romano-British town of Calleva Atrebatum, is rewarding. The walls are well-preserved. Finds are preserved in the Reading Museum.

Eating, drinking & accommodation

Astoria Restaurant X
Reading. 29 Cross Street. Tel 50632. French and Greek specialities. L 7s6d D 15s6d.

Bull Hotel 🍷
Reading. 23 Broad Street. Tel 53858. Snacks.

Caversham Bridge Hotel X 🍷 BB
Caversham. Tel Reading 53793. Riverside hotel. 24 rooms BB 35s. L 13s6d D 17s. International cooking with wine. Garage. Mooring.

European Coffee Grill X 🍷
Caversham. 32A Church Street. Tel Reading 77917. High quality English and Continental menu. Greek specialities. LD 6s to 20s. Licensed. Open until 24.00. Parking.

George Hotel X 🍷 BB
Reading. King Street. Tel 53445. C16th coaching inn. 40 rooms BB 35s. LD 12s to 18s. International cooking. Snacks. Parking.

Roebuck Hotel X 🍷 BB
Tilehurst. Oxford Road. Tel 27517. View over the river. 9 rooms BB 30s. D 12s6d until 21.30. English menu. Snacks. Fishing. Mooring. Parking.

Taj Mahal X
Reading. 115 King Street. Tel 53366. Specialises in Indian food. Also English and Continental menu. LD 8s until 21.30. No licence.

Natural history

Hobby and sparrow hawks are seen occasionally. At Cranesmoor Lake, Englefield, there is a large heronry. There are large flocks of mute swans and flocks of over 150 Canada geese. The cry of the curlew and the reeling trill of the grasshopper warbler can be heard.
Salix (willows) of various species and *Alnus glutinosa* (alders) line the banks. *Lychnis flos-cuculi* (ragged robin) with bright pink shaggy petals grows in damp places. *Silene dioica* (red campion), a near relative, often grows with *Endymion non-scriptus* (bluebell) and *Stellaria holostea* (greater stitchwort).

Fishing

Scenically, the surroundings are superb. The London Anglers hold the water for two meadows half a mile above Mapledurham Lock on the Berkshire bank.
The Oxfordshire bank is mostly private as far as Mapledurham where the Central Association of London and Provincial Angling Clubs have ¾ mile above the weir and 1½ miles downstream, as well as the mill stream and pool. Downstream of Tilehurst there is free fishing as far as Caversham. Here the Thameside Promenade is controlled by the Reading Council. Fishing is free for individuals but not for clubs.
The catch is mainly roach, dace and bream.
The Council also control the park stretch downstream of Caversham Bridge on the Oxfordshire bank.

Central Association of London & Provincial Angling Clubs
Secretary: J. Penn, 63 Cambridge Drive, Lee, SE12. Tel (01) 852 6375.

London Anglers Association
See Lechlade map page 27

Reading Council
Borough Surveyor, Town Hall, Reading.

Tackle shops

T. Turner & Sons
Reading. 21 Whitley Street.

Sonning *W J Howes*

Places of interest

Reading and Caversham
See previous map.

Sonning
Berks. EC Tue MD Sat. A desperately preserved village. Pretty, but it leaves an inescapable feeling that it is Hollywood's idea of a Thames-side village. Seen from the river the picture is formed round the eleven brick arches of the C18th bridge, with the wooded church in the background. Built largely in the C19th by Woodyer and Bodley, the church is remarkable for its monuments which date from all periods, starting with C15th brasses. The churchyard, walled with soft brick, is large and peaceful. It leads down to the river's edge and to a good walk along the south bank towards Reading. In the town the most interesting house is Lutyens' Deanery Gardens, built for Edward Hudson in 1901.
To the west of the town is Holme Park, now the Reading Blue Coat School. The wooded grounds drop sharply to the river.
A few shops, and post office.

Sonning Cutting
South of the town is a spectacular example of railway geology. A cutting, 60ft deep, through Sonning Hill, engineered by Brunel in 1839.

Archaeology

The large gravel pits at Sonning Eye have produced several mammoth tusks and teeth, dating from the latter part of the Ice Age.

Eating, drinking & accommodation

The Bull Hotel   ✕ ❗
Sonning. Tel 2201. An old inn by the churchyard with an atmosphere of Jaguars and expense accounts. Cold table L *Mon-Sat,* and snacks. Parking.

Sonning Lock *R R Bolland*

French Horn Hotel   ✕ ❗ B B
Sonning. Tel 2204. The hotel is in an attractive position, with lawns sloping to the river. 4 rooms BB 80s. French and English cooking LD 50s *daily until 21.30.* Mooring, fishing. Parking.

White Hart Hotel   ✕ ❗ B B
Sonning. Tel 2277. Founded in 1360, this inn boasts a fine view of the river across lawns and a rose garden. 23 rooms BB 60s. International cooking served in the Regency dining room. L 25s D a la carte, *daily until 22.30.* Snacks. Mooring, fishing. Parking.

Boatyards

White Hart
Sonning. Water, mooring.

Mooring

French Horn, Sonning.
White Hart, Sonning.
Official overnight mooring along towpath above Sonning Lock.

Refuse disposal

Sonning Lock.

Navigation

Maximum draught: Reading to Windsor 4ft6.

Bridges

Caversham Bridge, A4009, 15ft.

Reading Bridge, 17ft6.

Sonning Bridge, B478, 14ft2.

Locks
Caversham Lock, 131ft4 x 17ft11.
Sonning Lock, 156ft1 x 17ft11.
Blake's Lock on the river Kennet is the only lock under the control of the Thames Conservancy not actually on the Thames.

Natural history

Goldcrests (our smallest British bird) live in the coniferous woods, and wren and white-throat breed in woodlands.

Two deadly poisonous umbellifers grow near the river: *Oenanthe crocata* (hemlock, water drop-wort), a tall robust plant with tuberous roots, hollow stems and dark leaves; and *Conium maculatum* (hemlock), which is taller, paler green, with feathery leaves and a spotted stem. Both have large heads of small white flowers.

Fishing

Most of the Kennet is held by the Reading & District A.A., 3s per day for members' guests.

The Reading Council control the fishing on both banks between Caversham and Reading bridges. The towpath is generally free from the Kennet mouth to Sonning Bridge. The Kennet mouth was once noted for big barbel and trout. On the north bank the London Anglers have nearly a mile from opposite the Dreadnought Boat House downstream. There are plenty of sheltered swims with roach, dace and chub in these reaches and the Sonning-Dreadnought stretch has good bream shoals.

The Thames record roach of 3lb 9½oz was caught at Sonning in 1949.

London Anglers Association
See Lechlade map page 27

Emergency: see map 59

Reading Council
See previous map.
Reading and District Angling Association
Secretary: John Grantham,
16 Blenheim Gardens, Reading.

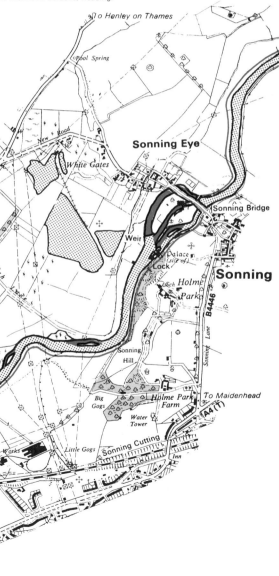

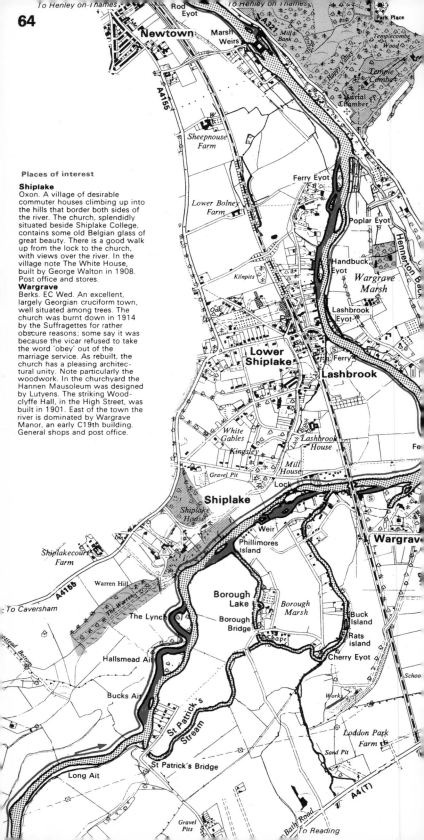

64

Places of interest

Shiplake

Oxon. A village of desirable commuter houses climbing up into the hills that border both sides of the river. The church, splendidly situated beside Shiplake College, contains some old Belgian glass of great beauty. There is a good walk up from the lock to the church, with views over the river. In the village note The White House, built by George Walton in 1908. Post office and stores.

Wargrave

Berks. EC Wed. An excellent, largely Georgian cruciform town, well situated among trees. The church was burnt down in 1914 by the Suffragettes for rather obscure reasons; some say it was because the vicar refused to take the word 'obey' out of the marriage service. As rebuilt, the church has a pleasing architectural unity. Note particularly the woodwork. In the churchyard the Hannen Mausoleum was designed by Lutyens. The striking Woodclyffe Hall, in the High Street, was built in 1901. East of the town the river is dominated by Wargrave Manor, an early C19th building. General shops and post office.

Harpsden

Oxon. An attractive village ½ mile west of the river. The centre is formed by the church, a tidy well restored building, and Harpsden Court, a C17th mansion with later additions. In the farm opposite the church the barns are walled with wooden wall-paper printing blocks, a most unusual and decorative effect. Worth the walk up from the river.

Park Place

An indifferent house set in splendid wooded parkland. The grounds contain a cyclopian bridge, built 1781-6, a grotto and a Megalithic tomb that came originally from Jersey. (See Archaeology section.)

Archaeology

Wargrave

In the grounds of Park Place stands a complete Megalithic chambered tomb, a monument remarkable for the Thames Valley, and indeed unique in Southern England. It was discovered in Jersey in 1785, and given as a present to Marshal Conway, the Governor at that time. On his

Shiplake Lock *R R Bolland*

retirement to Park Place, the monument was sent over for him, stone by stone on barges up the river, to be re-erected where it stands today. It can only be viewed by appointment.

Harpsden

On the edge of the golf course stood a Roman villa. Some foundations can still be seen, while some of the finds are on display in Henley Town Hall.

Eating, drinking & accommodation

Baskerville Arms Hotel X ♥ BB
Shiplake. Tel Wargrave 3332. 5 rooms BB 35s. LD 21s *until 21.30. Closed Tue and Sun.* Mooring. Parking.

St George & Dragon Hotel
X ♥ BB
Wargrave. Tel 2815. Note the hotel sign. 7 rooms. BB 40s. L14s6d D 15s6d *daily until 21.00. Fri and Sat until 21.30.* Mooring. Parking.

Boatyards

John Bushnell
Wargrave. Tel 216/2. Petrol, oil, gas, water, launches and cruisers for hire, repairs, launching, mooring, chandlery, lavatories, refuse disposal.

Hobbs & Sons
Shiplake. Tel Wargrave 137. Mooring, storage.

Swancraft
Wargrave. St George & Dragon Boathouse. Tel 577. Small boats and launches for day hire.

Wal Wyatt Marine
Wargrave. Tel 3211. Petrol, oil, gas, water, boat sales, repairs, Johnson distributor, launching, mooring, storage, chandlery, lavatories, yachting clothing, provisions.

Shiplake Lock
Water.

Mooring

Wargrave
John Bushnell's Boatyard.
Wal Wyatt Marine.
St George and Dragon.
Along towpath at Lower Lashbrook.

Shiplake
Official overnight mooring on Isingale towpath.

Sewage & refuse disposal

Shiplake Lock.

Public lavatories

Shiplake Lock.

Public launching slip

Wargrave. Ferry Lane.

Navigation

Maximum draught: Reading to Windsor 4ft6.

St Patrick's Stream
Navigation is not recommended because of the current.

Bridges
Shiplake Rail Bridge, 17ft10.

Locks
Shiplake Lock, 133ft4 x 18ft3.
Marsh Lock, 135ft2 x 21ft1.

Ferry
St George & Dragon Hotel, Wargrave.

Natural history

Water voles are common. Large flocks of collared doves, 200 or more, stay here in winter. First recorded at Cromer in 1955, this addition to the British list now breeds freely. There is a colony of over 300 sandmartins at Knowl Hill. The kingfisher breeds in this area.

Where the Loddon enters the Thames grow two rare plants: the first, *Leucojum aestivum* (summer snowflake, Loddon lily), grows in black swampy soil with willows and alders. (Curtis found it at Greenwich in 1788.) Although introduced in some places it is native here by the Loddon. The second is *Potamogeton nodosus* (Loddon pondweed) which grows in the water. It is known only from the rivers Avon, Loddon, Thames and Stour. Its submerged leaves are beautifully veined.

Fishing

From Sonning Bridge a long stretch on the Oxfordshire bank is held by the Old Comrades A.S. and is good for roach and chub. On the opposite bank the Standard Telephones A.S. have a beat up to St Patrick's Stream where barbel, chub, roach and dace can be caught.

The fishing on St Patrick's Stream and the River Loddon is reserved for members of the Hall Angling Scheme. Shiplake Weir can be fished on a Thames Conservancy permit.

Downstream of the weir the Twyford and District A.C. have a stretch. The second largest Thames tench of 5lb 12oz was caught from Shiplake in 1911. Marsh Weir can be fished on the Thames Conservancy permit. At Wargrave, the Thames record chub of 7lb 1oz was caught in 1897.

Old Comrades Angling Society
Secretary: J. Perring, 122 High Street, Tooting, SW17.

Hall Angling Scheme
Secretary: G. Bennett, RMC House, 53-5 High Street, Feltham, Middlesex. Tel (01) 890 1313.

Standard Telephones Angling Society
Secretary: E. Tenwick, c/o Standard Telephones, Oakleigh Road, New Southgate, N11.

Twyford & District Angling Club
Secretary: G. L. Addy, 15A Woods Road, Caversham, Berks.

A4 (T)
To Maidenhead

A321

Wokingham

Emergency : see map 69

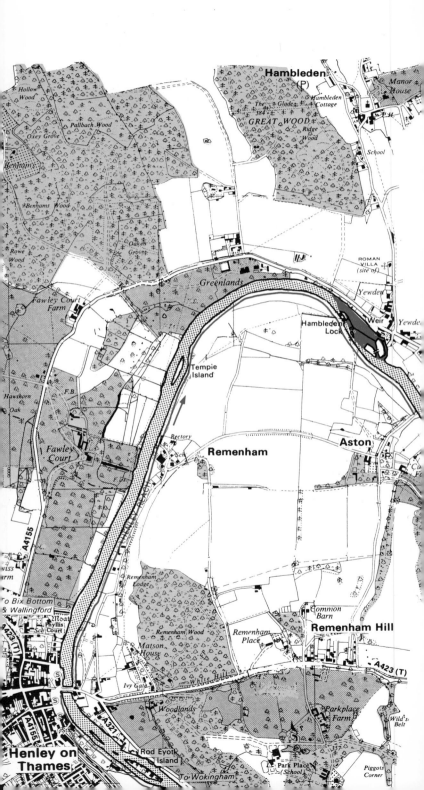

Places of interest

Henley
Oxon. EC Wed MD Thur. A fine market town; one of the most popular resorts on the river in summer. The main street, running down to the Thames from the Victorian town hall, has a feeling of timelessness and Edwardian elegance that is almost out of place today. From the river the most obvious features are the C18th stone bridge, and the Decorated and Perpendicular church, a very large and very gloomy building. General shops, banks, post office. Car park and public lavatories.

The Kenton Theatre
New Street. Repertory in a fine theatre, built 1805.

Remenham
Berks. An untidy village scattered along the south bank, backed by the woods of Remenham Hill.

Fawley Court
A fine riverside situation. The Court was built in 1684, and subsequently classicised by James Wyatt in 1771. Wyatt also built the Temple on Temple Island as a vista for the Court. It is a pretty ornament in its own right, with views down the river to Henley. The grounds were laid out by Capability Brown in 1770. It is now the Divine Mercy College.

Greenlands
A sumptuous C19th Italianate mansion, now an Administrative Staff College.

Henley Bridge *R R Bolland*

Hambleden
Bucks. Set back from the river and surrounded by heavily wooded hills, Hambleden is one of the most attractive villages in Berkshire. All mellow flint and brick with a marvellous original unity. The C14th church and the houses round the green make it a perfect village setting, with the C17th Manor House in the background. The church tower was built in 1721.

Note the excellent meat at A. Wheeler, Butcher and Game Dealer. Some general shops and post office.

Hambleden Mill
On the river the weatherboarded mill and mill house form a fine group around the lock.

Culham Court
A Neo-Classical red brick house of 1770-1. The five bays are well placed by the river.

Medmenham
Bucks. A village straggling up from the Thames into the woods behind. It is backed by RAF Medmenham, the headquarters of

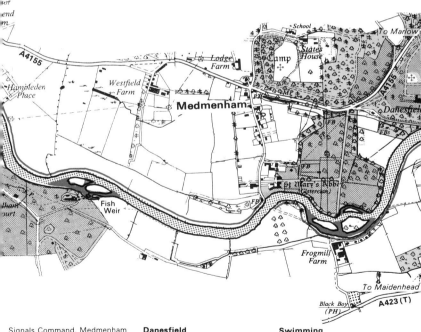

Signals Command. Medmenham Abbey (St Mary's Abbey), partly 1595, partly C18th Gothic and mostly 1898 was the home of the orgiastic Hell Fire Club, under the auspices of Sir Francis Dashwood. It was decorated in a suitably pornographic and sacrilegious style, but understandably nothing survived the C19th.

On the north bank by Medmenham is the last surviving windlass on the Thames, a relic of the days when barges had to be winched by hand through the weirs. Post office and stores.

Danesfield
A vast Tudor mansion built 1899-1901, commanding the river to the east of Medmenham.

Sport

Henley Regatta
Established in 1839 after the first university boat race had been held here in 1829. One of the first river regattas in the world, it was termed Royal in 1851. The regatta is very consciously an 'amateur' affair, glorious as a summer spectacle as much as a sporting event. *It takes place in the first week of July.*

Swimming
Henley. Public Baths, Wargrave Road. Tel 4742.

Archaeology

Medmenham
Medmenham and Danesfield Camps. Two Iron Age hill forts close to each other on the north bank. The ramparts and ditches are quite well preserved. Medmenham Camp is well worth a visit as it is well placed on the chalk cliff above the river.

Emergency: see map 69

Eating, drinking & accommodation

The Angel Hotel ✕ ☐
Henley. The Bridge. Tel 4977.
LD a la carte daily until 22.00.
Snacks. Mooring.

Flower Pot Hotel ✕ ☐ BB
Aston. Near Remenham. Tel
Henley 4721. 3 rooms 25s. LD
daily until 22.30. Snacks. Clay
pigeon shooting. Garage.

Little White Hart Hotel ✕ ☐ BB
Henley. Riverside. Tel 4145. 20
rooms 50s. English cooking and
snacks. LD daily until 21.00.
Mooring, fishing. Garage, parking.

The Red Lion Hotel ✕ ☐ BB
Henley. Tel 2161/3. C16th coach-
ing inn; has been much frequented
by royalty. 22 rooms BB 45s.
Old English dishes a speciality.
L 12s6d Mon–Fri, 17s6d Sat, Sun.
D 21s daily until 21.00, Sat until
22.00. Dinner-dance Sat 30s.
Mooring by prior arrangement.
Parking.

Two Brewers Inn ✕ ☐ BB
Henley. Wargrave Road. Tel 4375.
C16th inn with a Boat Bar for
river enthusiasts. 3 rooms 32s6d.
English and Spanish cooking,
snacks at the bar. L 10s6d D 20s
daily except Tue, until 22.00.
Mooring, fishing. Parking.

Ye Old Dog & Badger Inn ✕ ☐
Medmenham. Tel Hambleden 362
Lunches, snacks, coffee. Parking.

YHA
Henley. Friends Meeting House,
Northfield End. Tel 2060.

Boatyards

G. Allen
Henley. 5 Reading Road. Tel
12289. Groceries delivered to boat.

Hobbs & Sons
Henley. Station Road. Tel 2035.
Petrol, oil, gas, water, launches,
cruisers and rowing boats for day
hire, marine sales, repairs, launching, mooring, chandlery, refuse
disposal. Outboard motor
specialists.

J. Hooper
Henley. The Boathouse. Motor
punts and small craft for hire.

A. Parrott
Henley. Thames Side. Tel 2380.
Oil, gas, launches, punts, skiffs
and dinghies for day hire, repairs,
launching, mooring, storage of
outboard motors, chandlery,
parking.

Mooring
Angel Hotel, Henley.
Frogmill, opposite Medmenham.

Public launching slip
Wharf Lane, below Henley Bridge.
Aston. Old ferry site.
Medmenham. Old ferry site.

Navigation
Maximum draught: Reading to
Windsor 4ft6.

Bridges
Henley Bridge, A423, 14ft3.

Locks
Hambleden Lock, 135ft2 x 17ft9.

Natural history
There is a heronry in Oaken Grove,
at Hambleden
Mink, escaped from fur farms and
now living wild, are a danger to
birds. Chinese muntjac or barking
deer (about the size of a large
dog) live in the woods. Kept at
Woburn in the late C19th, they
escaped to live and breed in the
surrounding country. Badgers are
common in the Chilterns. Natterer's
bat, which flies in early evening
and feeds on moths, has been
found at Henley.
Asplenium adiantum-nigrum
(black spleenwort) grows on a
church wall at Medmenham. Malva
moschata (musk mallow), rose-
pink or white, is one of our
prettiest wild flowers and grows in
hedgerows and field borders.

The Warburg Reserve
At Bix Bottom, near Henley, is a
nature reserve belonging to the
Berks, Bucks and Oxon Naturalists'
Trust. Grasshopper warbler, redstarts and woodcock breed, and
muntjac, fallow and roe deer have
been recorded.
Seventeen species of orchid grow
here. Paris quadrifolia (herb paris),
Helleborus viridis (green helle-
bore), Aquilegia vulgaris (colum-
bine) and Alchemilla vestita (lady's
mantle) are interesting and uncommon plants also found.

Fishing
At Hambleden the London Anglers
have a short stretch downstream
of Hambleden Lock on the Berkshire bank and another stretch
from Aston Ferry to Culham Court.
Hambleden Weir can be fished on
a Thames Conservancy permit.
The occasional barbel can be
caught.
Downstream of Medmenham Ferry
the London Anglers again have
rights on the south bank from the
lane by the Black Boy Inn as far
as Temple. Campers can obtain
day tickets—3s for adults, 1s for
juniors. No fishing is allowed in
front of St Mary Abbot's Priory.
It is possible to catch roach, dace
chub, bream, perch, pike and the
occasional tench on all these
reaches.

London Anglers Association
See Lechlade map page 27

Emergency
Police. Market Place, Henley.
Tel 4602.
Hospital: War Memorial Hospital,
Peppard Lane, Oxford. Tel 2688.

The riverside at Henley R R Bolland

Places of interest

Hurley
Berks. A seemingly schizophrenic village. Part, hidden by trees, overlooks the Hurley backwaters where the river breaks its course around a number of islands. There are excellent river walks. The rest is given over to indiscriminate surburban development in the south, and to a huge riverside caravan sprawl in the east. In the old part the long dark and narrow nave of the church is all that remains of Hurley Priory (St Mary's), founded before 1087 for the Benedictine Order. Opposite the church are a C14th barn and dovecot; the barn was well converted into a house in 1950. Post office and general store.

Harleyford Manor
On the north bank opposite Hurley. The Manor was built in 1755 by Sir Robert Taylor for Sir William Clayton. The splendid grounds, reputedly by Capability Brown, sweep down to the river.

Bisham
Berks. A largely Georgian village. The church and the abbey both border the river, but are not in fact linked visually or historically. The partly Norman church contains the fine C17th Hoby monuments; note particularly the one to Margaret Hoby, one of the most unusual monuments of that period. The abbey, built mainly in the C14th and C16th, was a private house from 1540. It is now a national recreation centre of the Central Council of Physical Recreation (see Sports below).
The post office and store is set back from the river. Nearby is the War Memorial, a wayside crucifix by Eric Gill, 1917.

Temple Mills
A paper mill. Park of the building dates from 1790, reputedly by Samuel Wyatt.

Marlow
Bucks. EC Wed MD Mon. A fine Georgian town dominated by the spire of All Saints Church. The suspension bridge, built by Tierny

Clark in 1831-6, has a marvellous view of the weir. The bridge was completely restored in 1966, and is now subject to a five ton weight restriction. The town has much to offer. Marlow Place, Station Road, was built in 1720,

All Saints, Marlow

perhaps by Archer; its monumental splendour is now rather decayed. Holy Trinity Church is by Gilbert Scott, 1852, and the Roman Catholic church is a surprisingly uninspired design by Pugin. The main street is dominated by the Crown Hotel, 1807, formerly the town hall. To the east of the town is a good modern housing development by J. Seymour Harris. White weatherboarding and an unusual and effective use of rooflines, inspired by traditional mill buildings.

Marlow Weir *W J Howes*

General shops, banks and post office.
Regal Cinema: Station Road.

Winter Hill
Dominating the river on the south bank, Winter Hill is the climax of a long stretch of beechwoods. It has one of the best views over the Thames Valley, and is well worth the steep walk.

Sport

Bisham Abbey
The centre is a hive of sporting activities where young players and coaches come together under the aegis of their respective governing bodies of sport. They train in the activity of their choice, ranging from archery to weight lifting. River activities feature strongly in the training programme. The facilities include five 'tennis quick' courts and a large sports field. Those interested in taking part in training should write to the headquarters of the CCPR, 26 Park Crescent, London WIN 4AJ.

Because of the special nature of the training, it is *not* possible for the centre to be opened for casual visitors or tourists.

Eating, drinking & accommodation

Burgers X
Marlow. The Causeway. Tel 3389. Continental confectioners, caterers. L 6s coffee and teas, *closes 18.00. Closed Sun.* No licence.

La Chandelle X ♥
Marlow. 55 High Street. Tel 2799. English, French and Spanish specialities. L 10s6d D 25s *until 22.15. Closed Mon and Sun D, Chistmas to Easter.* Parking.

Compleat Angler Hotel X ♥ BB
Marlow. Tel 4444. Izaac Walton wrote his Compleat Angler in this district. There is a lovely view from the hotel over the river and weir. 31 rooms BB 60s. English and Continental cooking. L 30s D 35s *until 21.30.* Parking.

Hare & Hounds X ♥
Marlow. Henley Road. Tel 3343. C16th inn. International cooking. LD 25s *daily until 22.30 Sun-Thur, 23.00 Fri-Sat.* Parking.

East Arms Hotel X ♥
Hurley. Tel 280. Built about 1700. International cooking with good snacks. L 22s6d, L Sun 27s6d. D a la carte *until 22.00. Closed Sun D and all Mon.* Dinner-dance Sat. Parking.

The Old Farmhouse X ♥ BB
Hurley. Tel 271. 5 rooms 30s. English cooking. D 12s6d *daily until 20.00.* Licensed. Gardens. Parking.

Ye Olde Bell Hotel X ♥ BB
Hurley. Tel 244/282. Built in 1135 as the guest house for the monastery; there is still a connecting underground passage. Fine Norman porch. 9 rooms BB 84s. International cooking. L 27s6d D a la carte, *daily until 22.30.* Parking.

YHA
Bradenham. The Village Hall, Bradenham, High Wycombe.

Camping

Harleyford Manor
Marlow. Tel 3578. Booking essential. No tents.
Hurley Farm
Hurley. On A423. Tel Maidenhead 301. Tent 2s. Caravans.

Boatyards

P. Freebody
Hurley. Mill Lane. Tel 382. Specialist boatbuilders.
Harleyford Estate
Marlow. Harleyford Marina. Tel 3578. Gas, water, mooring, non-mechanical repairs, caravans, lavatories, sewage and refuse disposal.
J. G. Meakes
Marlow. Thames Marine Store, Bridge Works. Tel 2364/2171/2. Petrol, oil, gas, water, open motor boats for day hire. Main distributors for Newage/B.M.C. and DAF marine engines; Chrysler/ Evinrude/Seagull outboard motors; and U.K. Concessionaires for Fjord and Saga boats. Chandlery.
Woottens
Cookham Dean, Quarry Wood Boatyard. Tel Marlow 4244. Launching.
Hurley Lock
Water.

Mooring
Hurley, by permission Harleyford Estates. Tel Marlow 3578.

Refuse disposal
Hurley Lock.
Harleyford Marina.

Public launching site
Marlow Lock.

Public lavatories
Hurley Lock, Temple Lock, Marlow Lock.

Public launching site
Marlow St Peter's Road.

Navigation
Maximum draught: Reading to Windsor 4ft6.

Bridges
Hurley Upper Footbridge, 13ft1.
Hurley Lower Footbridge, 14ft5.
Marlow Bridge, A404, 12ft8.

Locks
Hurley Lock, 130ft8 x 19ft11.
Temple Lock, 134ft7 x 17ft11.
Marlow Lock, 151ft3 x 19ft11.

Natural history
The beech *Fagus sylvatica*, is native to the chalky Chiltern Hills and yields a strong hardwood timber which is in steady demand for furniture making. The woods (about 25,000 acres), are controlled so that the harvest of 100-year-old trees does not leave ugly scars on the hillsides. Beech is easily recognised by its smooth grey bark, oval leaves and slender brown buds; it is particularly lovely in its early spring greens or its autumn russet shades.
On Marlow Gravel Pits on the north bank, great crested grebe breed. In summer there are many buntings, reed and sedge warblers. In autumn and winter, pochard, goosander, sandpiper and red-shank can be seen.
There are also butterflies, among which are the pearl-bordered fritillary, hedge brown, comma and the clouded yellow.
Otters have been recorded, but they are under such threat that no locality can be given. Among the flowers growing in this area are *Geranium columbinum* (long-stalked cranesbill) which has pinkish purple flowers on very fine, long stems. The slender pointed seed pods, like a bird's beak, give it the name cranesbill. *Daphne*

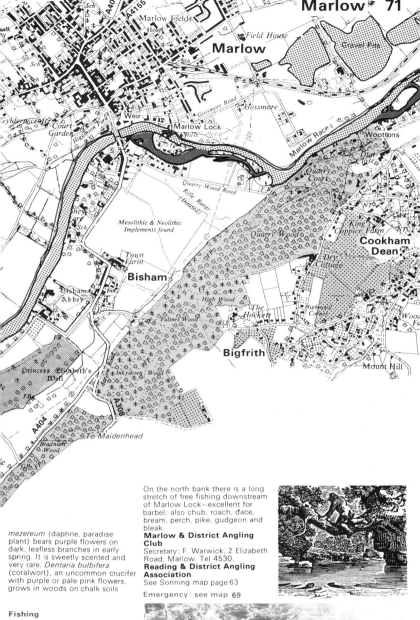

mezereum (daphne, paradise plant) bears purple flowers on dark, leafless branches in early spring. It is sweetly scented and very rare. *Dentaria bulbifera* (coralwort), an uncommon crucifer with purple or pale pink flowers, grows in woods on chalk soils

Fishing

On the north bank, the fishing rights from Temple Lock to the regatta enclosure near Marlow Bridge are held by the Marlow & District A.C., who also control a 50-acre lake at Marlow gravel pits. The Club headquarters is at the Chequers Hotel, but the waters are reserved for members except by arrangement. The river holds a good stock of chub, roach, dace, bream and barbel.
Marlow Weir is included on the Thames Conservancy permit.
At Bisham, Reading & District A.A. have a short stretch—3s for members' guests.
Weekend angling courses are sometimes organised by the Central Council for Physical Recreation at Bisham Abbey.
Free fishing is available to guests of the Compleat Angler Hotel (Marlow Weir pool is included)

On the north bank there is a long stretch of free fishing downstream of Marlow Lock—excellent for barbel; also chub, roach, dace, bream, perch, pike, gudgeon and bleak.

Marlow & District Angling Club
Secretary: F. Warwick, 2 Elizabeth Road, Marlow. Tel 4530.

Reading & District Angling Association
See Sonning map page 63

Emergency: see map **69**

R R Bolland

Places of interest

Bourne End
Bucks. EC Wed. A riverside commuter town famous as a sailing centre. General shops, banks, post office.

Hedsor
Bucks. A priory and an over-restored church on the hill. It is worth the walk up for the splendid views over the beechwoods.
Hedsor House was rebuilt in 1862 in an Italianate style.
Lord Boston's Folly, an C18th structure, faces the church from the opposite hill.

Cookham
Berks. EC Thur. An attractive, consciously preserved village famous as the home of Stanley Spencer. There is a permanent exhibition of his work in King's Hall. *Open Easter-Oct daily, winter Sat. Sun* 2s.
The iron bridge, built in 1867, overlooks the partly C12th church which contains fine C16th monuments. Spencer's 'Last Supper' painted in 1920, hangs in the church.
General shops and post office.

Cliveden
A most marvellous stretch of beechwoods from Hedsor to Maidenhead conceals the house.

Built by Sir Charles Barry in 1862 for the Astor family, it was the background to many C20th political intrigues and scandals ending with the Profumo case in 1963. Now owned by the National Trust it contains fine tapestries and furniture. *Open Apr-Sep, house 14.30-17.30, gardens Wed, Thur 11 00-18.00. Daily mid Aug-mid Sep.* House 2s6d, gardens 2s6d. The Canadian Red Cross Memorial Hospital is in the grounds.

Taplow
Bucks. Scattered high on the north bank. The church, in early C20th Gothic, contains unusually good brasses. Note also Nashdom, a house built by Lutyens in 1910. A few shops and post office.

Maidenhead
Berks. ED Thur MD Fri/Sat. A dormitory suburb of London, remarkable only for the architectural sterility of new development. All character has effectively been destroyed.
The town is best seen from the river. The beautiful balustraded

R R Bolland

bridge was built by Sir Robert Taylor in 1772-7. In the town there is an interesting group of church buildings by G. E. Street, built 1854-8. The splendid Edwardian police station, in red brick and terracotta, is by J. Morris & Son, 1906.
Excellent shopping centre, with banks and post office. Car park. Cinema: ABC, Bridge Avenue. Tel 23750.

Emergency: see map 74

Reitlinger Museum
Maidenhead. Guards Club Road.
Tel 21818. A miniature Victoria
and Albert Museum. *Open 10.00-
13.00, 14.00-16.30 Tue and Thur.*
Free.

Ray Mill Island
By Boulter's Lock. A public
pleasure garden with miniature
golf, public lavatories and telephone.

Sport

Maidenhead Regatta
On Sat before Autumn Bank
Holiday.

Swimming
Maidenhead. Market Street.
Outdoor, *open May-Sep.*
Odney Pool, by Cookham Lock.
For strong swimmers only.

Archaeology

Cookham
On Cook Marsh are five low
barrows, unusual survivors on the
flood plain of the river. Four were
opened in 1874, but little was
found save some cremated human
bones and a Saxon burial of later
date than the barrows themselves.
A fine Iron Age decorated dagger
with a bronze sheath, and a
Neolithic bowl were taken from
the river just below Cookham
Bridge. Both are in the British
Museum.

Hedsor
Large timbers found in the river
near here suggest that there may
have been a Roman Bridge at this
point, carrying the secondary road
from Silchester to St Albans.

Maidenhead
Palaeolithic finds have been made
in great numbers in this area
owing to the preservation of the
terraces of the Thames.
The largest hand-axe recorded in
Britain, 12½ inches long, was
discovered at Furze Platt; it is now
in the Natural History Museum.

Taplow
A rich pagan Saxon burial was
discovered in the barrow in the
grounds of Taplow Court in 1883.
It included weapons and shields,
drinking horns and other gold
finery. Most are now in the British
Museum.

Eating, drinking &
accommodation

Bear Hotel ✗ ⍨ BB
Maidenhead. High Street. Tel
25183. 12 rooms BB 45s. Good,
solid English fare with busy lunchtime buffet in Tyrol Bar. L 13s6d
D 15s6d *daily until 21.00 (Sat
21.30).*

Boulter's Lock Inn ✗ ⍨ BB
Maidenhead. Boulter's Lock. Tel
21291. Once an old mill, now
modernised; all bedrooms overlook the river. 14 rooms BB 50s.
International cooking. L 15s6d
D 21s *daily until 23.45.* Dancing
by candlelight nightly. Mooring,
fishing. Parking.

The Firefly ✗ BB
Bourne End. Tel 21197. 3 rooms
BB 35s. LD 17s6d until 21.30
Closed all Sun and Mon D.
Parking. No licence.

The King's Arms Hotel ✗ ⍨ BB
Cookham. Tel Bourne End 20146.
Has a Jacobean staircase with a
trip step. 6 rooms 40s. English
cooking. L 17s6d D 22s6d *until
20.30. Closed Mon.* Parking.

Kum Sam Chinese Restaurant ✗
Maidenhead. 71a High Street.
Tel 21670. Chinese and English
cooking. L 5s D *daily until 24.00.*
Hot meals (Chinese) to take away.

Red Lion ⍨ BB
Bourne End. Hedsor Road. Tel
21939. Friendly atmosphere in
this C16th inn. 4 rooms 27s6d.
Snack lunches at the bar. Bar

billiards and darts. Parking.

Riviera Hotel ✗ ⍨ BB
Maidenhead. The Bridge. Tel
25425. 36 rooms 48s6d. International cooking. L 15s D 21s
daily 21.30 (Sat 22.00). Mooring,
fishing. Parking.

Skindle's Hotel ✗ ⍨ BB
Maidenhead. Maidenhead Bridge.
Tel 25115. Attractive décor in this
riverside hotel. 13 rooms BB 60s.
International and English traditional cooking. L 25s (30s Sun).
D 37s6d (45s Sat) *daily until
22.30. Dancing nightly, tea
dances Sun.* Mooring (patrons
only). Garage, parking.

The Thames Hotel ✗ ⍨ BB
Maidenhead. Ray Mead Road.
Tel 28721. The dining room and
most of the bedrooms overlook the
river. 32 rooms BB 60s. English
and Continental cooking. L 17s6d
D 21s *daily until 22.30.* Garage,
parking.

Boatyards

Andrews' Boathouses
Bourne End. Hedsor Road. Tel
22314. Petrol, oil, gas, water,
cruisers and launches for hire,
mooring, repairs, agents for
Elysian and Seamaster; mooring
lavatories, sewage and refuse
disposal.

Andrews Bros.
Maidenhead. Ray Mead Road. Tel
24056. Cruisers and launches for
hire, repairs and renovations,
launching, mooring, storage.

Bert Bushnell
Maidenhead. Ray Mead Road.
Tel 24061. Petrol, oil, gas, water,
hire, launches and cruisers, repairs,
lavatories, refuse disposal.

Bourne End Marina
Bourne End. Tel 113/550. Petrol,
oil, gas, water, rowing boats, skiffs
and canoes on day hire, repairs,
agents for Elysian, Seamaster,
Freeman, Adamcraft, Mercedes
Benz (Marine Div), T. J. Cruisers;
lavatories, sewage and refuse
disposal, chandlery.

F. G. Emony
Maidenhead. Riverside Boatyard,
Ray Mead Road. Tel 20736.
Petrol, oil, gas, water; cruisers,
canoes, dinghies for hire, launch-
ing, mooring, chandlery.

W. J. Horsham & Son
Boulter's Lock Island. Petrol, oil,
motor boat hire, mooring.

Maidenhead Boat Services
Maidenhead. Ray Mead Road. Tel
24524. Oil, gas, water, cruiser
hire, repairs; agents for Johnson,
Crescent, Mercury, Seagull, Evinrude, Ailsa Craig. Mooring,
lavatories, chandlery.

Maidenhead Court Boathouse
Boulter's Lock. Tel Maidenhead
20723. Petrol, oil, gas, water;
cruisers and day launches for hire,
repairs, launching, mooring,
chandlery

Turk & Sons
Cookham. Ferry Boathouses. Tel
Bourne End 20110. Petrol, oil, gas,
water; day launches and small
boats for hire, repairs, moorings,
chandlery, camping, boatbuilders.

Boulter's Lock
Water.

Mooring
Boulter's Inn and Skindle's Hotel,
Maidenhead.
Above Cookham Bridge, south
bank. Bourne End, north bank.

Public launching slip
Cookham by Ferry Inn.

Refuse disposal
Boulter's Lock.

Navigation
Maximum draught: Reading to
Windsor 4ft6.

Bridges
Bourne End, Rail, 15ft6.
Cookham Bridge, A4095, 15ft2.

Cookham Foot Bridge, 12ft6.
Boulter's Lock Bridge, to
Ray Mill Island, 17ft3.

Locks
Cookham Lock, 183ft x 25ft.
Boulter's Lock, 199ft6 x 21ft3.

Natural history
In Cliveden Woods, which slope
for a mile to the water's edge, are
cuckoos, woodpeckers, tits,
warblers and nightingales. At
Taplow Court there is a heronry
near the river. At Cookham there
are flocks of fieldfares and redwings, winter visitors from Scan-
dinavia.
Many woodland flowers are to be
found in Cliveden Woods,
including bluebells. The bright
blue form of *Anagallis arvensis*
(scarlet pimpernel, poor man's
weather glass) has been found as
a garden weed in Taplow. The
flowers close in bad weather.
Myosotis scorpioides (water
forget-me-not) grows in the
marshes at Cookham.

Fishing
On the north bank the London
Anglers have fishing from opposite
Wootton's boathouse to Spade
Oak. Day tickets cost 3s for adults,
1s for juniors. There is a car park
at Spade Oak Farm, 2s6d.
On the opposite bank, the London
Anglers have a 300 yard stretch
downstream from Spade Oak.
From the Quarry Hotel Ferry to
Cookham Bridge on the south
bank, rights are held by the
Cookham & District A.C. Chub,
barbel, roach, dace, pike and the
occasional bream can be caught.
The Bourne End Community
Association Angling Club control
the fishing downstream from
Cookham Bridge to the weir at the
lower end of Cookham Lock on
the north bank.
The lock cutting and backwaters at
Cookham are held by the John
Lewis Angling Club. Chub, roach,
bream, dace, barbel, pike and
perch.
From the My Lady Ferry to
Boulter's Lock the fishing is free
on the south bank and the usual
species can be caught. Fishing is
also free from Boulter's Lock to
Maidenhead Bridge, but there are
few suitable swims.

Bourne End Community
Association Angling Club
Secretary: B. Spink, 70 Goddington
Road, Bourne End, Buckingham-
shire.

Cookham & District Angling
Association
Secretary: V. De'Ath, 38 Whyte-
ladyes Lane, Cookham Rise. Tel
Bourne End 22245.

London Anglers Association
See Lechlade map page 27

Tackle shops

J. Smith
Maidenhead. 4 High Street.
Tel 21038.

Emergency
Police: Broadway, Maidenhead
Tel 22311.
Hospital: St Luke's Hospital,
St Luke's Road, Maidenhead
Tel 20221.

Places of interest

Maidenhead Rail Bridge
The two beautiful arches, each 123ft long, are the largest brick-work spans in the world. Built 1839 by Brunel.

Bray
Berks. This section is dominated by the M4 motorway and the proximity of Slough. As a result there is much commuter development. Bray, surprisingly, still has a village centre. The well-preserved, largely C13th church is approached via a fine brick gatehouse of 1450. Simon Alwyn, the folk-heroic Vicar of Bray, held the living under Henry VIII, Edward VI, Mary and Elizabeth I. He is buried in the churchyard. Just outside the village is the Jesus Hospital, founded in 1627. There are alms-houses for twenty-six people who must be over fifty. A few shops and post office.

Ockwells Manor
About one mile SW of Bray. Built by Sir John Norreys between 1446 and 1466, it is one of the most elegant and refined timber-

framed buildings in England. A careful C20th restoration has left much original work. It contains a famous set of Armorial stained glass.

Monkey Island
Berks. On the island are the fishing lodge and pavilion of the Third Duke of Marlborough, built in 1744. Note the monkey paintings by Clermont. Now a hotel.

Down Place
A pretty C18th riverside mansion. Once the meeting place of the Kit Kat Club. Steele, Addison, Walpole and Congreve were members. Now rather decayed, it houses Bray Studios. Near by on the same bank is Oakley Court, a magnificent Victorian Gothic castle of 1859. All the elements of romantic

medievalism are present.

Dorney
Bucks. Buried among suburbia and C20th houses of all periods are Dorney Court and church. The court, all soft tudor brick, was built about 1500. Many subsequent restorations have not altered the original feeling of the house. The church forms a perfect unit with the court, and contains good work of all periods. Note the Norman font, the C17th woodwork and Garrard monument. There is a good modern stained glass window, 1965. Post office and stores.

Boveney
Bucks. A village scattered round a green. There are some over-restored tudor buildings, which still look good. A path by Boveney Place leads to the secluded river-side church. There are good walks all round.

Sport

Windsor Race Course
On an island opposite Boveney. Meetings in May, Jun, Aug, Sep, Oct.

Archaeology

Burnham
A hoard of 19 middle Bronze Age socketed axes was found in 1926 by Burnham Station (in Slough). As they were mainly damaged or broken, it was probably a metal founder's hoard.

Eating, drinking & accommodation

The Monkey Island Hotel   ✕ ♟
Bray. Tel Maidenhead 20849. The hotel is built on the island and has extensive gardens. French and English cooking. L21s D 32s6d *Sun-Thur.* D 37s6d *Fri.* D 47s6d *Sat. until 21.15. Dancing Wed-Sat.* Mooring. Parking.

Waterside Inn   ✕ ♟
Bray. Ferry Road. Tel Maidenhead 20691. The restaurant and terrace are beside the river. International cooking. LD 27s6d *until 22.00. Closed Sun D and all Mon. Dancing Sat.* Mooring, fishing. Parking.

Camping

Sunnybend Farm
Winkfield. Maidens Lane. 4 miles south of Windsor. Tel Winkfield Row 2846. Tent 7s6d.

Ivy Farm
Winkfield. Crouch Lane. Tel 2760. Caravans 5s.

Maidenhead Rail Bridge

Boatyards

Bray Marina
Bray. Monkey Island Lane. Tel
Maidenhead 23654. Petrol, oil,
gas, water, repairs, moorings,
storage, chandlery, boat sales,
lavatories, sewage and refuse
disposal for Marina customers
only, provisions, parking.

R. H. Messum
Bray. The Ferry. Tel Maidenhead
20567. Petrol, oil, gas, water;
fleet of cruisers and motor
launches for hire, mechanical
repairs, mooring, chandlery,
lavatories, sewage and refuse
disposal.

Willows Boat Services
Boveney. Maidenhead Road. Tel
Windsor 63768. Petrol, oil, gas,
water, cruiser hire, launching,
mooring, chandlery, provisions.

Boveney Lock
Water.

Mooring
Bray Marina
Willows Boat Services. Official
overnight mooring along towpath
above Boveney Lock.

Sewage & refuse disposal
Boveney Lock.
R. H. Messum.

Navigation

Maximum draught: Reading to
Windsor 4ft6.

Bridges

Maidenhead Bridge, A4, 18ft7.

Maidenhead Rail Bridge, 32ft2.
Motorway Bridge, M4, 25ft6.

Locks

Bray Lock, 134ft4 x 17ft11.
Boveney Lock, 149ft7 x 17ft10.

Ferry

R. H. Messum, Bray.

Natural history

There is a rookery at Dorney.
Pheasants and partridges are fairly
common.

Small damsel flies, bright metallic
blue or green, rest on reeds and
rushes, and larger dragonflies
hover over ponds.

On Dorney Common can be found
Trifolium fragiferum (strawberry
clover): the fruiting heads
resemble strawberries in both
shape and colour. Two of our
largest native grasses are common
by rivers: *Glyceria maxima* (great
reed grass) which stands up to
eight feet in height and has a
large head of flowers, and
Phragmites (reed), which can be
even taller, and has shaggy, silky
flower tassels of a soft purple
colour.

Carex riparia (great pond-sedge)
is also common in or by the water.
It is three feet or more high, and
has large dark-brown flower spikes
in early spring.

Bray Lock *R R Bolland*

Fishing

From Maidenhead Bridge there is
free fishing on the Buckinghamshire bank as far as Boveney Lock.
The Wall stretch, below the railway
bridge, is noted for its barbel,
dace, roach and occasional chub.
The Dorney Reach is good for
roach and dace. Maidenhead A.C.
have two short stretches downstream of Bray Lock on the south
bank from just above the motorway bridge to the mouth of the
Cut. Fishing tickets are available
for members' guests. Bray Weir is
included in the Thames Conservancy permit. The London Anglers
have a stretch on the south bank
opposite Queen Island. Chub and
roach fishing is particularly good
where the reach and the main
channel meet at either end of the
Island. T.C. permit covers Boveney
Weir. Downstream of Boveney
Lock free fishing extends along the
north bank through the Brocas

Meadow. Pike are caught in winter.
A short stretch on the south bank
upstream of Windsor Racecourse
is held by the Windsor A.C. —
containing the usual species. The
Race course stretch belongs to the
Civil Service A.S. On the north
bank fishing from Boveney to
Windsor Bridge is free. A Thames
record carp of 18lb 1oz was
caught at Windsor in 1894.

London Anglers Association

See Lechlade map page 27

Maidenhead Angling Club

Secretary: R. Henwood, 14
Cumbria Close, Maidenhead.
Tel 28402.

Windsor Angling Club

Secretary: Mr Joncy, 2 Bradshaw
Close, Windsor, Tel 61565.

**Civil Service Angling Associa-
tion**

Secretary: E. Cooper, 52 Brixton
Hill Court, SW2.

Tackle shops

R. Harding

Windsor, 6 St Leonards Road.

Emergency: see map 74

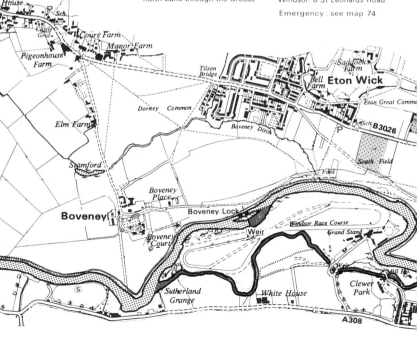

Emergency: see map 74

A331

Datchet

B376

Southlea

Sandled Court

Southlea Farm

Welley Farm

Double Cottages

Albert Bridge

Nickcroft Ait

Ham Fields

Ham Island

Old Windsor Weir

Works

Ham Bridge

Sunnymeads

Ham Lane

Manor Farm

Trafalgar Place

Oram House

The Tapestries

Pol Sta

The Manor

Works

Old Windsor Lock

Remenham House

Saxon Royal Palace (site of)

Ferry

Diana Farm

Nursery

Wd Pp

Nursery

Old Windsor

Hotel

Manor Farm Estate

THE GREEN

Wraysbury

Sch

Mill Buildings

Long Bridge

Burfield Lodge

Sand & Gravel Pits

Pelling Place

Woodside

RC College

Ferry

Runnymede House

A308 Runnymede

Priest Hill

Ankerwyke

B376

Sanatorium

To Virginia Water

To Sonninghill

To Egham

Remains of

School

Places of interest
Windsor
Berks. EC Wed MD Thur. Largely Victorian, the town owes its existence to Windsor Castle, both historically and visually. The castle, the largest and grandest in England, was first built by Henry II, 1165-79. Most succeeding monarchs have left their mark, notably Charles II, and Queen Victoria who spent over one million pounds on modernisation. The result is a fairy palace superbly sited up above the river, dominating the landscape for miles around. The building falls into three sections:
The Lower Ward
St George's Chapel, the finest

town hall, built by Wren in 1689-90 after a design by Sir Thomas Fitch, has the usual open ground floor. The ceiling is supported by four Tuscan columns which stop two inches short; a private joke of the architect's at the expense of a doubting mayor. To the west of the town there is a fine riverside park, with tennis courts, miniature golf and a swimming pool. All shops, banks, post office and parking.
Theatre Royal: Tel 61107. Repertory.
Cinema: Regal. Peascod Street.
Eton
Bucks. EC Wed. Separated from Windsor only by the Thames. Eton is essentially a single narrow High

Wraysbury
Bucks. After Datchet there is much bungaloid development along the north bank, culminating in Wraysbury, a small scattered village with little to offer. General shops and post office.
Ankerwyke
Built on the site of a Benedictine nunnery is Ankerwyke Priory, a low, early C19th mansion surrounded by trees; among them the Ankerwyke Yew whose trunk is 33ft in circumference.

Sport
Swimming
Windsor. Riverside Park.
Slough. Community Centre, Farnham Road. Tel 24508.
Slough. Slough Lido, Baylis House, Stoke Poges Lane. Tel 20339.

Cinemas
Slough. Granada, Windsor Road. Tel 21212.
Slough. Adelphi, Bath Road. Tel 20470.

Archaeology
Windsor
The original Saxon palace and settlement was at Old Windsor. The site was excavated in 1954-5.
Datchet
Mesolithic and Neolithic flint axes and Bronze Age tools and weapons have been dredged from the river opposite Datchet in fairly large numbers. Some are now in the Eton College Museum.

Eating, drinking & accommodation
Bells of Ouzeley X Ⴒ
Old Windsor. Tel 65179. Pleasant outlook over the river. English and Continental cooking, sea foods and cold meats. Extensive wine list. Buffet counter. LD a la carte *until 22.00. Closed Xmas.* Mooring. Parking.
Castle Hotel X Ⴒ BB
Windsor. High Street. Tel 61891, 65031. Georgian posting inn, modernised. International cooking and snacks. 41 rooms BB 56s. L15s D 18s6d *until 20.30 daily.* Resident dance band. Parking.
The Crown & Cushion Ⴒ BB
Eton. High Street. Tel Windsor 61531. Modernised 400 year old hotel. 9 rooms BB 30s. Hot snacks. Parking.
Donkey House Hotel Ⴒ BB
Windsor. Tel 60644. This was once a bargees' inn. 5 rooms BB 30s. Cold buffet lunches in summer. Snacks *until 21.30.* Mooring. Parking.
The House on the Bridge X Ⴒ
Eton. 71 High Street. Tel Windsor 60914. Italian and English cooking; background music. L 13s6d D 19s6d *until 22.30 daily.* Parking.
The Manor Hotel Ⴒ
Datchet. The Green. Tel Slough 43442. International cooking. Specialities: tournedos rossini and escalope 'Lavender'. LD a la carte *daily until 21.30, Sat until 22.00.* River garden.
The Old House Hotel X Ⴒ BB
Windsor. Thames Street. Tel 61354. 40 rooms BB 49s6d. Built and lived in by Wren in 1676. Cocktail and dining terrace overlook the Thames. French and English cooking. L 19s6d D 25s *daily until 21.15.* Mooring. Parking 2s6d a night.
Ye Harte & Garter Hotel X Ⴒ B
Windsor. High Street. Tel 63426. Opposite the main entrance to the castle. The hotel comprises a Grill room, Cellar Bar with pop music, Bierkeller and Coffee House, where hot meals (from 8s6d) are served all day. LD 16s6d *until 23.30, Sun 23.00.* Parking.

Windsor Castle from the air *Aerofilms*

example of Perpendicular architecture in the country. The Albert Memorial Chapel, built by Henry VII, and then turned into a Victorian shrine.
The Middle Ward
The Round Tower, with a panoramic view over a dozen counties.
The Upper Ward
The private apartments and the State Apartments containing a collection of paintings.
The castle is surrounded by parks; Home Park, borders on the river and contains Frogmore, built by

St George's Chapel / Eton College Chapel

Wyatt in 1792 out of an earlier house, and Royal Mausoleum. The Great Park, linked to the castle by the famous Long Walk, is 4800 acres in size; it extends as far as Virginia Water in the south. Admission: Castle precincts *10.00 until dusk daily. Free.* Sections open Apr-May 11.00-16.00 (Sun May 13.30-17.00), Jun-Sep 11.00-17.00 (Sun 13.30-17.00), Oct 11.00-16.00 (Sun 13.00-16.00), Nov-Mar 11.00-15.00. Closed Sun Nov-Mar and when the Queen is in residence. 2s to each section.
In the town there are buildings of all styles, most of them C19th. The church of St John the Baptist, in the High Street, built 1820-2. The three galleries are supported by delicate cast iron piers. The

Street with an inordinate number of antique shops. At the end of the street lies Eton College, founded by Henry VI in 1440. The buildings date from 1441 up to present day, and are dominated by the C15th chapel.
Admission: *term time 14.30-17.00. Holidays 10.30-12.30, 14.30-17.00. Closed Sun.*
Ceremonies: The Wall Game, The Glorious Fourth of June. All shops, including some traditional tailors, and post office.
Datchet
Bucks. EC Wed. Datchet is now buried in a large dormitory suburb, but the centre around the green still has a village feeling. General shops and post office.
Old Windsor
At first sight a misnomer, as Old Windsor seems to be nothing but an expanse of suburban development. However, the old village exists by the riverside, built around the site of a Saxon Royal Palace. The C13th church, hidden among trees, was restored by Gilbert Scott in 1863. To the right of the village lies Beaumont College, a Roman Catholic school established in 1861. The mansion was built by Henry Emlyn in 1790. General shops and post office.

YHA

Windsor. Edgeworth House, Mill Lane, Clewer. Tel Windsor 61710.

Camping

Willows Caravan Park
Windsor. Maidenhead Road. Tel 61785. Caravans. All year.

Boatyards

H. Chambers
Wraysbury. Ferry Lane. Tel 2051
Cruiser hire, launching, mooring.

Cooke's Boatyard
Wraysbury. Old Ferry Drive. Tel 2569. Petrol, oil, diesel, water, marine stores, launching, storage, provisions. Apr-Sep.

Crevalds Services
Old Windsor. 105 Straight Road. Tel Windsor 60393/4. Petrol, oil, gas, water, repairs, launching, mooring, chandlery, lavatories, sewage and refuse disposal.

John Hicks Boatyard
Datchet. The Waterfront. Tel Slough 43930. Gas, water, cruisers for hire, boat building and sales, mechanical repairs, mooring, chandlery.

H. Hill & Son
Windsor. 120 Oxford Road. River trips.

Golding Bros.
Windsor. No. 4 Arch, Goswell Hill. Tel 65468. Rowing and motor boats, camping boats for hire and passenger craft, chandlery. Good Fri-end Oct.

Tom Jones
Windsor. Romney Lock Boathouse. Tel 60699. Oil, gas, repairs, mooring, chandlery.

Waterways Hire Service
Windsor. Goswell Hill. Tel 65739. Day hire.

Old Windsor Lock
Water.

Mooring

Wraysbury
Crevalds Services, Cooke's Boatyard.

Datchet
John Hick's Boatyard.

Windsor
C. Hill & Son.
The Old House Hotel, Windsor. Also baths for river users 5s, above Romney Lock, 2s6d a day.

Public launching slip

On the promenade above Windsor Bridge. Apply to the car park attendant.

Sewage & refuse disposal

Crevalds Services.

Navigation

Maximum draught:
Reading to Windsor 4ft6.
Windsor to Staines 5ft6.

Bridges

Windsor By-pass Bridge links with M4, 20ft6.
Windsor Rail Bridge, 17ft9.
Windsor Bridge, A332, 13ft2.
Black Potts Rail Bridge, 19ft6.

Victoria Bridge, A331, 20ft3.

Albert Bridge, A328, 18ft8.
Old Windsor Lock Cut Bridge, to Ham Island, 14ft3.

Locks

Romney Lock, 132ft10 x 18ft1.
Old Windsor Lock, 179ft5 x 24ft2.

Ferry

By the Bells of Ouzeley, Old Windsor. *Summer only.*

Natural history

In Windsor Great Park there has been a starling roost for over 100 years. Hawfinches, nightingales and redstarts breed, and there is a small heronry at Fort Belvedere, where large flocks of wintering fieldfares can be seen. There is a roost for over 1000 black headed gulls; waxwings are occasional winter visitors and crossbills breed here from time to time. On Virginia Water (at the southern end of Windsor Park) mandarin ducks breed freely and flocks number more than 150. They come from the Far East and are not yet on the British list, although here they are well established. Ducks which breed here include pochard, shoveller and teal. The occasional bittern, ring ouzel and black tern can be seen. There is a heronry at Wraysbury, and at Winkworth, Canada geese flock in large numbers. Dabchick breed on the gravel pits. Siskins winter here. Permits are required to visit the Wilkinson Bird Sanctuary at Eton and also the marshy area of Ham Island Bird Sanctuary at Windsor.
Ham Island bird sanctuary covers 100 acres and one can observe Canada goose, plover, sandpiper and dunlin. Permits from the Warden, 24 Queens Close, Old Windsor.
Ophioglossum vulgatum (adder's tongue) is a fern which grows in Windsor Great Park, also *Scutellaria minor* (lesser skullcap), an uncommon little pink relative of the familiar blue one which grows by the river.

Fishing

At Windsor, on the north bank, free fishing extends through the Brocas Meadow. The fishing on the backwater which rejoins the Thames at this point is held by the Salthill A.S. Here the Thames is noted for dace, chub, roach, perch, gudgeon and the occasional carp.
In Windsor Great Park, Virginia Water and the smaller ponds are fishable on season permits obtainable from the Deputy Ranger. The fishing is for roach, rudd, tench, carp, pike and perch. Romney Weir, downstream from Windsor Bridge, can be fished on a Thames Conservancy permit. Below the weir the fishing is free from Romney Island and the Lock cutting as well as along the recreation ground on the south bank as far as Victoria Bridge.
From Datchet on the north bank the Civil Service A.C. have a 1½ mile stretch from above Albert Bridge to below Old-Windsor Weir. The south bank from Albert Bridge to Old Windsor Weir is held by the Old Windsor A.C. T.C. permit covers Old Windsor Weir. The Thames record gudgeon of 4¼oz was caught at Datchet in 1933. There is free fishing in the Runnymede meadows downstream to Runnymede road bridge. Between the bridge and Bell Weir Lock it is good for barbel. At Wraysbury on the north bank two gravel pits are available to holders of the Hall Angling permit.

Civil Service Angling Association
See Bray map page 77

Crown Estate Office
The Great Park, Windsor. Tel 602. Apply to the Deputy Ranger.

Hall Angling Scheme
See Wargrave map.

Old Windsor Angling Club
Secretary: A. Heather, Newton Lane, Old Windsor.

Salthill Angling Society
Secretary: H. Cownley, Greatlands Crescent, Maidenhead. Tel 29191.

Tackle shops

R. Harding
Windsor. 6 St Leonards Road.

Emergency: see map 74

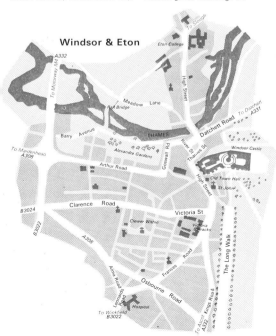

Windsor & Eton

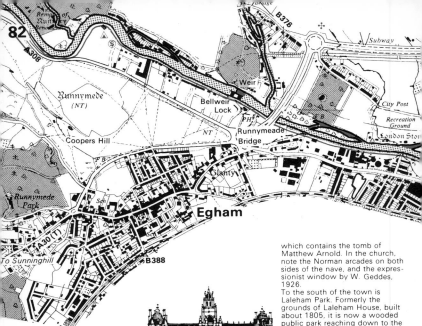

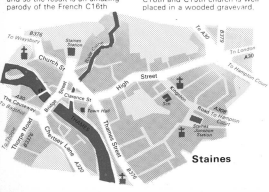

Places of interest

Runnymede

Surrey. Beside the river on the south bank is Runnymede, a stretch of parkland backed by Cooper's Hill. The paired gate-houses, by Lutyens, introduce an area of memorials. The inspiration is the sealing of the Magna Carta in 1215. On top of the hill is the Commonwealth Air Forces Memorial. This quadrangular structure, built by Sir Edward Maufe, 1953, perfectly exploits its situation. Below are the Magna Carta Memorial and the Kennedy Memorial, the latter built on an acre of ground given to the American people. There are many good walks. The area is owned by the National Trust. *Parking summer only.* 1s6d.

Egham

Surrey. EC Thur. A characterless town set back from the river. The most imposing structure is the Gas Works, London Road, built in 1928; an interesting piece of industrial architecture. All shops, banks, post office. Parking.

Royal Holloway College

West of Egham. Built by W. H. Crossland in 1879-87 for Thomas Holloway, to celebrate the success of Holloway's Pills. The mansion is based on Chambord on the Loire and so the result is an amazing parody of the French C16th

Renaissance style. The building is successful because of Crossland's decorative skill and because of his total belief in his ability to carry out so unlikely a project. The sky-line and the front (on A30) are the most impressive elements.

Staines

Bucks. EC Thur MD Wed/Sat. A commuter town which has expanded hugely over the last thirty years. However, the area around the pleasantly situated church has remained virtually unchanged. Clarence Street, which culminates in Rennie's stone bridge, built 1829-32, still has the feeling of a C18th market town. Just above the bridge stands the London Stone. This marks the former limit of the jurisdiction of the City of London over the Thames.
Staines is surrounded by the huge reservoirs of the Metropolitan Water Board.
All shops, banks, post office. Parking.
Cinema. ABC Clarence Road.

Laleham

Middx. The first impression of Laleham is one of bungalows and houseboats. The village does not exploit the river at all, and the centre lacks the riverside feeling of some Middlesex towns. The C18th and C19th church is well placed in a wooded graveyard,

which contains the tomb of Matthew Arnold. In the church, note the Norman arcades on both sides of the nave, and the expressionist window by W. Geddes, 1926.
To the south of the town is Laleham Park. Formerly the grounds of Laleham House, built about 1805, it is now a wooded public park reaching down to the river.
Public lavatories and parking.
A few shops and post office.

Sport

Staines. Amateur Regatta is held *in July.*

Archaeology

Staines

A Neolithic causewayed camp, an enclosure with roughly circular interrupted ditches, was excavated in 1961-2. Such camps are usually found on the chalk downs, and not low down in the valley.
Staines, the Roman town of Pontes, grew up around the river crossing point of the Roman road from London to Salisbury and the west.
There are the remains of a Roman bath south of the High Street.

Laleham

Excavation of gravel pits around Laleham has revealed Iron Age, Roman and Saxon settlements.

Eating, drinking & accommodation

Angel ✗ ♟ BB
Staines. High Street. Tel 52509. 11 rooms BB 40s. English cooking, buffet and snacks. L 11s6d D 13s6d *daily until 21.00.* Parking.

Anglers Hotel ✗ ♟ BB
Egham. Runnymede. Tel 3544. A Thames-side situation. 12 rooms BB 45s. International cooking. L 12s6d *daily until 22.30.* Dinner-dance *Sat until 24.00.*

Great Fosters ✗ ♟ BB
Egham. Stroude Road. Tel 3822. An outstanding example of a brick C16th house, built on an older site. Moat, formal gardens. Splendid antique furniture and hangings. 26 rooms BB from

52s6d. English and Continental cooking, buffet and snacks. L 21s D 25s *daily until 21.30. Sat 22.00* with dinner-dance. Heated swimming pool, hard tennis court. Garage, parking.

Staines

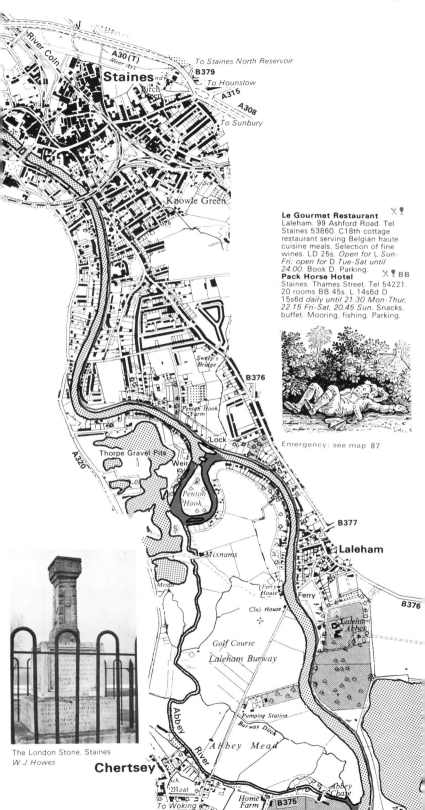

To Staines North Reservoir

To Hounslow

To Sunbury

Le Gourmet Restaurant ✗ ▾
Laleham. 99 Ashford Road. Tel
Staines 53860. C18th cottage
restaurant serving Belgian haute
cuisine meals. Selection of fine
wines. LD 25s. *Open for L Sun-
Fri; open for D Tue-Sat until
24.00.* Book D. Parking. ✗ ▾ B B
Pack Horse Hotel
Staines. Thames Street. Tel 54221.
20 rooms BB 45s. L 14s6d D
15s6d *daily until 21.30 Mon-Thur,
22.15 Fri-Sat, 20.45 Sun.* Snacks,
buffet. Mooring, fishing. Parking.

Emergency: see map 87

The London Stone. Staines
W J Howes

Penton Hook Weir *R R Bolland*

Camping

F. Nicholes & Sons
Egham. Tel 2342.
Laleham Park
Apply on site.
Penton Hook Lock.

Boatyards

Biffens Boathouse
Staines. Punts and motor boats for hire. Boatbuilder.
Marine Trimming Co
Penton Hook Yacht Basin. Staines Lane. Tel Chertsey 3779. Tailor-made boathoods, covers, etc. Service at your moorings.
Maratime Motors
Chertsey. Penton Hook Marina, Staines Lane. Tel 4224. Mechanical repairs, Perkins' diesel distributors London-Oxford, agents for Evinrude, Seagull, Avon Campari; chandlery.
F. Nicholes & Sons
Egham. Runnymede Boathouse. Tel 2342. Motor and rowing boats for hire, non-mechanical repairs, moorings, camping.
Penton Hook Marina
Chertsey. Staines Lane. Tel 2145, 2661. Petrol, oil, gas, water, boat sales and brokerage, repairs, launching, mooring, storage, chandlery, lavatories, sewage and refuse disposal, parking, licensed clubhouse, hot showers, provisions.
J. Tims & Sons
Staines. The Boathouse. Tel 52093. Petrol, oil, gas, water, cruisers for hire, repairs, launching, mooring, chandlery, lavatories, sewage and refuse disposal.
Penton Hook Lock
Water.

Mooring

Egham
Anglers Hotel.
Chertsey
Penton Hook Marina.
Staines
J. Tims & Sons.
Pack Horse Hotel.
Swan Hotel.
Near Staines Town Hall steps.

Sewage & refuse disposal

Penton Hook Marina. Customers only.
J. Tims & Sons. Customers only.

Refuse disposal

Bell Weir Lock.

Public lavatories

Bell Weir Lock.
Penton Hook Marina.
Laleham Park.
By Staines Town Hall steps.

Navigation

Maximum draught:
Windsor to Staines 5ft6.
Staines to Teddington 6ft6.
Bridges
Runnymede Bridge, Staines By-pass, 23ft.

Staines Bridge, A30, 19ft6.
Staines Rail Bridge, 21ft.
Locks
Bell Weir Lock, 132ft5 x 18ft.
Penton Hook Lock, 266ft8 x 24ft10.
Ferry
Laleham.

Natural history

Dabchick breed in Thorpe Gravel Pits, and common sandpiper and turtle doves are often heard. Collared doves can be found near Staines. Metropolitan Water Board reservoirs in the London area have huge populations of rousting gulls; there are 7,000 at Staines. Duck counts on all reservoirs total over 5,000.
At Staines there is a small colony of coypu, a large rodent kept formerly for the production of nutria fur, now living wild.
At Laleham there are numerous red admiral, small tortoiseshell and large white butterflies in July and August on sedum flowers. *Veronica filiformis*, an introduced speedwell with sky blue flowers on thread-like stems, carpets the grass banks in May and June. At Runnymede meadows *Primula veris* (cowslip) flowers.

Fishing

Between Bell Weir Lock and Staines Bridge there is excellent free fishing for barbel, bream, chub, roach, dace and gudgeon. Bell Weir, which holds trout, can be fished on a TC Permit. Downstream of Staines Bridge there is free fishing on all accessible banks. The Colne is good for dace, small chub, gudgeon and bleak.
The island at Penton Hook is popular and the fishing is rewarding and free through to Chertsey Lock for the usual species.
The swims by the reservoir intake at Laleham can produce good chub, barbel, bream and roach. Laleham Green is overcrowded in the summer and the best fishing is in the early autumn.
Staines North Reservoir is held by the London Anglers, Staines South Reservoir is held by the Civil Service A.S. and both are noted for big roach, bream, perch and pike.

London Anglers Association
See Lechlade map.

Tackle shops

Johnson & Clarke's (Tackle Dept)
Staines, High Street.

Places of interest
Chertsey
Surrey. EC Wed MD Sat. From the river the first sight of Chertsey is James Paine's rather uneasy stone bridge of 1780-2. This sets the pattern for the town which just manages to retain a feeling of the C18th. This is particularly true of the area around Windsor Street, which runs past the site of the abbey. Today nothing remains of what was one of the greatest abbeys in England. Founded in 666, rebuilt during the C12th, it was finally destroyed during the Reformation. It is likely that materials from the abbey were used in the construction of Hampton Court. In the town centre the large and airy church is mostly C19th. The interior is painted in pleasing Adamesque colours. Next to the church is the Italianate Town Hall, now a local museum. *Open 16.00-17.00 weekdays, 11.00-13.00 Sat. Closed Wed.* All shops, banks, post office.

Weybridge
Surrey. EC Wed. A commuter town rich in 'stockbroker' tudor. It is built around the confluence of the River Wey and the Thames. The junction is marked by a pretty iron bridge of 1865. Weybridge represents the frontier of the suburbia that now spreads almost unbroken to London.
Behind Weybridge lay Brooklands, the doyen of motor racing circuits in the early C20th. It is now an aircraft factory, but part of the legendary banking of the track can still be seen from the London-Portsmouth railway.
All shops, banks, post office.

Shepperton
Middx. Recognisable from the river by the lawns of the C19th Manor House, Shepperton is a surprising village survival. The square contains a number of relatively intact C18th inns. The church, with its fine brick tower, was built in the C17th and C18th. Note the box pews. To the north of the church is the rectory, which has an excellent Queen Anne front of about 1700.
General shops and post office.

Walton-on-Thames
Surrey. EC Wed. The river approach to Walton is lined with horrific tin and wood shacks on the north bank. These decide the shape of the town, a huge straggling shopping centre of little merit. However, Roubiliac's huge monument to Viscount Shannon is worth a visit. Erected in 1755, it wholly dominates the church. There is much new development, but only the multi-storey car park has any quality. The new Town Hall breaks all records for civic anti-architecture. The C19th bridge can no longer bear heavy loads, and so is accompanied by a permanently temporary steel structure alongside. All shops, banks, post office.

Conway Stakes
A stretch of parkland to the west of Walton Bridge. It is a famous courting area, but, being marshy, many a night of passion has ended with a bogged down car and muddy feet!

Sunbury
Middx. EC Thur. The appearance of the riverside at Sunbury suggests that Middlesex cares more about the river than Surrey. Perhaps the north bank has always been more socially desirable. Sunbury has a pleasant village feeling, but the parish church is a C19th disaster. Sunbury Court, the grand mansion of the town, was built in 1770. It is now the Salvation Army Youth Centre. General shops and post office.

Sport
Enterprise School of Sailing
Sunbury. 95 Kenton Avenue. Tel 83834. Individual, practical sailing instruction based on eight one-hour lessons.
Associated coastal sailing course. *Weekdays and week-ends. Closed Tue.*
Swimming
Walton. Kings Road. Tel 22984.
Sunbury. 1 Rivermead. Tel 83194.

Archaeology
Shepperton
War Close. So named because of the finds of human bones, swords and spears from a Saxon burial ground.
Walton
A Saxon cemetery was discovered in 1750 on Walton Bridge Green.

Eating, drinking & accommodation
The Anchor Hotel ✕
Shepperton. Church Square. Tel Walton 21618. International cooking and snacks. LD 18s grill, 25s restaurant, *daily until 21.45.* Licensed. Parking.
Ashley Park Hotel ✕ ♥ BB
Walton. Tel 20196. 8 rooms BB 42s6d. L from 10s6d, D from 14s6d *daily until 21.00 Sun-Thur, 21.30 Fri-Sat.* Parking.
Oatlands Park Hotel ✕ ♥ BB
Weybridge. Oatlands Drive. Tel 47242. Built on the site of a royal palace, this hotel offers every luxury. English cooking. 160 rooms BB 53s6d. LD 18s6d *daily until 2.00.* Table licence only. Golf course, swimming pool, bowls, squash racquets, games room, children's playground. Ladies hairdresser. Garage, parking.
The Ship Hotel ✕ ♥ BB
Weybridge. Tel 48364/6. Parts of the hotel date from C16th, but most of it is modern. 16 rooms BB 70s. English and French cooking, buffet lunches in the bar. L 15s6d D a la carte, *daily until 22.00.* Parking.
The Swan Hotel ✕ ♥ BB
Walton. Manor Road. Tel 20326. 10 rooms 30s. Bar lunches; D residents only. Mooring, fishing. Parking.
Thames Court Hotel ✕ ♥ BB
Shepperton. Tow Path, Ferry Lane. Tel Walton 21957. This hotel, which overlooks Shepperton Lock, has some Delft tiling. 8 rooms BB 42s6d. French cooking. L 13s6d (Sun 15s) D a la carte, *until 21.30. Closed to non-residents D Sun, Mon.* Mooring. Parking.
The Weir Hotel ✕ ♥
Walton. Sunbury Lane, Towpath. Tel Sunbury 84530/82078. The cocktail bar overlooks the river. International cooking. LD from 15s *until 22.00. Closed Sun.* Mooring, fishing, shove halfpenny. Parking.

Boatyards
W. Bates & Son
Chertsey. Bridge Wharf. Tel 2255/6, 5600. Petrol, oil, gas, water, cruisers for hire, repairs, mooring, chandlery, launching, lavatories, sewage and refuse disposal, yacht brokerage.
Bridge Marine Services
Walton Bridge. Tel 24407. Gas, repairs, mooring, launching, builders, surveys.
Horace Clark & Son
Sunbury. Vjer Line Cruisers, Thames Street. Tel 82028. Petrol, oil, gas, water, diesel, cruisers and launches for hire, repairs, mooring, chandlery.
Geo. R. Dunton & Co.
Shepperton. Ferry Lane. Tel Walton 21378. Oil, gas, water, repairs, launching, mooring, chandlery.
Eyot House
Weybridge. D'Oyley Carte Island. Tel 48586. Repairs, mooring, launching, chandlery, insurance, flats, towage.
Kenneth M. Gibbs & Co.
Shepperton. Sandhills. Tel Walton 20926. Gas, mooring, non-mechanical repairs, chandlery, boat builders. Parking.
Meads Cruisers
Chertsey. The Meads. Tel 3803, for moorings Tel 4699. Mooring, launching, cruisers, launches and dinghies for hire, agents for Colvic fibreglass hulls, engine installation, repairs, chandlery, storage.
Old Ferry Boatyard
Shepperton. Tel Walton 23013. Gas, water, cruiser and launch hire, repairs, mooring, launching, yacht brokerage, insurance, 24 hour service.
James Taylor Yacht Co.
Walton. Tow Path. Tel 23600. Oil, gas, motor boat and cruiser hire, repairs, agents for Ailsa Craig, launching, mooring, chandlery, boat transport and trailer hire.
Weybridge Marine
Weybridge. Tel 47453. Petrol, oil, diesel, water, gas, boat hire, boat builders, mooring, launching.
George Wilson & Sons (Boatbuilders)
Sunbury. Thames Street. Tel 82067, 82954. Gas, water, fishing punts and dinghy hire, launching, mooring, repairs.

Emergency: see map 87

Above Chertsey Lock *R R Bolland*

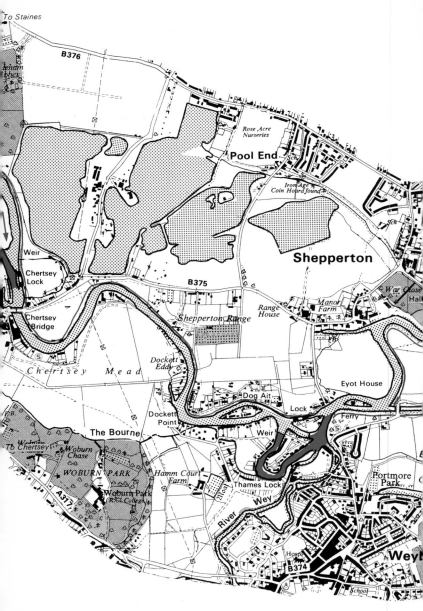

To Staines

B376

Rose Acre Nurseries

Pool End

Iron Age Coin Hoard found

Shepperton

Weir

Chertsey Lock

B375

Chertsey Bridge

Shepperton Range

Range House

Manor Farm

War Close

C h e r t s e y   M e a d

Dockett Eddy

Eyot House

Dog Ait

Lock

Dockett Point

The Bourne

Weir

Ferry

Tb Chertsey

Woburn Chase

WOBURN PARK

Woburn Park R.C. College

Thames Lock

Eyot House

Portmore Park

Hamm Court Farm

Wey

River

Wey

A317

B374

School

Hosp

Shepperton Lock
Water.
Sunbury Lock
Water.

Mooring
Chertsey
W. Bates & Son
Meads Cruisers.
Sunbury
Horace Clark & Son.
George Wilson & Sons.
Weir Hotel.
Along towpath below Sunbury
Lock.
Shepperton
Old Ferry Boatyard.
Geo. R. Dunton & Co.

Walton
Towpath at Swan Inn.
James Taylor Yacht Co.
Weybridge
Weybridge Marine.
Official overnight mooring along
towpath at Weybridge (opposite
Shepperton Lock).

Sewage & refuse disposal
W. Bates & Son, Chertsey.
Shepperton Lock.

Refuse disposal
Chertsey Lock.

Public lavatories
Shepperton Lock.
Sunbury Lock.

Old Ferry Yard, Shepperton.
Weybridge Marina, Weybridge.
Anglers Hotel, Walton.
Thames Street, Weybridge.

Navigation
Maximum draught: Staines to
Teddington 6ft6.
River Wey is navigable as far as
Godalming. Apply River Wey
Navigation, Friday Street, Guild-
ford Wharf, Weybridge.
Bridges
Chertsey Bridge, B375, 19ft1.

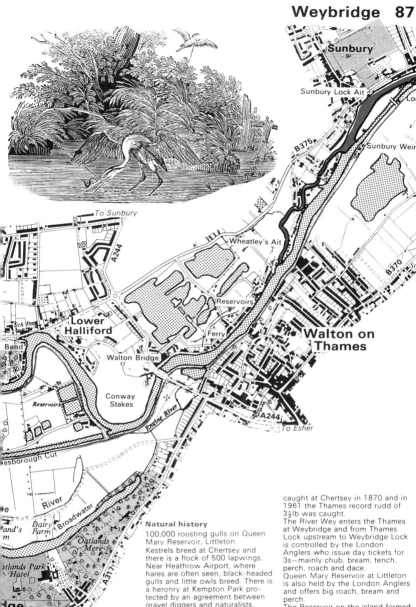

Natural history

100,000 roosting gulls on Queen Mary Reservoir, Littleton. Kestrels breed at Chertsey and there is a flock of 500 lapwings. Near Heathrow Airport, where hares are often seen, black-headed gulls and little owls breed. There is a heronry at Kempton Park protected by an agreement between gravel diggers and naturalists. *Iris pseudacorus* (wild iris, flag) and *Typha latifolia* (great reedmace) grow in ditches near Walton Bridge, as does *Impatiens capensis* (orange balsam), a plant from the eastern part of North America. This plant was first recorded in Britain in 1822 by the river Wey. Its American name is jewel weed. It is doubtful whether *Geranium pyrenaicum* (mountain cranesbill) is a native plant. It was first recorded in 1762, and comes from the Pyrenees. It has magenta flowers and can be found all along the banks below Walton Bridge.

Fishing

Almost all the fishing on the main river is free in this area and on as far as London.
Between Chertsey Lock and bridge there are some good roach swims. Shepperton weir is on T.C. permit.
The record trout of 14lb 9oz was caught at Chertsey in 1870 and in 1961 the Thames record rudd of 3½lb was caught.
The River Wey enters the Thames at Weybridge and from Thames Lock upstream to Weybridge Lock is controlled by the London Anglers who issue day tickets for 3s—mainly chub, bream, tench, perch, roach and dace.
Queen Mary Reservoir at Littleton is also held by the London Anglers and offers big roach, bream and perch.
The Reservoir on the island formed by the Desborough Cut, near Walton, is owned by the Woking & District Water Company. The cut fishes well for chub, bream, roach, dace, perch and pike.
From Walton Bridge down to the Angler's Hotel can also be rewarding. An eel of 6½lb was caught in 1966.

London Anglers Association
See Lechlade map page 27
Thames Conservancy
See Kelmscott map page 29

Tackle Shops

H. Robson
Chertsey. 93 Guildford Street.
Walton Tackle
Walton. 15 Bridge Street.

Emergency
Police. New Zealand Avenue, Walton on Thames. Tel 21314
Hospital. Walton on Thames Hospital, Sidney Road. Tel 20060

Desborough Cut Upper Bridge, 17ft.
Desborough Cut Lower Bridge, 17ft.
Walton Bridge, A244, 18ft3.
Sunbury Lock Cut Footbridge, 19ft6.

Locks
Chertsey Lock. Keep close to north bank. 200ft8 x 21ft.
Shepperton Lock, 174ft5 x 19ft10.
Sunbury Locks:
154ft8 x 19ft3. Old lock.
206ft x 24ft4. New lock.

Desborough Cut
Opened in 1935, the canal cuts off Shepperton. The old main stream is still navigable.

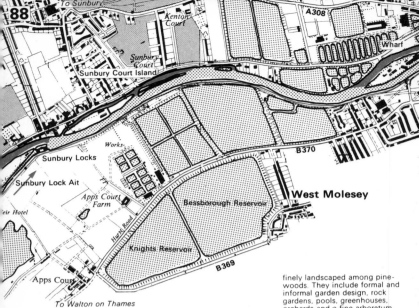

To Sunbury
To Walton on Thames

Kenton Court

Sunbury Court

Sunbury Court Island

Works

Sunbury Locks

Sunbury Lock Ait

Apps Court Farm

Knights Reservoir

Bessborough Reservoir

West Molesey

eir Hotel

Apps Court

A308

Wharf

B370

B369

Hurst Road

Places of interest

West and East Molesey
Surrey. Named after the River Mole which joins the Thames opposite Hampton Court.
The least attractive area on the Thames, a characterless sprawl that makes no use of the river whatsoever. The lack of civic enterprise is epitomised by the new Hurst Park estate. This drab new slum, built on the old race course, has destroyed a potentially exciting riverside area.
General shops and post office.

Hampton
Middx. EC Wed. An attractive late C18th village whose heart remains intact despite much new development.
The riverside is dominated by the church, built 1831 by Lapidge. It contains a good modern window by Eric Fraser. Despite the proximity of Hampton Court, the village owes its existence to Hampton House. Bought by David Garrick in 1754, the house was subsequently altered by Adam.
By the river is Garrick's Temple, built to house Roubiliac's bust of Shakespeare. Nearby, the incongruous Swiss chalet owned by Hucks and Son really is Swiss; it was brought over in 1899.
To the west of the town the river bank is taken up by the Metropolitan Water Board. The buildings range in style from impressive official Italianate of 1853 to plain C20th brick.
General shops and post office.

Chessington Zoo
Leatherhead Road, Chessington, Surrey. Tel Epsom 27227. A zoo of 65 acres 5 miles south of East Molesey. Most animals are on show in pleasantly free and open surroundings. *Open 9.30-dusk.* 5s (2s6d in winter).

Hampton Court
Probably the greatest secular building in England. Cardinal Wolsey, son of an Ipswich butcher, was graced by ambition and ability to such an extent that at the age of forty he had an income of £100,000 a year. He was thus able to build the grandest private house in England. Work began in 1514. Henry VIII was offended by the

unashamed ostentation of his lieutenant. In 1529 he caused Wolsey's downfall, and took over

the house. Henry spent more on Hampton Court than on any other building, establishing it as a Royal Palace. Subsequently Wren added to it, but little work has been done since.
Unlike Windsor, Hampton Court survived the C19th relatively intact. Today it is occupied by 45 Royal pensioners.
In the formal gardens are the Great Vine, planted in 1769, and the Maze which is rather broken down and disappointing now. *Open May-Sep 9.30-18.00 (Sun from 11.00), Nov-Feb 9.30-16.00 (Sun from 14.00), Mar-Apr 9.30-17.00 (Sun from 14.00).* 2s6d.
Behind the palace is Bushey Park, enclosing 2000 acres. A formal park reminiscent of Versailles, it is famous for deer.

Hampton Green
A fine series of buildings round the green. Most are C18th, but some are earlier. Seen together they make a pleasing whole.
By the green is Hampton Court Bridge, built by Lutyens in 1933.

Thames Ditton
Surrey. The centre of this unspoilt riverside village has somehow kept at bay the usual careless development of the Surrey bank. The church is in the midst of an excellent graveyard and garden where the peace is only broken by the eternal jets from Heathrow. Inside are several good brasses. The huge pendulum of the tower clock swings exceedingly slowly and exceedingly loudly, guaranteed to throw any vicar out of his stride. By the river there are some pretty whitewashed houses around the suspension bridge to Thames Ditton Island.
General shops and post office.

Wisley Gardens
The gardens of the Royal Horticultural Society are situated ten miles from Hampton Court, off the A3. Covering 156 acres beside the River Wey, they have been

finely landscaped among pinewoods. They include formal and informal garden design, rock gardens, pools, greenhouses, orchards and a fine arboretum. *Open 10.00-19.30 or sunset. Closed Sun.* 3s6d. Restaurant in summer.

Sport

Molesey Regatta
Held in mid-June.

Kempton Park
Race Meetings are held in Feb, Mar, Nov, Dec.

Swimming
Hampton. High Street. Tel (01) 979 2599. Open air pool, *open summer only.*
Teddington. Vicarage Road. Tel Teddington Lock 5157. Open air pool, *open summer only.*

Eating, drinking & accommodation

Albany Hotel ♥ ✕ BB
Thames Ditton. Queens Road. Tel (01) 398 1747. 6 rooms BB 30s. Grills *Mon-Fri* L, snacks. Mooring. Parking.

The Greyhound Hotel ✕ ♥ BB
Hampton Court. Hampton Court Road. Tel (01) 977 1878/3831. Near Hampton Court Palace. 22 rooms BB 48s. English cooking. LD 15s, *daily. Restaurant until 20.15,* grills *until 22.30.* Garage, parking.

The Mitre Hotel ✕ ♥ BB
Hampton Court. Tel (01) 979 2264. Built about 1665 to house some of the courtiers of King Charles II. 7 rooms BB 70s. International cooking, all meals à la carte. LD *daily until 24.00.* Parking.

Queen's Arms Hotel ✕ ♥ BB
Hampton Court. Tel (01) 977 3998. 15 rooms BB 38s6d. International cooking, and snacks at the bar. D 15s6d *until 23.00. Closed Sun, Mon.*

The Swan ♥
Hampton Wick. 22 High Street. Tel (01) 977 1445. Opposite Cardinal Wolsey's cottage. Snacks large and varied wine cellar. Parking.

The Tudor Rose ✕
Hampton. 2 High Street. Tel (01) 979 4935. English cooking, specialities prepared by the proprietor. L *Mon-Fri* 7s6d D à la carte *until 24.00. Closed Mon.* No licence, but customers may bring their own wine. Mooring. Parking.

Camping

J. Martin & Son, East Molesey.

Camping equipment
C. Nielson & Son, sale and hire.

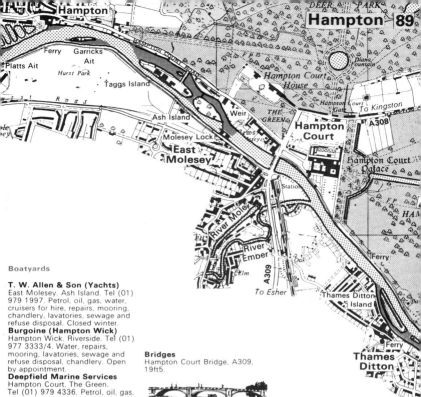

Boatyards

T. W. Allen & Son (Yachts)
East Molesey. Ash Island. Tel (01)
979 1997. Petrol, oil, gas, water,
cruisers for hire, repairs, mooring,
chandlery, lavatories, sewage and
refuse disposal. Closed winter.
Burgoine (Hampton Wick)
Hampton Wick. Riverside. Tel (01)
977 3333/4. Water, repairs,
mooring, lavatories, sewage and
refuse disposal, chandlery. Open
by appointment.
Deepfield Marine Services
Hampton Court. The Green.
Tel (01) 979 4336. Petrol, oil, gas,
water, mechanical repairs, agents
for Evinrude, Johnson; mooring,
launching, lavatories, boat transport, chandlery.
Hucks & Son
Hampton. The Chalet. Tel Molesey
2135. Diesel, water, gas, repairs,
mooring, chandlery.
G. Kenton
Hampton. Hampton Ferry Boathouse, 12 Thames Street. Tel (01)
979 4712. Gas, camping skiffs,
dinghies and fishing boats for hire,
mooring, storage.
Maid Boats
Thames Ditton. Ferry Yacht Station
Tel (01) 398 0271/3. Petrol, oil,
diesel, water, gas, cruisers for hire,
moorings.
J. Martin & Son
East Molesey. River Bank (near
Molesey Lock). Tel (01) 979 5515
Rowing boats and fishing punts
for hire, repairs, mooring.
Molesey Lock
Water.

Mooring

Hampton
G. Kenton, Hampton Ferry Boat-
house. At wharf by Hampton
church.
Hucks & Son, The Chalet.
Small island above Taggs Island.
Thames Ditton
Albany Hotel.
G. H. Wood (Marina).
Swan Hotel.
E. & A. Tagg.
Maid Boats, Ferry Yacht Station.

Sewage & refuse disposal
Molesey Lock.

Public lavatories
Molesey Lock.

Public launching slip
Lower Sunbury Road, Hampton.
Swan Hotel, Thames Ditton.
Drawdock, East Molesey.

Navigation
Maximum draught:
Staines to Teddington 6ft6.

Bridges
Hampton Court Bridge, A309,
19ft5.

Locks
Molesey Lock, 268ft4 x 24ft10.
Ferry
Hampton.
Thames Ditton.

Natural history
House martins nest under the
eaves of Hampton Court Palace.
Mallard, coot and moorhen breed
in the park, and so do kestrel, little
owl and jackdaw. The wheatear
and whinchat can be seen on
migration.
There is a herd of fallow deer in
the park.
Acorus calamus (sweet flag) from
southern Asia grows in the park
and by the river. The iris-like
leaves give off a sweet scent when
crushed, so it was grown for
strewing on the palace floors to
mask less agreeable odours. It was
recorded as naturalised as early
as 1660.
Viscum album (mistletoe) grows
on hawthorn and lime trees.
Chenopodium bonus-henricus
(good King Henry) grows in the
park. It is a spinach-like plant and
may have been used as a vegetable,
but it is not particularly palatable.

Fishing
All the fishing on the main river in
this map section is free. A noted
stretch is from Hampton Court
Bridge to Kingston Bridge. Sunbury
weir can be fished on a Thames
Conservancy permit. Between
Sunbury Lock and Molesey Lock
the MWB reservoirs, the Knight and
Bessborough, can be fished on a
1s6d day ticket or a permit.
The Civil Service AA hold the
fishing on the two Lambeth
reservoirs. One of these produced
the British rod-caught record
roach of 3lb 14oz.
At Hampton the Grand Junction
Reservoir is reserved for MWB
members. Carp of 15½lb have been
caught in the Hampton area.
Molesey Weir pool is included in
the Thames Conservancy weir
permit. A record barbel of 14lb 6oz
was caught here in 1888.
There is some free fishing on the
Mole at Molesey—mainly roach,
dace, chub and gudgeon.
The Hampton Court Palace
Home Park ponds can be fished on
application to the Superintendent
of Hampton Court and Bushy
Parks, Hampton Court. The ponds
hold tench, carp, perch, roach and
pike.
**Civil Service Angling
Association**
See Bray map page 77
Metropolitan Water Board
The Clerk of the Board,
Metropolitan Water Board,
Rosebery Avenue, EC1.
Thames Conservancy
See Kelmscott map page 29

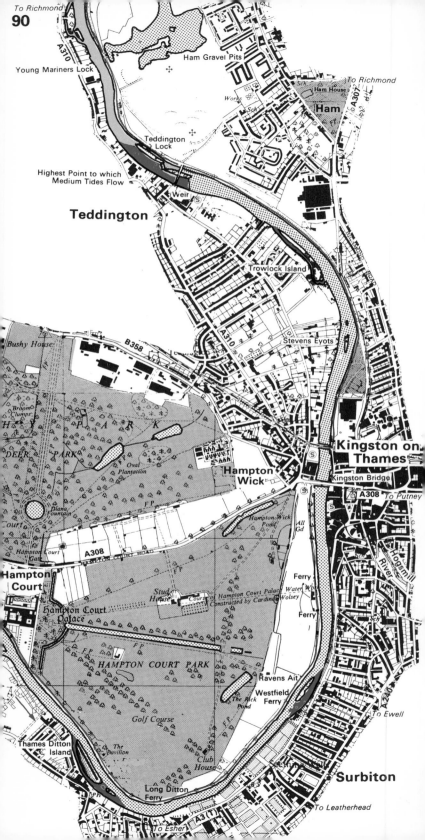

Boatyards

The Boat Shop
Hampton Wick. Kingston Bridge.
Tel (01) 977 4670 (chandlery)
(01) 977 5010 (clothing).
Oil, gas, agents for Avon dinghies,
Tyne canoes, Johnson & Seagull;
chandlery, yachting clothing.

F. D. Brown
Ham. 71 Lock Road. Tel (01) 940
8611. Mooring.

H. Gibbs & Son (Boatbuilders)
Trowlock Island. Teddington.
Tel (01) 977 2759. Cruisers and
motor yachts for hire.

Hart & Co (Boats)
Surbiton. Portsmouth Road.
Tel (01) 399 2113. Repairs,
mooring, launching, lavatories,
sailing dinghies, motor launches,
cruisers for hire. Closed winter.

Kingston Bridge Boatyard
Hampton Wick. Tel (01) 546 3212.
Water, repairs, mooring, chandlery,
boat designers and builders.

Kingston Slipways
Kingston. Tel (01) 546 0303.
22 High Street. Repairs, mooring,
launching, chandlery, brokerage,
special joinery.

W. Mould
Kingston. 41 High Street.
Tel (01) 546 2368. Petrol, gas.

Tough Bros
Teddington Wharf. Tel (01) 977
4494. Petrol, oil, diesel, water,
gas, mooring, launching, chandlery,
footwear, boat builders.

R. J. Turk & Sons
Kingston. Thames Side Boathouse.
Tel (01) 546 2434. Sales (01) 546
6385. Oil, gas, water, hire dinghies,
motor boats and canoes, repairs,
agents for Evinrude, Chrysler;
mooring, launching, chandlery,
technical advice for marine films.

Teddington Lock
Water.

Mooring

Hart & Co, Surbiton.
H. Gibbs & Son, Trowlock Island
Kingston Bridge Boatyard,
Hampton Wick.
R. J. Turk & Sons, Kingston.
Twickenham drawdock
(embankment).
Ham Landing.
Ham Fields (Public Car Park).
Official overnight mooring
at Stevens Eyot. Kingston.

Navigation

Maximum draught:
Staines to Teddington 6ft6.

Bridges
Kingston Bridge, A308, 23ft11.
Kingston Rail Bridge, 22ft4.
Teddington Lock Footbridge,
19ft4.

Locks
Teddington Locks
There are three locks:
Barge Lock, 650ft x 24ft9.
Old Lock, 177ft11 x 24ft4.
Skiff Lock, 49ft6 x 5ft10.
Traffic moving upstream must
observe light signal at end of
lock island.
*1. Vertical red lights: Barge and
Old Lock closed.*
*2. Sloping left blue lights: Barge
Lock only open.*
*3. Sloping right blue lights: Old
Lock only open.*
Skiff Lock is always open, so
ignore lights.

Ferry
(Westfield ferry) Hart & Co,
Surbiton, to Hampton Court.

Emergency: see map 87

Teddington Weir *R R Bolland*

Places of interest

Surbiton

Surrey. The archetype of a suburb: a dense residential area with good shops, built round an excellent train service.

Surbiton Station, built 1937 by J. R. Scott, epitomises the Modern Movement in England, both architecturally and socially.

The town sits back from the river, leaving a fine promenade towards Kingston. This echoes the Hampton Court riverside on the opposite bank. General shops, banks and post office.

Kingston

Surrey. EC Wed. MD Mon, Sat. A Royal Borough where seven Saxon kings were crowned. The Coronation stone is displayed outside the Guildhall.

There is a good river frontage, centred round the stone bridge, built 1825-8 by Lapidge. Away from the river, the Market Place is the centre of the town. It suffers badly from traffic but still looks pretty. It contains buildings of all periods, but the Italianate Town Hall, 1838-40 is the most striking. London Road includes good C18th buildings and the largely Tudor Lovekyn Chapel. Note also the five conduit houses built by Cardinal Wolsey to supply water to Hampton Court. Coombe, to the east of Kingston, has some interesting C20th houses; Miramonte by Maxwell Fry, 1937, is notable. All shops, banks and post office.

Teddington

Middx. The least interesting of the Middlesex towns. The tiny parish church, largely C18th, is dwarfed by the incomplete bulk of St Alban's, a church of unnecessary size.

There are good walks by the river, which can be crossed by the lock footbridge. One of the most impressive sights is the weir, especially when the river is full. The largest on the river, the weir marks the boundary between the tidal and non-tidal Thames. The official boundary between the Thames Conservancy and the Port of London Authority is 265 yards below Teddington Lock, and is marked by an obelisk on the Surrey bank. General shops and post office.

Ham

Surrey. Built round the common, Ham has houses of all periods, but, apart from Ham House, the most interesting are the C20th. Parkleys Estate, by Eric Lyons, 1954-6, is one of the most striking housing developments in Surrey. Note the refreshing use of projecting floors at different levels. The ground plan of the estate has had a lasting influence on projects of a later date. General shops and post office.

Ham House

(See next map also.) A superb C17th riverside mansion, the exterior largely by Sir John Vavassour. Inside, the C17th plasterwork is remarkable. It contains a collection of period furniture. *Open Apr-Sep 14.00-18.00, Oct-Mar 12.00-16.00. Closed Mon.* 1s. Parking.

Twickenham

Middx. One of the most elegant and desirable areas in the C18th, Twickenham has since disappeared under waves of suburbia. However, the area around St Mary's church remains relatively intact. The vigorous church, with its three-storey tower, dates largely from 1714. Alexander Pope has many connections with Twickenham. In the church there are monuments to him and to his parents.

Set in parkland by the river is Marble Hill, a rather plain Palladian mansion built in 1720 by George II for his mistress, Henrietta Howard. It is being lavishly restored by the GLC.

In the grounds are York House, built about 1700, and the Octagon of Orleans House. York House is now the Municipal Offices. Nearby is a rather astonishing group of statuary: a life-size representation of either Birth of Venus or the Pearl Fishers (see Richmond map).

The surviving glory of Twickenham is Strawberry Hill, Walpole's essay on the Gothic revival. The most important Gothic building surviving, it is still as charming and convincing a case for the revival as when it was built. Designed first by John Chute and Richard Bentley between 1753-63, and later by Thomas Pitt, the house has a strong feeling of unity. It well expresses Walpole's appreciation of Gothic forms and spirit. The interior is the most successful part. It now houses St Mary's Training College and can be viewed only by appointment. All shops, banks and post office. Cinema: Odeon, Heath Road, Twickenham. Tel (01) 892 5005.

Eel Pie Island (Richmond map)

Twickenham. In Edwardian days the hotel ran tea dances. More recently, in the early 1960's it was the most spectacular beat and jazz club in London. The Rolling Stones started off at Eel Pie Island.

Sport

New Horizon School Camps

Sec. Gary Borrett, 15 Manor Court, Manorgate Road. Tel (01) 546 9269. *from 7.30-8.30.* A varied list of camps including winter sports in Scotland, work camps, fruit picking, waterway holidays.

Swimming

Twickenham. The Embankment. Tel (01) 892 4466. Open air pool *summer only.*

Ice Skating

Sports Drome, Cleveland Road, Twickenham. Tel (01) 892 3436.

Kingston Head of the River

End of March.

Twickenham Regatta

End of May.

Archaeology

Kingston

Although a Saxon and medieval town, excavations on the banks of the river Hogsmill have produced proof of Neolithic and Iron Age occupation. Finds in Kingston Museum.

Ham Fields

One of the richest areas for archaeological discoveries in the London area, evidence of occupation from the middle Stone Age to the Saxons has been found, including the remains of a Saxon village.

Twickenham

Dredging in the backwater between Eel Pie Island and Twickenham has produced Prehistoric tools and weapons, indicating that the island was occupied in Prehistoric times. Neolithic pottery fragments and flints discovered in Church Street, Twickenham.

Eating, drinking & accommodation

Contented Plaice

Kingston. 60-62 High Street. Tel (01) 546 9755. English cooking. L 15s D 20s *daily until 23.45.*

The Kouzina

Kingston. 6 Vicarage Road. Tel (01) 546 1336/8541. Continental food served to a background of Greek music. Greek specialities. LD 15s *until 23.00, 23.30 Sat. Closed Sun.*

London Steak House

Kingston. 17 High Street. Tel (01) 546 3788. LD from 12s6d *until 23.00 Mon-Sat, 22.30 Sun.*

Milano Restaurant

Kingston. 22 Wood Street. Tel (01) 546 2413. Italian cooking with background music and candles. L 8s D 21s *until 24.00. Closed Sun L.*

Griffin Hotel

Kingston. 1 Market Place. Tel (01) 546 0924. Situated on the river Mole, this inn still has the old stables, used when it was a coaching inn. 6 rooms BB 37s6d. L 10s6d D 12s6d *daily until 21.00.* Parking.

Camping

Surrey Car & Caravan Company

Kingston. 44 Richmond Road. Tel 6340. Equipment.

Natural history

Great crested grebe nests on local gravel pits.

Scilla autumnalis (autumnal squill), an uncommon blue flower with dark violet anthers, has been known in meadows beside the Thames for over a hundred years. *Saxifraga granulata* (meadow saxifrage), also uncommon in London, grows at Ham. *Impatiens glandulifera* (Indian balsam, policeman's helmet), with flowers of every shade from white to deep pinkish purple, grows in masses along the banks. This native of the Himalaya, which grows to a height of five feet or more, escaped from cultivation in 1855 and is now widely distributed. The seed capsule explodes at a touch when ripe.

Another escape from cultivation is *Angelica archangelica* (giant angelica), whose stems are used for crystallised angelica. This tall, robust plant with large, almost globular umbels of small greenish flowers, is naturalised on river banks. The young stems may be eaten like rhubarb.

Fishing

The main river is free fishing in this section. A good stretch is from Hampton Court Bridge to Kingston Bridge. Along this stretch are the Galleries swims, famed for holding a good head of barbel. The 1968 London Anglers Thames championship winner caught 22lb 8¾oz of barbel here.

On the Surrey bank at Kingston, the Canbury Gardens is popular for roach, bream, dace, perch, bleak, gudgeon, eels and carp. The power station outlet sometimes produces big carp. An eel of 5lb 12½oz was caught at Kingston in 1932. From Kingston to Teddington Lock the river is noted for roach and dace. Teddington Weir is included in the Thames Conservancy permit. The river at Radnor Gardens, Twickenham, is good for the occasional carp.

Thames Conservancy

See Lechlade map page 27

Places of interest

Petersham
Surrey. But for the traffic, this would be one of the most elegant village suburbs near London. It is exceptionally rich in fine houses of the late C17th and C18th. These are not visible from the river, but Douglas House, 1700, close to the east drive of Ham House, Rutland Lodge, 1666, and Petersham Lodge, 1740, both in River Lane, are not far away from the Thames.

Richmond
Surrey. EC Wed. One of the prettiest riverside towns in the London area. Built up the side of the hill, Richmond has been able to retain its Georgian elegance. It still has the feeling of a C18th resort.
Richmond Green is the centre, both aesthetically and socially. Perhaps the most beautiful green in any town in England, it is surrounded by early C18th houses. Only the brick and terracotta theatre, built in 1899, breaks the pattern; so deliberately that it is almost refreshing.
By the green is the site of Richmond Palace, a Royal Residence built by Henry VII after 1497 out of the earlier Sheen Palace. It was largely derelict by the mid C17th and today nothing survives but the gateway. Behind the gate, in Old Palace Yard, is The Trumpeter's House. This magnificent building of eleven bays is of about 1708 and shows a strong Wren influence.
Richmond Hill continues the C18th tradition. Dominated by the Neo-Georgian bulk of the Star and Garter Home, the hill has marvellous views over the river and the scenery around. All shops, banks and post office.
Richmond Theatre, The Green, Richmond. Tel (01) 940 0088.

Richmond Park
2000 acres in size. The park was first enclosed by Charles I. Stocked with deer, it remained a favourite hunting ground till the C18th. Private shooting stopped in 1904 but hunting lodges can still be seen. White Lodge, built for George II in 1727, now houses the Royal Ballet. Today the park is a recreation area, famous for walking and riding. *Open 8.15-17.00.*
The Observatory, 1729 by William Chambers, in the Old Deer Park is a building of scientific interest. The three obelisks nearby were used to measure London's official time.

Richmond Bridge
See London Bridges and Tunnels.

Isleworth
Middlesex. This village with its C17th and C18th houses is at its prettiest from the river before Syon House is reached. Church Street with the C15th tower of All Saints Church, the London Apprentice Inn and a few Georgian houses, makes a charming setting.

Syon House
Isleworth. Built on the site of a C15th convent, the present square structure with its corner turrets is largely C16th, although the house was entirely refaced in 1825. The house is mainly of interest on account of the interior decoration by Robert Adam, 1761. Close to the house is the new Garden Centre, whose only contribution aesthetically has been to fill the

fine C18th glasshouse by Fowler with exotic plants. The grounds of the house extend to the river where there is an elegant boathouse with ionic columns, attributed to Capability Brown. *Open May-mid Oct 11.00-16.30 weekdays.*

Garden Centre
Syon House. The centre is of great value to amateur and professional gardeners. Almost every kind of plant, greenhouse equipment and garden furniture can be bought here or just admired. *Open May-Oct 10.30-17.30. Nov-Feb Sat and Sun 10.30-16.00.*

Royal Botanic Gardens
Kew. Apart from their exceptional botanic interest which is covered under *Natural History*, the gardens are of historic importance, being the consecutive work of two ages, the mid C18th and the mid C19th. As a national institution, they originated when part of the gardens of Richmond Lodge, 1700, by Capability Brown, and of Kew Palace, mid-C18th, by Chambers, were taken over by the State and enlarged under Sir William and Sir Joseph Hooker in 1841.

A large part of the charm of the Gardens today lies in the presence amongst the rare species of the C18th temples and glasshouses the Orangery and Kew Palace. The Palace, or Dutch House, built by the merchant, Samuel Fortry, 1631, is a gabled brick house close to the river and typical of the style favoured by London merchants at this period. *Open 10.00-20.00 or dusk.*

Kew
Surrey. Old Kew centres round the Green with its C18th houses and the entrance to the Botanic Garden at one end. The Church of St Anne is partly C18th but greatly altered in the C19th.

Chiswick
Middlesex. Chiswick stretches between Kew Bridge and Hammersmith Terrace and provides some of the most picturesque scenery anywhere on the river near London. Its Georgian houses extend along Strand on the Green and again at Chiswick Mall. Between these points the grounds of three large C18th mansions originally extended to the river: Grove House, Sutton Court and Chiswick House. Only Chiswick House remains. The site of Grove House has been built over. Duke's Meadows, part of the grounds of Chiswick House, is now a Recreation Ground by the river. Chiswick Cemetery backs on to St Nicholas' Church where Lord Burlington and William Kent are buried.

British Piano and Musical Museum
Brentford. St George's Church, High Street. Housed in a church, this is a fascinating collection of automatic, old and odd musical instruments. *Open April-Sep Sat and Sun 10.30-18.00. Oct-Mar 1st and 3rd Sat and Sun 14.30-18.00. Closed Dec and in bad weather.*

Gunnersbury Park Museum
Gunnersbury Park. A local history museum containing material relating to Chiswick, Brentford and Ealing. This includes social history and archaeology. The topographical collection is of interest in connection with the Thames. *Open Oct-March Sun, Wed and Sat 14.00-16.00. April-Sep Sun 15.00-20.00, other days (not Fri) 11.00-13.00, 14.00-17.00.* Underground Acton.

Chiswick House
Chiswick. In 1720 Lord Burlington's admiration for Palladio was publicly acclaimed in his building of Chiswick House,

which was modelled on Palladio's Villa Capra. The interior decoration is by Kent. The gardens, by Kent and Bridgeman, still have fine statuary. *Open Apr-Sep 10.30-19.00. Oct-Mar Wed-Sun 10.30-16.00.*

Mortlake
Surrey. In the C17th Mortlake was famous for its tapestry works of which little remains. But some of the tapestries can be seen in the Victoria & Albert Museum. A pottery works developed in the C18th. The riverside is picturesque along Thames Bank where there is a fine group of C18th houses.

Cinemas
ABC, Sheen Road, Richmond. Tel (01) 940 4148
Gaumont, 5 Hill Street, Richmond. Tel (01) 940 1760.
Odeon, Hill Street, Richmond. Tel (01) 940 5759.
Odeon, Heath Road, Twickenham. Tel (01) 892 5005.

Sport

Swimming
Richmond. Old Deer Park, Twickenham Road. Tel (01) 940 8461. Open air pool *open summer only. indoor and learners' pool all year.*
Twickenham. The Embankment. Tel (01) 892 4466. Open air pool *summer only.*

Ice skating
Sports Drome, Cleveland Road, Twickenham. Tel (01) 892 3436.

Water Ski-ing
The Prince Water Ski-ing Club, Secretary: D. Spier, 236 Earl's Court Road, SW5. The club operates on a gravel pit leased to them by the Ready Mixed Group at Bedfont.

Chiswick Regatta
Held mid-June.

Richmond Regatta
Held end of June.

Mortlake Sculling Race
Held early May.

Archaeology

Isleworth
Three dug-out canoes found on the Surrey foreshore. Date uncertain.

Syon Reach
Many Prehistoric and Saxon finds from the river and the north foreshore. Finds of rich metalwork of 900-600 BC have come from Old England, near the junction of Syon Park and Brentford Dock. Now in the London Museum.
A Roman hut was excavated in 1928, also on the foreshore.
Oak stakes observed on the bed of the river and on the north bank are thought to be those planted in the river to hinder the crossing of Julius Caesar's army.

Mortlake
Neolithic pottery from the river and foreshore indicate a settlement. Finds in London Museum and British Museum.

Chiswick Eyot
A Saxon spearhead of the C5th or C6th found on the foreshore in 1931.

Emergency: see map 95

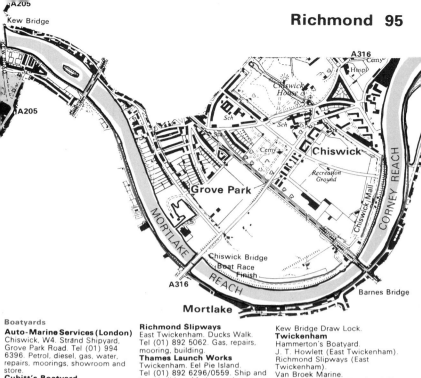

Boatyards

Auto-Marine Services (London)
Chiswick, W4. Strand Shipyard,
Grove Park Road. Tel (01) 994
6396. Petrol, diesel, gas, water,
repairs, moorings, showroom and
store.

Cubitt's Boatyard
Chiswick, W4. Cubitt's Lock Basin,
Hartingdon Road. Tel (01) 994
2093. Gas, mooring, launching.

Hammerton's Boatyard
Twickenham. Marble Hill Boathouse. Tel (01) 892 9620. Skiffs
for hire, mooring, ferry.

J. T. Howlett
East Twickenham. Richmond
Bridge. Tel (01) 892 3183. Diesel,
oil, water, gas, mooring, launching,
marine stores, footwear, yacht
agent.

Richmond Slipways
East Twickenham. Ducks Walk.
Tel (01) 892 5062. Gas, repairs,
mooring, building.

Thames Launch Works
Twickenham. Eel Pie Island.
Tel (01) 892 6296/0559. Ship and
boat builders. Marine engineers.

Van Broek Marine (London)
Twickenham. 1 Strawberry Vale.
Tel (01) 892 2861. Diesel, gas,
water, repairs, mooring, boat sales,
launching.

Mooring

Off north bank with access from
Kew Pier: apply to PLA.

Chiswick
Auto Marine Services.
Cubitt's Boatyard.
Landing stairs right bank upstream
of Barnes railway bridge.

Kew Bridge Draw Lock.

Twickenham
Hammerton's Boatyard.
J. T. Howlett (East Twickenham).
Richmond Slipways (East
Twickenham).
Van Broek Marine.
Hammersmith Pier. Tel (01) 748
8607. Mooring by arrangement.
Ship Drawdock, Mortlake, by
Mortlake Brewery.

Public launching slip

By Richmond Bridge.

Ferry
Below Eel Pie Island.

Emergency
Police: Red Lion Street, Richmond.
Tel 1113
Hospital: Royal Hospital, Kew
Foot Road, Richmond.
Tel (01) 940 3331.

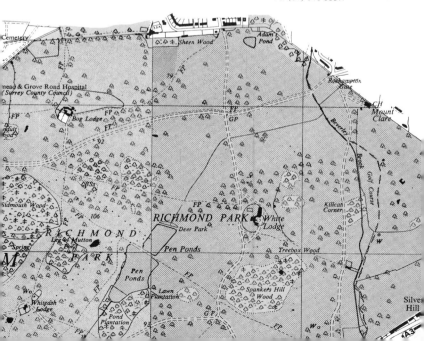

Navigation

From Richmond to the sea navigation on the tidal Thames is far more complex than on the upper reaches. Below Richmond the Thames is a commercial river first and foremost and so users of pleasure craft must take very much greater care.
The Port of London Authority has control over the tidal river. Anyone considering a trip on this part of the river should study their regulations.
The following publications are essential for any navigation on the tidal Thames:
Port of London Authority River Byelaws. Published by the PLA, Trinity Square, London, EC3. 12s6d.
Stanford's Charts for Coastal Navigation. No. 5 The Thames Estuary. 15s6d. No. 6 The Lower Thames. 15s6d. Published by Edward Stanford Ltd, 12-14 Long Acre, London, WC2.
The Pilot's Guide to the Thames Estuary. Published by Imray. 38s6d.
A set of tide tables.
As these publications will answer every query about the tidal Thames, we are giving no navigational information below Richmond.
Facilities for private boats are limited below Richmond. The details we give are designed to help the experienced boat users who wish to reach the estuary.
For tidal information apply to Assistant Harbour Master, The Toll House, Kew, Richmond Surrey. Tel (01) 940 8288.

Locks
Richmond Lock. The only lock on the river operated by the Port of London Authority. For about four hours the weir gates are lifted and the river is fully tidal. When the gates are shut a red disc is shown below the centre arch of the footbridge. Red light in the same position at night. Rollers for small craft. 250ft x 26ft8.

Eating, drinking & accommodation

Brown Bear X🍷
Richmond. 50 The Quadrant. Tel (01) 940 3058. Good grills and snacks. LD from 15s *daily until 23.30*. Darts.

City Barge X🍷
Chiswick, W4. 27 Strand on the Green. Tel (01) 994 2148/8649. Built in 1484, rebuilt 1955, the inn used to serve bargemen on the Thames. L 25s *Mon-Fri*, evening snacks. Darts. Parking.

Ham Brewery Tap X🍷
Ham Common. Ham Street. Tel (01) 940 8699. Lunches and snacks. Parking.

Ivy Hall Hotel XBB
Richmond. Petersham Road. Tel (01) 940 0435. Built 300 years ago, and once the home of King William IV, the hotel has its own garden down to the river. 40 rooms BB 32s6d. LD 10s hotel guests only. Fishing. Parking. No licence.

London Apprentice X🍷
Isleworth. 62 Church Street. Tel (01) 560 6136 (restaurant bookings (01) 560 3538). Apprentices from Livery Companies of London used to row up the river and land here for refreshment. The inn is about 500 years old. English cooking, specialities steaks and Dover soles. LD à la carte *until 21.30*. Closed Sat L and Mon D. Fishing. Parking.

Richmond Hill Hotel X🍷BB
Richmond. Richmond Hill. Tel (01) 940 2247. Good position at the top of Richmond Hill, overlooking the valley, and close to Richmond Park. 133 rooms BB 70s. L 15s D 21s *daily until 21.00*. Swimming pool. Garage, parking.

Richmond Rendezvous X🍷
Richmond. 1 Paradise Road; annexe 1 Wakefield Road. Tel (01) 940 5114/6869/0579. Peking style cooking of very high standard. LD from 25s *daily until 23.30*. Licensed.

The Ship X🍷
Mortlake. Riverside, SW14. Tel (01) 876 1439. Right on the river; close to the boat race finishing post. Part of the parking space is liable to flooding. Lunches, snacks. Darts. Parking.

La Veranda Trattoria X🍷
Richmond. 102 Kew Road. Tel (01) 940 9044. Italian cuisine. LD from 17s6d *until 23.30 (Sun 23.00). Closed Mon.*

Natural history

At the Royal Botanic Gardens, Kew the common wild birds such as blackbird, song thrush, chaffinch and tits are so fearless that they feed from the hand. There are fine collections of native and foreign waterfowl, and nesting birds include coal tit, nuthatch, chiffchaff, goldfinch and great green woodpecker. At dusk our smallest British bat, the pipistrelle, hawks for flies over the lake. Special beds contain many plants arranged according to their families. Wild gardens show *Endymion non-scriptus* (bluebell), *Cardamine pratensis* (lady's smock), *Primula vulgaris* (primrose) and many others in natural surroundings. A striking alien (from the Caucasus) to be seen here in May is *Smyrnium perfoliatum* (golden alexanders). The flowers, bracts and upper leaves are a bright greenish yellow, making it very conspicuous. It is also naturalised in Battersea Park.

Syon House water meadows are a Site of Special Scientific Interest, designated by the Nature Conservancy. There is a roost of cormorants, possibly the only one in Britain, in the tall poplar trees.
In Richmond Park there are herds of fallow and red deer and numerous grey squirrels. Cuckoo, stock dove, barn owl, greater spotted woodpecker and many jackdaws are known to breed.
Bats frequent Pen Ponds, where a number of waterfowl nest.
At Riverside Gardens in Richmond there is a very good Ginkgo (Maidenhair Tree), and some of the finest London planes.
At Petersham Common frothy white *Anthriscus sylvestris* (hedge parsley, Queen Anne's lace) forms wide borders along both sides of the road in spring.
Marble Hill, Twickenham, has a historic Black walnut and the tallest Lombardy poplar (118ft) in Britain. Radnor Gardens have the biggest Weeping Willow in the country.

Fishing

The river from Teddington Weir to the sea is controlled by the Port of London Authority. Near Eel Pie Island some fair bags of roach, bream, dace and perch may be taken—usually from a boat.
North bank. The Radnor Gardens stretch at Twickenham is popular for roach, dace and eels. It is sometimes possible to catch a good carp. At the lower end of the TAPS water below Richmond sluice gates at Isleworth, there is some fine fishing for roach, bream, dace and carp. In 1968 three carp were caught—a 9lb common carp and two mirror carp of 10¼lb and 12lb.
South bank: From the Young Mariner's lock at Ham one can reach the Ham gravel pits, noted for roach, dace, bream, tench, perch and pike. The mouth of the lock is good for bream and roach. Petersham meadows are noted for quality roach.
A few rainbow trout are caught at Richmond every season, whilst at Kew anglers prefer to fish at low tide when they may catch a roach, dace, bream or eel.
The Pen Ponds in Richmond Park can be fished for roach and perch on a permit from the Superintendant, Richmond Park.

Port of London Authority
EC3. Trinity Square.

Thames Angling Preservation Society
Secretary: S. Porter, 10 Station Road, Harlesden, NW10. Tel (01) 965 7247.

Tackle shops

Morgan's Tackle
Kingston. Kingston Bridge.

E. Charman
Teddington. 190 High Street.

E. Thurston
Twickenham. 360 Richmond Road. Tel (01) 892 4175.

The frozen Thames in 1963 *W J Howes*

North Bank: Places of interest

Hammersmith

Hammersmith Terrace
These sixteen identical houses with their gardens running down to the river were built as a block in 1750. The veteran of the Thames, Sir A. P. Herbert, lives in the Terrace.

Upper Mall
The early Victorian buildings of the Metropolitan Water Board by W. Tierney Clark, 1812, stand out. The Engine House is a vast warehouse of yellow stock brick. Next door is the C17th Ship Inn. Further down are some fine C18th houses. William Morris lived in Kelmscott House between 1878-96.

Lower Mall
This is prettier than the Upper Mall and characterised by the Rutland and Blue Anchor pubs, C18th cottages and a dilapidated Victorian boathouse with a wrought iron balcony.

St Peter's Church
St Peter's Road. Shabby and neglected by the main road, this church by Lapidge, 1827-9, is a memory of better days. Its pleasing yellow stock brick facade has a classical portico and cupola. St Peter's Square nearby, probably 1825-30 by an unknown architect, was obviously conceived as part of a scheme and its houses are large and elegant.

Hammersmith Flyover
This feat of modern engineering was designed by G. Maunsell & Partners, in association with the GLC architects' department.

Hammersmith Bridge
See London Bridges and Tunnels.

Fulham

In the C18th and C19th Fulham was the 'fruit and kitchen garden north of the Thames', but today little of the fertile village with its great houses is left and most of Fulham is sprawled building. The river bank with Fulham Palace and Hurlingham House still holds attractions.

Fulham Palace
The Palace lies behind the long avenues of Bishop's Park, stretching to the river. Until the C19th the Palace was one of the country estates of the Bishop of London, but today it is his main residence. The building, a typical manor, is of varied architecture: the courtyard is C16th, the east front late C18th with C19th alterations, and the chapel by Butterfield, 1867.

Church of All Saints
Putney Bridge. This church by Blomfield, 1880, is mainly of interest for the C17th monuments, C16th Flemish brass and the C18th and C19th sarcophagi. Behind the churchyard are the Powell Almshouses by Seddon, 1869. These are exquisite, and even enemies of Victorian architecture should respond to their charms.

Hurlingham House
Ranelagh Gardens. This is the only large C18th residence still surviving in Fulham. The house has a fine river front with corinthian columns and is now the centre of the Hurlingham Club. Members play tennis, golf and croquet in the grounds.

Fulham Power Station
This four-chimneyed edifice by G. E. Baker & Preece, Cardew & Rider, 1936, is a striking landmark.

Chelsea (before Albert Bridge)

Lots Road Power Station
Lots Road. This huge and dominating structure was built in 1904 to provide electricity for the new underground railway.

Crosby Hall
Cheyne Walk. The hostel of the British Federation of University Women is of interest for its hall which was once part of the residence of Sir John Crosby, a C15th wool merchant, in Bishopsgate. The hall, 1466-75, was brought here from Bishopsgate almost entire. It has a sumptuous painted roof and is hung with tapestry and a painted cloth screen. The leather emblazoned chairs are Spanish. *Open 10.00-13.00, 14.00-18.00. Sun 14.00-18.00.*

Chelsea Old Church
Cheyne Walk. The church was bombed during the war and rebuilt in 1964. Its interior is of great interest on account of Sir Thomas More's private chapel, 1528, and the many C17th monuments, all of which escaped destruction.

Cheyne Walk
The walk is characterised by the houseboats and the C18th houses of riverside village type, nos 46-48, and terraced architecture, nos 19-26.

Carlyle's House
24 Cheyne Row. Once the haunt of writers such as Dickens and Tennyson, the house is *open daily except Tue, 10.00-13.00, 14.00-18.00. Sun 14.00-18.00.* William de Morgan had his pottery at no 34 Cheyne Row from 1872-82.

South Bank: Places of interest

Barnes

Barnes Terrace
Close to the river an attractive village atmosphere pervades. The C18th houses with their cheerful iron verandas and balconies contrast with the iron railway bridge, 1849, crossing the river at this point. Near the Church of St Mary, Church Road, are more good early C18th houses.

Castelnau
Barnes is rich in Victorian houses and some of the best are to be seen in Castelnau. Remarkably standardised, they are largely semi-detached and typical of Early Victorian villa architecture with their arched windows.

Barn Elms Park
Barn Elms was originally the mansion of Sir Francis Walsingham, Secretary of State to Elizabeth I. Nothing remains of the house apart from the ornamental pond and the ice house. Until recently the Park was used by the Ranelagh Polo Club, but it is now used exclusively as school playing fields and the goal posts can be seen from the river.

Wandsworth

The Embankment is picturesque. The London Rowing Club and Westminster School have their boathouses here and the eights and sculls can be seen practising in the afternoon amidst the swans. Each spring the Oxford and Cambridge boat race is rowed between Mortlake and Putney. The first race was held at Henley in 1829. Beside Putney Bridge, the badly sited ICL building entirely dwarfs the Church of St Mary, rebuilt by Lapidge in 1836.

Putney

Until the C19th Wandsworth was a village oasis on the River Wandle, a good fishing river, and was noted for a local silk and hat industry. The course of the Wandle can still be traced near the Church of All Saints. The Surrey Iron Railway, whose wagons were drawn by horses, stretched beside the river. The remains of the windmill which was part of the pumping station for the railway can be seen at the corner

Emergency: see map | 95

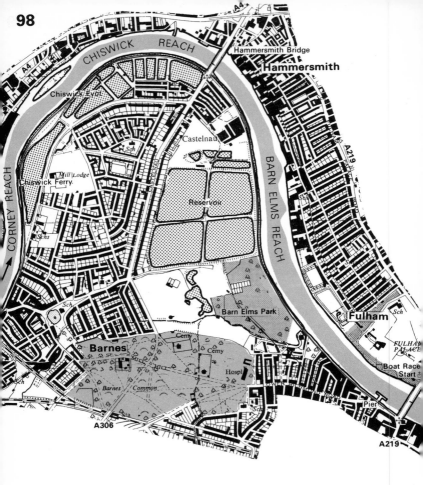

of Windmill Road. Today, little
remains to point to the past. There
are a few Georgian houses in
Church Row, but the river bank is
a grimy industrial scene. Inland,
particularly near West Hill, is
some notable post 1930 building:
Mayfield Comprehensive School
with new buildings by Powell &
Moya, and Whitelands Training
College, Sutherland Grove, by
Giles Gilbert Scott 1930.

Battersea (before Albert Bridge)

Almost all that can be seen from
the river is a mass of warehouses,
notably Hovis and Mayhews Bell
Flour, and the Church of St Mary.
Further inland are many Victorian
buildings, in particular by
Mountford.

St Mary's Church

Church Road. The church is one
of the few relics of Battersea's
C18th village. Built in 1775 by
Joseph Dixon, it is strangely
Dutch in character. Inside is some
good C17th glass. From the porch
is an outstanding view of Lots
Road Power Station and the
industrial Thames.

GLC Somerset Estate

Church Road. All of dark grey
brick and concrete, this estate
is a credit to the GLC architect
Hubert Bennett, 1962-6. Two
tower blocks dominate small
maisonettes and courtyards.

Old Battersea House

Vicarage Crescent. Home of the
potter, William de Morgan, in the
late C19th. this C17th house will
reopen as a Museum of De Morgan
Pottery and Pre-Raphaelite
paintings in 1970.

Sir Walter St John's School

High Street. A dignified red brick
Victorian building in Tudor style
by Butterfield, 1859.

Sport

University Boat Race

End of March or early April,
from Putney Bridge to Mortlake.

Putney Amateur Regatta

Held early May.

Hammersmith Amateur
Regatta

Early May.

Archaeology

Hammersmith

Prehistoric finds by the bridge
indicate an Iron Age Settlement.

Putney

Roman pottery discovered on the
foreshore by the bridge.
Excavations by Wandsworth
Historical Society have found
traces of a Roman settlement to
the west of Putney High Street.

Eating, drinking &
accommodation

The Bull's Head

Barnes, SW13. 373 Lonsdale Road.
Tel (01) 876 5241. Snacks,
modern jazz nightly *except Mon.*

Castle

Putney, SW15. 220 Putney Bridge
Road. Tel (01) 788 0972. Conti-
nental and English cooking.
LD 30s *until 22.30.* Closed Sun.
Parking.

The Black Lion

Hammersmith, W6. 2 South Black
Lion Lane. Tel (01) 748 7056.
English cooking and snacks.
L 12s6d *Mon-Fri.* Parking.

The Dove

Hammersmith, W6. 19 Upper Mall.
Tel (01) 748 5405. Built over 300
years ago, it is still a pub where
watermen and writers can chat
together over a pint. Buffet
counter. LD 5s *until 22.00. Closed
Sun.* Parking.

The Eight Bells

Fulham, SW6. 89 High Street.
Tel (01) 736 6307. Before Putney

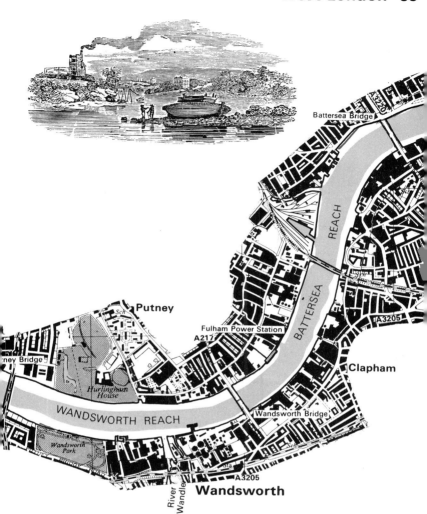

Bridge was built, this was the ferry inn. Good snacks. Parking.
Pier Hotel
SW3. 31 Cheyne Walk. Tel (01) 352 3800. Roomy riverside inn with pleasant beer garden. LD.
YHA
Earl's Court, SW5. 38 Bolton Gardens. Tel (01) 373 7083.
Kensington, W8. King George VI Memorial Youth Hostel, Holland House, Holland Walk. Tel (01) 937 0748.

Boatyards

Chelsea Yacht & Boat Co.
Chelsea, SW10. Cheyne Walk. Tel (01) 352 1427. Gas, non-mechanical repairs, mooring.

Mooring

Putney Pier. Convenient landing for Putney. Tel (01) 788 5104.
Putney Drawdock.
Putney Bridge.
Chelsea Yacht & Boat Co.

Navigation

See previous section.

Natural history

The main feature of London's riverside parks is the remarkable growth of the London plane trees, *Platanus hybrida*. These first arose about 1780 through the chance cross-breeding of the North American plant *P. occidentalis*, and the *Oriental* plane from Asia Minor *P. orientalis*. The offspring, which is increased by cuttings, shows great vigour, stands up to town smoke well, and throws welcome cool shade on hot days; the dappled yellow and brown bark is most attractive. First noticed at Oxford, London plane is now planted in Paris, Brussels and many other European and American cities. Many large riverside specimens are now 150 years old; those in Berkeley Square were planted in 1789 and are now 100 feet tall.
At the end of the towpath in Putney there are many mute swans, and on Putney Footbridge *Parietaria diffusa* (pellitory of the wall) grows. Black-headed gulls feed from the hand in winter. House martins nest near Hammersmith Bridge. Ducks and gulls roost and sometimes feed on Barn Elms reservoirs; as many as 20,000 gulls have been counted in January.
Rumex patientia (patience dock), a large alien dock, grows near Barnes Footbridge. Tall, handsome, often reddish in colour and with very large leaves, it is a native of Asia Minor.
Here also is a colony of rare snail, *Laciniaria biplicata*—its shell is about ¾ inch tall, thin and spirally twisted. It lives in willow roots by day and on the trunks by night. Threatened by building, part of the colony was moved elsewhere in the area to preserve it.
Chrysanthemum vulgare (tansy), with its fern-like aromatic leaves, has been used in medicine for hundreds of years. Its yellow, button shaped flowers may be seen in many places by the water.

Fishing
There is some fishing in the reaches between Barnes to Hammersmith where it is tidal. This is mainly for roach, dace, bream and eels.
In Barn Elms at Barnes are a group of reservoirs, famous for big roach and perch. Reservoirs 5-8 can be fished on a 1s6d day ticket or a £1 season permit.
Metropolitan Water Board
See Hampton map page 89
Tackle shop
Cooper's Fishing Tackle
Hammersmith. 204 King Street. Tel (01) 748 6920.

Emergency: see map 101

North Bank: Places of interest

Chelsea

Chelsea Embankment
Chelsea Embankment was made in 1871. No 17 is Norman Shaw's famous Swan House. At the west end is the Physic Garden, established by the Apothecaries Society in 1673. In it is a statue of Sir Hans Sloane by Rysbrack, 1733.

Royal Hospital
Royal Hospital Road. The Hospital was founded by Charles II as an institution for invalid and veteran soldiers and built by Wren. Alterations were made in the C18th by Robert Adam and John Soane. The 200 in-pensioners and the 100,000 out-pensioners wear scarlet frock coats in the summer and dark blue overcoats in the winter—a uniform dating from the C18th. On Sundays the pensioners parade at 10.30 in the forecourt in Royal Hospital Road. Visitors may attend the Chapel service at 11.00. The museum, hall and chapel are *open 10.00–12.00, 14.00–18.00. Sun 14.00–17.00.*

Chelsea Barracks
Chelsea Bridge Road. The barracks were built in 1962 by Tripe and Wakeham. Suitably military, they are long, low, regular blocks.

Westminster

Churchill Gardens
Grosvenor Road. One of the first council estates of this type to be built, the architects, Powell & Moya, were chosen by competition in 1946. The contrast of heights and layout is pleasing. All social amenities—schools, shops, playgrounds—are provided and the development is both socially and architecturally successful. Hot water and heating is piped from Battersea Power Station.

Dolphin Square
Grosvenor Road. The social amenities of this huge block of flats—there is an underground swimming pool and squash courts—far outweigh its architectural merits. Built in 1937, by Gordon Jeeves, its facade is flat and dreary. It is the largest self-contained block of flats in Europe and covers 7½ acres.

Riverwall House
Vauxhall Bridge. This modern building, 1966, by Farmer and Dark, houses part of the Foreign and Commonwealth Office. In the foregarden stands Henry Moore's bronze, 'Locking Piece', 1968.

Tate Gallery
Millbank. The Gallery was founded by Sir Henry Tate, the sugar manufacturer, in 1897 and built by

Sidney R. J. Smith in the classical style. It contains one of the best collections of Impressionist and post-Impressionist paintings and sculpture in the country.
Open 10.00–18.00. Sun 14.00–18.00

Millbank Tower
Millbank. The Vickers building. The traditional balance of the river bank has been overturned by this office building by Ronald Ward and Partners, 1963, and occupied by Vickers Ltd. Whereas the Houses of Parliament originally dominated the Thames, the Vickers building—34 storeys and 387ft high—now rules the north bank as the Shell building rules the south. Inside the Tower are car parks, a cinema and ten hotel suites for Vickers visitors. Note the green floodlighting at night.

Victoria Tower Gardens
Abingdon Street. The gardens are memorable for their sculpture. Rodin's 'Burghers of Calais', 1895, are close to the river and near the entrance stands a monument to Mrs Emmeline Pankhurst and Dame Christabel Pankhurst, champions of the women's suffrage movement in the early 1900's. In Abingdon Street Gardens opposite, Henry Moore's bronze, 'Knife Edge', should be noticed.

Houses of Parliament
Parliament Square. Despite their authentic medieval appearance, the Houses of Parliament were in

fact completed in 1860. Attributed to Charles Barry, it is certain that his assistant, Pugin, had a strong influence on the designs. The medieval Palace of Westminster, seat of the Norman kings, once stood on the site. Of this only Westminster Hall remains.

Westminster Abbey
Parliament Square. The Abbey has been the burial place of the Kings of England since the C10th, but the existing Gothic building dates from the C13th. It has been greatly restored. It is so rich in architectural and historic interest that

the visitor should buy a guide at the door. In its shadow shelters the Church of St Margaret, the parish church of the House of Commons since 1614, and very fashionable for weddings.

Old Scotland Yard
Victoria Embankment. Scotland Yard has now moved to new buildings in Victoria. The old building, by Norman Shaw, 1888, has fine iron gates by Reginald Blomfield. It now houses government departments and Cannon Row Police Station.

Ministry of Defence
Horse Guards Avenue. This colossal stone building by Vincent Harris, 1913, typical of Edwardian imperialism with its colonnades and pediments, occupies the site of the medieval Palace of Whitehall. Henry VIII's wine cellar still lies beneath the giant block and can be visited. In the fore-garden can be seen part of the 280ft river terrace and steps to the water built by Wren for Mary II. The steps mark the edge of the river before the building of the Victoria Embankment in 1869. Opposite the Defence Building on the Embankment, a golden eagle crowns the Air Force Memorial by Sir Reginald Blomfield and Sir W. Reid Dick, 1923.

[Map of the Chelsea/Battersea/Pimlico area of the Thames, with labels:] Belgravia, Pimlico, Vauxhall Br, Chelsea, Royal Hospital, Chelsea Bridge, Grosvenor Bridge, NINE, Albert Bridge, CHELSEA REACH, Battersea Power Station, QUEENSTOWN ROAD, Battersea Park, Battersea

---

Emergency
Police
City of London Police, 26 Old Jewry, EC2. Tel (01) 606 8866.
New Scotland Yard, Victoria Street SW1. Tel (01) 230 1212.
Thames River Police, 98 Wapping Lane, E1. Tel (01) 709 9976.

Hospitals:
Battersea General Hospital, Prince of Wales Drive, SW11. Tel (01) 228 0123.
Charing Cross Hospital, Agar Street, WC2. Tel (01) 836 7788.
Fulham Hospital, St Dunstan's Road, W6. Tel (01) 748 2050.
Guy's Hospital, St Thomas's Street, SE1. Tel (01) 407 7600.
Hammersmith Hospital, Du Cane Road, W12. Tel (01) 743 2030.
Putney Hospital, Lower Common, SW15. Tel (01) 788 0055.
St Thomas' Hospital, Lambeth Palace Road, SE1. Tel (01) 928 9292.
Westminster Hospital, Dean Ryle Street, SW1. Tel (01) 834 8161.

Holborn

Covent Garden

Somerset House

Waterloo Bridge

Cleopatras Needle

Charing Cross Station

ungerford Bridge

Whitehall Stairs

Westminster Bridge

Big Ben

Houses Parliament

tminster Abbey

Lambeth Bridge

Vickers Building

Millbank Barracks

Vauxhall

Kennington

South Lambeth

Inner & Middle Temple

President

Discovery Wellington

Chrysanthemum

Pier

KINGS

South Bank Arts Centre

Royal Festival Hall

Shell Building

Waterloo Station

County Hall

Pier

St Thomas's Hospital

Hospl

Lambeth Palace

Lambeth

Fire Brigade H.Q.

St Pauls Cathedral

The City

Blackfriars Station

REACH

Cannon Street Station

Fishmonger Ha

Blackfriars Bridge

Bankside Power Station

Southwark Bridge

London Bridge

Southwark

Whitehall Court
Whitehall Place. More Chambord than Chambord with all its pyramid roofs, balconies and loggias typical of a French chateau, Archer & Green's building, 1884, is the seat of various London clubs. In the foregardens are C19th statues of Tyndale, Sir Bartle Frere, and Sir James Outram.

Victoria Embankment Gardens
Summer lunchtime concerts and plays are performed here. There is a vulgar yellow and maroon seaside bandstand. But of considerable interest in the gardens is the York

Water Gate by Nicholas Stone, 1625. The Water Gate was the entrance from the Thames to York House, London residence of the Duke of Buckingham in the C17th. Also of note is the Screen wall

---

with seats and pond by Lutyens. Behind is the Belgian War Memorial with an exceptionally fine and unusual bronze group by V. Rousseau, facing on to the Embankment.

Cleopatra's Needle
Victoria Embankment. One of a pair erected about 1500 BC at Heliopolis, the ancient Egyptian centre of sun-worship, the Needle was presented to Britain by Mohammed Ali in 1819 and erected here in 1878.

The Adelphi
John Adam Street. The new Adelphi, an ugly office building with two projecting wings, all in greyish concrete by Collcutt & Hamp, 1936-8, makes a mockery of the earlier Adelphi, a magnificent river facade of residences by the brothers Adam, 1772. Forty-nine windows long above an arched substructure and terrace, the old Adelphi was demolished in 1936, and the Embankment thus denuded of one of its most splendid buildings.

Savoy Hotel
Strand. The hotel was founded by Richard D'Oyley Carte and built to the designs of T. E. Colcutt. When it opened in 1889 it represented a revolution in comfort and had 70 bathrooms. The builder is reputed to have inquired whether the guests were amphibians! The name was taken from the fact that it was built on part of the site of the old Savoy Palace.

Somerset House
Strand. Built in 1776 by Sir William Chambers on the site of Protector Somerset's house, 1547, this magnificent building with its arches, terrace and river entrances decorated with lions and Tuscan columns, was intended to compete

with the splendour of Adam's Adelphi. Today it is mainly occupied by the General Register Office whose records of birth and death go back to 1836. In the East wing is King's College, part of the University of London. On the corner of the gardens following the building on the Embankment is a bronze statue of Brunel by Marochetti, 1886. Brunel was the engineer in charge of the building of the Great Western Railway. His ship, the

---

Great Eastern, was launched on the Thames, at Millwall.

No 2 Temple Place
This exquisite two-storeyed white building in early Elizabethan style, 1895, by J. L. Pearson is a gem of its period. Originally the Astor Estate Office, it is now the headquarters of Smith & Nephew Associated Companies.

The Temple
The name derives from the Order of Knights Templars who occupied the site from 1160-1308. In the C17th the Temple was leased to the benchers of the Inner and Middle Temple, two Inns of Court. These inns, together with Lincoln's Inn and Gray's Inn, hold the ancient and exclusive privilege of providing advocates in the Courts of England and Wales. To appreciate the Temple Buildings, only a few of which are visible from the river, a visit should be made on foot. On the Embankment Sir Joseph Bazalgette's arch and stairs mark the C19th acess to the Temple from the river.
Close by is moored *HMS Discovery,* the sailing ship which Scott used on his expedition to the Antarctic in 1901-4. *It is usually open to visitors from 10.00-16.30 daily.* For training courses for youth organisations here, apply to D. Clayton, 155 Notting Hill Gate, W11.

City of London

Between Blackfriars, whose name recalls the C13th monastery of the Dominicans, and London Bridge, almost all that is visible from the river is a row of decaying warehouses and the dome of St Pauls in the distance. But behind the warehouses, in Upper Thames Street, are a number of Wren churches: St Benet's, St Mary's Somerset (tower only), St James Garlickhythe and St Michael Peternoster Royal. The following buildings are of immediate interest on the river:

Mermaid Theatre
Upper Thames Street. The theatre is in a warehouse converted in 1959 by Devereux and Davies. The interior is unpretentious and attractive. Bernard Miles, the founder, aimed to reintroduce drama to City audiences. Apart from the popularity of the restaurant and snack bar, the theatre has achieved success with its productions.

Vintners Hall
Upper Thames Street. Although the Hall is hidden by a warehouse, it is important because of its connections with the Thames. Built in 1671, but altered in 1870 and 1910, the fine wrought iron entrance bears two swans. The swans reflect the ancient privilege the Company shares with the Dyers Company of possessing

a game of Swans on the Thames. Each July a census of the swans on the reaches up to Henley is made. This is known as the 'Swan Upping'. The cygnets are marked with one nick for the Dyer's Company and two nicks for the Vintners. The Queen's swans are unmarked. Occasionally a swan feast is held. The Swan Warden, with a retinue of officials and musicians playing woodwind instruments, presents roast cygnets to the Master.

Cannon Street Station
Only the murky red brick arched train sheds with their monumental towers remain of the great Victorian station by J. Hawkshaw and J. W. Barry. These extend into the river at the railway bridge. The rest of the station has been rebuilt further inland.

Fishmongers Hall
Built in the grand classical manner in 1831-4 by Henry Roberts, the Company administers the annual Doggett's Coat and Badge Race for Thames Watermen. This race, the oldest annual contested sporting event and the longest rowing race in the world (1 furlong short of 5 miles), was introduced in 1715. Doggett, an Irish comedian and staunch Hanoverian, who used the services of the watermen to ferry him to and from the theatres, decided to mark the anniversary of the accession of George I to the throne by instituting an annual race for watermen. The race is from London Bridge to Cadogan Pier, Chelsea, and is usually held at the end of July. The victor is presented with an orange-red coat, breeches and cap, and a silver arm badge bearing the words 'The Gift of the late Thomas Doggett'.

London Bridge
See London Bridge and Tunnels.

South Bank, Places of interest
Battersea

Festival Gardens
Part of Battersea Park since the Festival of Britain in 1951, the piers and pleasure palaces of the Fun Fair decorate the river bank. Here the big wheel turns from *14.30-22.30 from Easter until the end of Sept.* It is the largest amusement centre in England—side-shows, roundabouts and big dipper. The *News of the World* Gala day for Charity is *held on the second Saturday in May at 14.30.* For 3s6d it is possible to obtain the autographs of many famous theatre and screen celebrities who attend the Gala.

Battersea Park
The Park was laid out by Sir James Pennethorne as a public garden and opened by Queen Victoria in 1858. There is a boating lake, a sub-tropical garden and sculptures by Moore, Hepworth and Epstein. A triennial exhibition of modern sculpture is held. *On Easter Sunday* the Park is gladdened by the Easter Parade of floats *at 15.00,* and on the *Sun before the Royal Tournament, towards the end of June,* there is a march-past of Tournament performers. Jazz concerts are given in the summer. Inland, Battersea now houses the University of Surrey and the Battersea Home for Lost Dogs.
In the future it will include Covent Garden Market whose new premises are being built on the site of the old Nine Elms Station.

Battersea Power Station
One of the most potent buildings on the river bank, this vast oblong of brick with its four chimneys was designed by Sir Giles Gilbert

Scott, 1932-4, and was one of the first examples of contemporary industrial architecture.

Lambeth
Albert Embankment
Designed as a broad footwalk by Sir Joseph Bazalgette, 1867, the Embankment stretches between Vauxhall and Westminster Bridges. The upper Embankment was the site of the C18th Vauxhall Gardens, whose Chinese pavilions and walks were the envy of Europe, but today it is mainly a display of C20th commercial architecture. The most interesting buildings are included here.

London Telecommunications Centre
Albert Embankment. Built in 1962 by T. P. Bennett & Partners, this building houses the administrative headquarters of the London telephone service, whose regional network covers 1300 square miles.

National Dock Labour Board
Albert Embankment. The NDLB is responsible for implementing the Dock Workers' Employment Scheme, 1967, which ended the system of casual labour in the Docks. The building was constructed in 1956 by Frederick Gibbard.

London Fire Brigade
Albert Embankment. Housed in a grey regular building by E. P. Wheeler, 1937, the Brigade responds to more than 28,000 calls a year and numbers over 2000 firemen.

Doulton House
Albert Embankment. Doulton House is the main office of Doulton & Co, makers of ceramics. The Thames-side was famous for its potteries in the C16-C19th, but the Royal Doulton Works, established in 1815, are the sole survivors of this tradition. Their C19th premises were demolished and the present building by T. P. Bennett was erected in 1939. It is interesting in its use of materials. The exterior is faced in ivory terracotta made by Doulton, the doorways are bronze with four pilasters in gold terracotta and above the entrance is a frieze of pottery depicting 'Pottery through the Ages'.
Inside, the hall is decorated with nine coloured tile panels hand-painted with the coat of arms of each city where Doulton has factories. These details make this an original building of the 1930's.

Lambeth Bridge House
Lambeth Bridge. Headquarters of the Ministry of Public Buildings and Works, this elephantine grey building, 1939, with its air of officialdom, entirely dwarfs the delightful grouping of Lambeth Palace and the Church of St Mary.

Lambeth Palace
Lambeth Palace Road. The Palace is probably the most important medieval building in London and

has been the site of the Archbishop of Canterbury's residence since the C12th. The red brick gatehouse, 1495, and the Great Hall, rebuilt about 1660 and now housing the library, can be seen from the road, but owing to shortage of staff the picture gallery, including pictures by Holbein, Van Dyck and Reynolds, and the Chapel are only open to the public on a few days a year: the Garden opening for the National Gardens Scheme in June (Tel 01-730-0355) and the Lambeth Parish Church Garden

Party (Tel 01-928-3409), also in the summer. The hall and library are *open 10.00-12.00 daily except Sun.*

St Thomas Hospital
Lambeth Palace Road. Only the Medical School with its Italianate tower and three of the seven brick pavilion blocks of Currey's buildings, 1868, remain, and these will soon be demolished and replaced by the modern buildings of the new hospital. So far only a tall oblong ward block has been built, but the plan for the new Hospital is ambitious and will transform this section of the Embankment. The scheme envisages fairly high buildings in concentrated blocks. Prepared by W. F. Howitt, staff architect, and Yorke Rosenberg Mardall, it allows for the most up-to-date use of medical equipment. St Thomas' was founded in Southwark in the C12th and is not only a teaching hospital and the centre of the Nightingale Training Scheme for Nurses, which Florence Nightingale began there, but also a district hospital. The lamp-stands on the Embankment below the hospital are worth a glance. They are entwined with dolphins and acanthus.

County Hall
Westminster Bridge. The imposing headquarters of the Greater London Council by Ralph Knott, 1921-3, reflects the architect's admiration for Piranesi. The central feature is the concave giant colonnade and the niches filled with sculpture. Visitors can attend the Council meeting on *alternate Tuesdays at 14.30.* There are also conducted tours of the building on *Sat 10.30-12.00, 13.30-15.30.* The magnificent lion beside County Hall was formerly the trademark of a brewery. Erected in 1837, the lion is made of Coade stone, an artificial stone impervious to weather. For many years it stood outside Waterloo Station and was moved to its present position on Westminster Bridge in 1966.

Shell Centre
Part of the area known as the South Bank, the Shell Centre was designed by Sir Howard Robertson, 1962. Of greyish white concrete with monotonous little square windows, the flat surface is totally unrelieved—it seems more in character to view it as a physical feature rather than as architecture. The central 351ft-high skyscraper rises like a huge grey mountain. On the top is a public viewing gallery with magnificent views of London. The largest office building in the world, the Centre covers 7½ acres and is a self-contained empire of shops, garages, cinemas, squash courts and swimming pool. Long corridors make the interior as dead as the exterior.

The South Bank Development
The Festival Hall, the Queen Elizabeth Hall, the National Film Theatre and the Hayward Gallery are the buildings included in the GLC's recreational and cultural scheme for the South Bank which probably originated with the Festival of Britain in 1951. These buildings will soon be joined by the National Theatre, which will be built to designs by Denys Lasdun. The Festival Hall, completed in 1951 and built by Sir Robert Matthew and Sir Leonard Martin, has seating for 3400. The Queen Elizabeth Hall by Hubert Bennett, 1967, is much smaller and intended for recitals. Bennett also designed the Hayward Gallery, opened in 1968.

The Arts Council are to exhibit travelling exhibitions and their own collection of sculpture and paintings here. The overall social conception for the South Bank is admirable, and architecturally the best use is made of the river position through raised terraces, but the visitor is overwhelmed by the maze of tunnels and winding staircases which lead to the terrace area and by the blind corners to the buildings which in many instances block the view and lead to a sense of social isolation. The buildings are at their best when viewed from the river as a unit.

Southwark
Upper Ground
Here the river bank becomes a line of decrepit warehouses. The yellow hoarding of the *Daily Mail* warehouse stares across the water, then comes Bowater's warehouse and 'Youngers Tartan Bitter'. In Barge House Street, once the site of the Royal Barge sheds, looms the Oxo warehouse, 1928, by A. W. Moore, its tower advertising 'Oxo' in Disney letters.
Next, Sainsbury's warehouses by Sir Owen Williams, 1935. Beside Blackfriars Bridge rises the modern block, United Africa House.
Bankside
Until the C19th Bankside was the site of amusement gardens and theatres. In the C16th the Rose Theatre, the Swan and the Globe were all around Bankside and it was also the scene of bear-baiting. Close to the theatres were the inns, Spurre, Christopher and Bull. Today almost all is warehouses apart from the Bankside Power Station and a few remaining C17th and C18th houses, nos 49-52. Wren lived in no 49 and watched the building of St Pauls. At the far end of Bankside is the delightful C17th Anchor Inn.
Bankside Power Station
This predatory one-chimneyed brick edifice by Sir Giles Gilbert Scott, 1935, may be compared with Battersea Power Station by the same architect.
Hopton Almshouses
Hopton Street. In their dank surroundings, these C18th brick almshouses surrounding a small garden with lawns and rose bushes stand out like jewels.
Winchester Square
Clink Street, the site of the old Clink Prison burnt down in the Gordon Riots of 1780, leads to the Square. This was once the main courtyard of Winchester Palace, seat of the Bishops of Winchester. This C13th house was burnt down in 1814 and only a few fragments amongst the warehouses of J. Sims and Pickfords remain.
Southwark Cathedral
Cathedral Street. From the river all

that can be seen is the four-pinnacled tower. The best approach is inland through Winchester Walk, and past the Borough Market, *open at 04.30* for fruit and flowers.
In the middle ages the Cathedral was part of the Augustinian priory of St Mary Overie. Despite its C19th additions, it is still one of the most impressive Gothic buildings in London and is so rich in historic and architectural interest that the visitor should buy a Guide at the door. Apart from

the wealth of monuments, the model in the retro-choir showing the Priory and Winchester Palace in 1540 is of special interest and also the collection of carved wooden bosses from the C15th roof.
London Bridge
See London Bridges and Tunnels
Craft Centre
WC2. 43 Earlham Street. Pottery, glass, silver and china made in craft workshops all over England are exhibited here.

Archaeology
Battersea
Bronze Age and Iron Age swords, and the famous Battersea Shield taken from the river. Now in British Museum.
Roman pottery and Prehistoric worked flints found on the foreshore by Battersea Park.
Vauxhall
During the rebuilding of the bridge a Viking sword with gold and silver inlay of about the C11th was found.
Lambeth
A Roman boat was discovered on the site of County Hall.
Waterloo
From the river near the bridge: A hoard of 100 Saxon silver coins, found in 1884, and an Iron Age horned helmet. Now in British Museum.
The City
Londinium, the city now, was the Roman capital of Britain. The western wall reached the river between Blackfriars and Puddle Dock, while the east lies under the Tower of London.

Eating, drinking & accommodation
L'Aiglon ✗ ❢
Chelsea, SW3. 44 Old Church Street. Tel (01) 352 8650. Run by the same two actors who run the Chichester Festival Theatre Restaurant. International cooking. D only, 33s *until 23.15 (Sun 22.45)*. Licensed. Parking.
Anchor ✗ ❢
Southwark, SE1. 1 Bankside. Tel (01) 407 1577. The original pub was destroyed by fire, and the present one dates from 1750, renovated in 1963. Minstrel's gallery, view of the river, plenty of 'antiques' on the walls. L 10s6d *Mon-Fri*, D 12s6d *Mon-Sat*. Snacks. Parking.
Charing Cross Hotel ✗ ❢ BB
Strand, WC2. Tel (01) 839 7282. 217 rooms BB 67s. English and

French cooking. L 25s D 28s6d *daily until 22.00 (Sun 21.00)*. Parking.
The Savoy ✗ ❢ BB
WC2. The Strand. Tel (01) 836 4343. World famous in reputation and clientele. Edwardian in atmosphere and service. 500 rooms. LD. Outstanding cuisine. Secretarial service.
The Black Friar ❢
EC4. 174 Queen Victoria Street. Tel (01) 236 5650. Overshadowed by Blackfriars Rail Bridge, the pub has a unique Art Nouveau interior. Snacks.
The Mermaid ✗ ❢
EC4. 8 Upper Thames Street. Tel (01) 248 2835. Both restaurants have a view of the river. Meals are synchronised with Mermaid Theatre times; it is essential to book.
Mermaid Tavern. English cooking. LD 25s (Thur, Sat 16s6d). All-in theatre ticket and dinner 40s. *Closed Sun*.

Riverside Restaurant. International cooking. LD 40s. After theatre D *Thur, Sat until 23.00. Closed Sat L and all Sun*. Snack bar.
YHA
Highgate, N6. 84 Highgate West Hill. Tel (01) 340 1831.

Boatyards
Barge Good Service
Moored mid-stream off County Hall. Tel (01) 228 1612. Diesel and lubricants.

Mooring
PLA moorings with access from Westminster Pier and Charing Cross Pier. Apply Assistant Harbour Master, Toll House, Kew, Richmond. Tel (01) 940 8288. Cadogan Pier. Convenient landing for Chelsea district. Tel (01) 352 4604.
Battersea Church Drawdock, Battersea.
Natural history
There are enclosures for deer and other animals in Battersea Park. Grey squirrels are plentiful, and many wildfowl live and breed on the lake. Chelsea Physic Garden was founded in 1673 by the Society of Apothecaries, and here many native and foreign plants are grown in natural order beds. Experimental greenhouses and a laboratory are on the site, and many specimens from them are supplied every year to botanical workers. Permission must be obtained to visit. Canada geese, once kept in Royal Parks, now live wild and may often be seen near Westminster Bridge.
There is a fine collection of waterfowl, started by Charles II, in St James's Park. Jays may be seen in the central parks, and numerous feral (or 'London') pigeons and wood-pigeons. Kestrels bred on County Hall in 1968 and raised two young, then visible from the Shell Centre's viewing platform. Many thousands of starlings fly into London at dusk, perhaps attracted by the greater warmth of the city centre, to roost. Vast flocks wheel and turn in the sky before settling for the night on buildings and trees, particularly in Trafalgar Square and along the Embankment, where their noisy chattering can be heard above the traffic. In 1951 their numbers were estimated as at least 10,000 and possibly as many as 100,000 at times.
In Palace Yard at the Palace of Westminster there is a row of *Catalpa bignonioides* which includes the biggest specimen in Britain.

Fishing
There is a strong tidal flow through the Chelsea, Blackfriars and Southwark reaches and although not fished, these stretches are known to hold some roach, eels, bream, perch, dace, barbel and tench.
Until the early C19th salmon were regularly caught and as the river grows cleaner it is possible that in the future they may return to these waters.
Battersea Park Lake has roach, perch, pike and a few carp.
The fishing in lakes and ponds in and around London can be rewarding, although almost all waters are overfished and the serious angler should avoid holiday times and weekends.

Tackle shops
Tookes Tackle
614 Fulham Road, SW6.
Tachbrook
244 Vauxhall Bridge Road, SW6. Tel (01) 842 5179.
Emergency: see map 101

Bridges

Richmond Bridge
This fine stone bridge with its five arches and parapet is one of the most handsome on the Thames and was frequently the subject for paintings in the C18th-C19th. Built in the classical style by James Paine, 1777, it replaced the earlier horse ferry and was a toll bridge until 1859. In 1937 it was skilfully widened without loss of character.

Richmond Railway Bridge
Typical of the early railway period, this iron and concrete bridge by Locke was built in 1848 as part of the Richmond-Staines-Windsor line. It should be compared with Barnes Bridge by the same designer.

Twickenham Bridge
This wide concrete structure by Maxwell Ayrton carries the Chertsey Arterial Road and was opened in 1933.

Richmond Footbridge
Beneath the arches of this handsome double footbridge, 1894, are three weir gates. When the gates are lowered they form a complete barrier across the river, making a lock.

Kew Bridge
The bridge was opened by Edward VII in 1903 and is officially called the King Edward VII bridge. Designed by Sir John Wolfe Barry and Cuthbert Brereton, it replaced the earlier C18th bridge and is a fine stone structure with three spans.

Kew Railway Bridge
When it was opened to traffic in 1869, this five-span lattice girder bridge was part of the London and South-Western Railway extension. It was designed by W. R. Galbraith.

Chiswick Bridge
Built in 1933, this bridge has the longest concrete arch of any bridge on the Thames. The centre span measures 150ft. Designed by Sir Herbert Baker, it was opened by the Prince of Wales.

Barnes Railway Bridge
This light and elegant iron bridge by Locke was opened in 1849 to connect with the Richmond line. Its design is similar to Richmond Railway bridge.

Hammersmith Bridge
Sir Joseph Bazalgette's suspension bridge, 1887, has a distinct personality of its own. This flows from the partly gilt iron pylons crowned with fussy pavilion tops, all of which bestow a sense of frivolity on the bridge.

Putney Bridge
The wooden toll bridge of 1729 which had become unsafe was replaced by this bridge by Sir Joseph Bazalgette in 1884.

Fulham Railway Bridge
This trellis girder iron bridge was part of the Metropolitan extension to the District Railway. Designed by William Jacomb, it was opened in 1889 and connects with a footbridge running parallel to it. It is part of the London Transport underground system.

Wandsworth Bridge
In 1938 the C19th bridge was replaced by the existing structure by E. P. Wheeler.

Battersea Railway Bridge
The West London Extension Railway, of which this bridge was a part, was opened in 1863 to connect the south of England directly with the north. The line was the only one which did not end at a London terminus and was therefore a target for bombing in the Second World War in the hope that this direct link between north and south England might be broken.

Battersea Bridge
The old Battersea Bridge of 1772 was a picturesque wooden structure much painted by Whistler and Turner. But this bridge of 1890 by Sir Joseph Bazalgette is a grimy iron structure without aesthetic pretension.

Albert Bridge
Over spiky and over-strutted, this combined cantilever and suspension bridge by R. W. Ordish was opened in 1873 and named after Prince Albert.

Chelsea Bridge
The suspension bridge of 1858 was replaced in 1934 by this concisely designed structure by G. Topham Forrest and E. P. Wheeler.

Victoria Railway Bridge
When it opened in 1859, this was the widest railway bridge in the world—132ft wide and 900ft long—and it provided ten separate accesses to Victoria Station. It has recently been widened further to meet the demands of modern transport.

Vauxhall Bridge
By 1900 when this bridge was built, J. Walker's iron bridge which it supplanted had become the most hazardous on the river. This structure is by Sir Maurice Fitzmaurice and W. E. Riley.

Lambeth Bridge
The site was first occupied by a horse ferry, then the ugly suspension bridge of 1862, and finally in 1932 by this steel bridge by G. Topham Forrest. It has just been attractively repainted.

Westminster Bridge
Westminster Bridge by Thomas Page, 1862, is at its best at high tide. At low tide the lanky piers are drab with mud. It was built when the stone bridge of 1749 was demolished.

Charing Cross Railway Bridge
This bridge is, also known as the Hungerford bridge. Its ugliness holds a certain curiosity when seen against the palatial splendour of Whitehall Court. It replaced the C19th suspension bridge. A separate footbridge runs alongside to Waterloo Station.

Waterloo Bridge
Sir Giles G. Scott's concrete bridge, 1945, is plain and elegant. It replaced John Rennie's early C19th bridge, a beautiful design of Greek columns and nine elliptical arches.

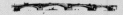

Blackfriars Bridge
Although the general outline is bold, it has rather a dwarfed and stunted look. It was built by William Cubitt in 1899 from the designs of Thomas Page and took the place of the C18th bridge by Robert Mylne.

Blackfriars Railway Bridge
Built in 1886 for the London, Chatham and Dover Railway, this elegant iron bridge, with its high parapet and decorative coat of arms at each end, can best be seen from the road bridge.

Southwark Bridge
This bridge, which is rather lifeless, replaced Rennie's early C19th iron bridge, considered one of the finest on the river. It is by Sir Ernest George, 1919.

Cannon Street Railway Bridge
Built in 1866 as part of the extension of the South-Eastern Railway, the bridge's engineers were J. Hawkshaw and J. W. Barry. It is a prominent structure on account of the C19th train shed which juts out on one side of the bridge. The shed's monumental towers and gloomy brick edifice lends character to the whole.

London Bridge
Until 1749 London bridge was the only bridge over the river in London. The first wooden bridge recorded was built by the Saxons, but it is possible that the Romans may also have had a bridge here.

In 1176 the wooden bridge was replaced by a stone structure. This had houses, shops and a church built along it and was very similar in appearance to the Ponte Vecchio in Florence. The heads of traitors were displayed on the spikes of the fortified gates at either end. In 1831 this bridge was demolished and a new bridge by John Rennie replaced it. This granite bridge with its five arches is now, in its turn, being rebuilt. It had become too narrow to meet the additional demands of modern traffic and because of structural faults could not be widened. The new bridge, whose construction is under the direction of the City Engineer, Harold K. King, will have an elegant flat arched profile in three spans carried on slender piers.

The foundation structures will be sunk 70ft into the river bed. Work is expected to be completed by 1972. But Rennie's bridge will be reconstructed in Los Angeles where a concrete bridge to the same design will cross from a newly formed island in Lake Havasu to the Arizona mainland. The McCulloch Corporation have paid 2,460,000 dollars for the materials of Rennie's bridge and, as the Corporation of London build the new London Bridge, they are carefully dismantling the granite parapets and face work of the old bridge. Each stone is carefully marked for shipping to Los Angeles for facing the new Los Angeles bridge.

Tower Bridge

This bridge with its two Gothic towers was built by Sir John Wolfe Barry and his assistant Isambard Brunel, the younger, in 1894.

The towers are not purely ornamental. Inside is part of the machinery which operates the bascules or drawbridges and there are also stairs to the upper latticework footbridge which is now closed to pedestrians.

About twenty ships pass through the bridge each day. The bascules, which also provide a roadway, separate in the middle and are lifted upwards to allow a headway of 140ft. Ships signal their intention to pass through by flying a ball and pennant in the daytime and by showing two red lights vertically by night. In addition, one long and three short blasts are blown on the siren. The traffic lights are then turned to red and bells are rung to warn traffic and pedestrians. Only on a few occasions has the system failed. In 1952 a bus was trapped on the bridge as the bascules rose and had to leap several feet, but there were no serious injuries. In 1968 during the hot weather, the pistons swelled and it was not possible to operate the bridge. All the original machinery is still in use and the bascules are operated hydraulically.

Tunnels

London Underground Tunnels

Five of the tunnels beneath the Thames are part of the London Transport underground system. The Northern, Bakerloo and City lines each have their separate tunnels crossing the Thames near Waterloo Station; the Northern line crosses again by London Bridge. But the most famous of the London Transport tunnels is the Thames Tunnel which carries Metropolitan trains between Rotherhithe and Wapping (see below).

Tower Subway

The top of the tunnel's 60ft shaft can be seen on Tower Hill. Designed by Henry Greathead, the tunnel was opened in 1845 as a subway to carry passenger traffic from Tower Hill to Bermondsey. It worked on the principle of a cable tramway. Carriages were pulled to and fro by stationary engines at either end. Nowadays the tunnel is used for water pipes.

Thames Tunnel

This tunnel which now carries the underground trains between Rotherhithe and Wapping was the first underwater pedestrian tunnel in the world when it opened in 1843. It was largely the achievement of the famous engineer, Isambard Brunel. Building took eleven years, during which time both he and his men risked their lives. Twice the river broke into the tunnel and the project had to

be abandoned. In 1827 Brunel held a banquet in the tunnel to celebrate the renewal of work. It was a financial failure, and in 1865 the tunnel was bought by the East London Railway Company and extended to connect with the Great Eastern Railway. The Company was finally absorbed by the Underground, and in 1913 the line through the tunnel was electrified. The old tunnel shaft can be seen in Brunel Road.

Rotherhithe Tunnel

The circular air vents of this road traffic tunnel connecting Rotherhithe and Stepney can be seen on either side of the river. The tunnel was opened in 1908. 6278ft long, it carries two lanes of traffic. The maximum safety level of carbon monoxide is 250 PPM. Robert Vazie's early C19th tunnel was close to the site. This tunnel was almost completed in 1808

when it collapsed under the stress of an exceptionally high tide. Work was then abandoned.

Greenwich Tunnel

The Blackwall tunnel which had opened in 1897 was designed as a road traffic tunnel. In 1902 it was therefore decided to build a pedestrian subway to link Greenwich with the Isle of Dogs. Opposition was met from the Watermen and Lightermen who feared that their services would no longer be required. The southern entrance to the footway is in Cutty Sark Gardens, Greenwich, and the northern in Island Gardens, Isle of Dogs.

Blackwall Tunnel

Built between 1889 and 1897, this is London's oldest tunnel for road traffic. It is a 6116ft long tube, 16ft wide, and runs parallel to the new Blackwall road tunnel which was opened in 1967. Originally designed to carry two lanes of traffic, the old tunnel will now become one way. Traffic will pass down the new tunnel in the opposite direction.

Woolwich Tunnel

This foot tunnel has linked Woolwich with North Woolwich since 1912. The inconvenience caused by interruptions in the Woolwich Free Ferry Service during the hard winters lead to the decision to build the footway. The tunnel cost only £78,000.

Dartford Toll Tunnel

Opened in 1963, the tunnel links Dartford with Purfleet. As early as the C18th there was a plan to build a tunnel in the lower reaches of the Thames. Work was started on a tunnel between Tilbury Fort and Gravesend but was soon abandoned for lack of funds. In 1924 the Tilbury-Gravesend site was rejected in favour of the present site and the pilot tunnel had been completed by 1938 when war intervened. Work on the full bore tunnel was revived in 1955.

The main tunnel is 28ft in diameter and carries a two-lane highway 100ft below high water in the river. The control room of the tunnel can be seen on the Kent side of the river as can the ventilation building near the tunnel portal. In the summer queues build up at the entrances, but it is hoped that these may be reduced when the North Orbital and South Orbital roads are built with which the tunnel will form an important link.

Tideway Race, 1966 R R Bolland

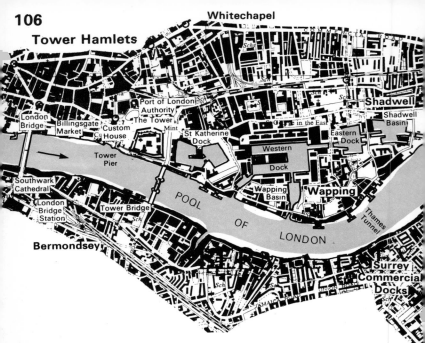

Whitechapel

Shadwell

Port of London
Authority

The Tower

Shadwell
Basin

London
Bridge

Billingsgate
Market

Custom
House

Mint

St Katherine
Dock

'...in the East'

Eastern
Dock

Western

Dock

Tower
Pier

Southwark
Cathedral

Wapping
Basin

Wapping

London
Bridge
Station

Tower Bridge

POOL

OF

LONDON

Thames
Tunnel

Bermondsey

Surrey
Commercial
Docks

North Bank: Places of interest

Port of London

The Port of London effectively
begins at London Bridge. Here the
Pool of London stretches down-
river to Limehouse Reach and the
river with its wharves and docks
and vast ships is a hive of
industry. Customs launches and
tugs ply up and down. Vessels of
up to 10,000 tons can go up to
London Bridge, and London is the
biggest oil port in Britain. It has
been a port for 2000 years and
was already exporting goods in
AD 30. Nowadays the docks are
overcrowded and need either to
be reorganised or closed completely and re-established at
Tilbury.

St Magnus the Martyr

Lower Thames Street. This Wren
church, 1687, has an imaginatively
detailed steeple, added in 1706
and reaching 185ft high. This contrasts with the sheer modern wall
of Adelaide House. The ornate
black and gold clock dates from
1709. In the churchyard, once part
of the approach to old London
Bridge, destroyed in 1831, can be
seen stones from the old bridge
and also the remains of a Roman
wharf. The interior of the church
has some of the most sumptuous
woodwork to be seen anywhere in
the city.

Billingsgate Market

Lower Thames Street. The market
is a yellow brick Victorian building
with arcaded ground floor and was
built by Sir Horace Jones, 1875.
The first reference to a market at
Billingsgate was made in AD 870.
A free-fish market was established
by statute in 1699, but until the
C18th coal, corn and provisions
were also sold. Today about
250 tons of fish pass through the
market on a normal trading day.
To see the market in full operation,
one should be there *between
05.00 and 09.00*. The fish-porters
wear curious leather hats with flat
tops and wide brims, formerly
known as 'bobbing hats'. Bobbing
was the charge made by the porter
to carry fish from the wholesaler
to the retailer. These hats enable
the porter to carry about a
hundredweight of fish on his head.

The Custom House

Lower Thames Street. A custom
house has stood beside Billingsgate since 870. The present
building is by Laing, 1813-17, but
the river facade was rebuilt by
Smirke in 1825. Badly bombed in
the war, the building has been
restored. It is suitably official and
all of Portland stone and yellow
brick. In front of it is *HMS Harpy*,
a double-decked floating structure
from which the Customs men
depart in their launches.

Tower Place

EC3. Tower Hill. This modern
pedestrian centre was designed by
George Trew & Dunn and the
City of London Real Property
Company with Sir Basil Spence as
consultant. Completed in 1965, it
won a Civic Trust award in 1967.
There is three-storey car-parking,
offices, shops and a pub. A large
open courtyard has good views
of the Tower and river.

The Tower of London

EC3. Tower Hill. Tel (01) 709
0765. Although greatly restored
and altered over the centuries, the

Tower is probably the most
important work of military architecture in Britain and has been
used as a palace, a fortress and a
prison since William the Conqueror
built the White Tower in 1078.
Apart from the historic and architectural interest of the building,
there are the Crown Jewels and
the museum of armament to see.
The uniformed yeoman warders
who act as guides lend colour to
the scene. On the riverside, Gun
Wharf displays trophy guns and
there is a children's beach. At
lunchtime, Tower Hill, like
Speaker's Corner, Hyde Park,
enjoys the voracious harangues of
anyone who chooses to make a
speech. *Open mid-Mar-Oct 10.00-
14.30. Oct-Mar 10.00- 16.00.
Sun mid-Mar-Nov 14.00-17.00.*
Entrance 2s.

Port of London Authority

EC3. Trinity Square. Edwin
Cooper's building, 1912-22, is a
lasting monument to Edwardian
optimism. Vast and vulgar, it is
nevertheless most impressive.
The Port of London Authority not
only controls and administers the
Port of London, but also the tidal
river from Teddington to the sea.

Tower Bridge

Boat trips of the London docks
depart from here in the summer
months. It is advisable to book the
dock trip with the Port of London
Authority, Trinity Square, EC3.
Tel (01) 481 2000, Ext. 96-260.

Tower Bridge

See London bridges and tunnels.

St Katharine and London Docks

E1. These docks were built during
the wave of industrialisation and
trade of the early C19th. Con-
veniently placed by the Limehouse
Cut, they connected with the
national canal system. Until their
closure in 1968 they were mainly
associated with long-term storage,
especially of wine and wool. Both
docks are of architectural value.
St Katharine's, built in 1828, was
designed by Thomas Telford, the
engineer of the Menai Straits
Bridge and the Holyhead Road.
The doric columns and the office
building by Hardwick make it the
most attractive of the dock
buildings. London Docks, built
1805 by Asher Alexander, have an
entrance bounded by a symmetrical
terrace of houses. The docks have
recently been bought by the GLC
for £1½ million, to be developed as
a residential area with a yacht
marina and a commercial
exhibition centre.

Wapping High Street

E1. It is almost all wharves, but
no. 93 is a characteristic early
C19th wharf owner's house.
A garden occasionally breaks the
pattern, and little blind alleys lead
off to the Thames, among them
Wapping Stairs.

Rotherhithe Tunnel

See London Bridges and Tunnels.

Regent's Canal Dock

E14. Narrow Street. The Regent's
Canal, a branch of the Grand
Union Canal, was opened in 1820
to connect Paddington with the

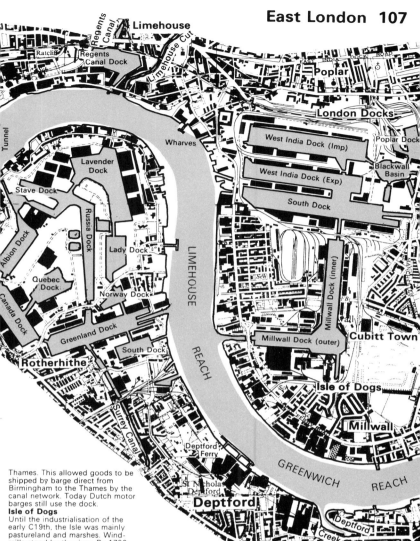

Thames. This allowed goods to be shipped by barge direct from Birmingham to the Thames by the canal network. Today Dutch motor barges still use the dock.

Isle of Dogs
Until the industrialisation of the early C19th, the Isle was mainly pastureland and marshes. Windmills stood by the river. By 1799 the Port of London had become so overcrowded that Parliament authorised the building of a new dock on the Isle of Dogs, under the auspices of the West India Company. Built by William Jessop, the two West India Docks were opened in 1802. The plain brick warehouses are noteworthy.
In 1870 the South Dock was added. It was built on the site of the City Canal which had connected Limehouse Reach and Blackwall Reach between 1805 and 1829. The Millwall Docks, the most southern, were completed in 1864. For many years these docks had a monopoly of all West India goods. Recently they have been greatly modernised with new transit sheds, electric cranes and fork-lift trucks. They handle regular services from all parts of the world. Fruit, hides, rubber and hemp are typical imports.

South Bank: Places of interest
Hays Wharf
SE1. Hays Lane. Standing alone amongst the surrounding Victorian warehouses, the wharf was built in 1931 by H. S. Goodhart-Rendel and shows a strong Scandinavian influence with its figure of St Olave. The reliefs are by Frank Dobson.

Shad Thames
SE1. The warehouses are linked by iron bridges at all levels. The area is dominated by the smell from the Courage Brewery, founded in 1789.

Cherry Garden Pier
Here the ships sound their signal if they want Tower Bridge to be raised. Private boat trips can be arranged for parties up to twelve from here upon application to the Harbour Master, PLA, Trinity Square, EC3. Tel (01) 481 2000.

Rotherhithe Street
SE16. Amidst the tall warehouses and damp alleys the street has an atmosphere all of its own. There are several C18th and early C19th buildings, including a C18th shipowners mansion inside Nelson Wharf. Note also the C17th Angel Inn, and the good Modern Movement warehouse in Horseferry Wharf. Built 1937 by J. Hill. The street can be seen from a P1 or P2 Red Arrow bus.

Surrey Commercial Docks
SE16. The only docks on the south side of the river. Built in 1807 and later enlarged by the addition of the Greenland Dock. Today the eleven docks can berth fifty-three ships. Part of the Quayage includes the surviving 6½ miles of the Surrey Canal. Built at the same time as the docks, the canal was designed originally to link London and Portsmouth. In fact it only went as far as Camberwell.
The docks deal mainly with timber. 200,000 tons are handled by over 3,500 barges every year. A fully mechanised transit shed connects the Greenland and the South Docks.

Royal Naval Victualling Yard
SE8. Grove Street. The site of the Victualling Yard, an army supply depot till 1961, indicated the importance of Deptford as a naval and shipbuilding centre from the C16th to the C19th. Founded in 1513 the yard became the principal naval dockyard in the kingdom, rivalling Woolwich. Sir Francis Drake was knighted at the yard after his triumphant return.

Emergency: see map 101

108 East London

Archaeology

Southwark
Opposite the city, Southwark formed the extra-mural settlement of Roman London. It grew up round the Roman road to the south coast.

Eating, drinking & accommodation

The Angel ✕ ♟
SE16. 21 Rotherhithe Street. A popular old riverside pub. Lunch and snacks.

The Baked Potato ✕
EC3. 16 Tower Place. Tel (01) 626 0923. The restaurant is filled with interesting things to look at: statues, busts, marble pillars, chain-mail, etc. Large round oak tables. Meals *from 10.00-17.30*, from 6s. *Closed Sun.*

The Copper ✕ ♟
SE1. 206-208 Tower Bridge Road. Tel (01) 407 0968. The name derives from the police station nearby and from the brewery close to the pub. L *3s9d-7s6d Mon-Fri.* Snacks. Folk singing *Tue 5s.* Juke box, one-armed bandit. Parking.

George Inn ♟
SE1. 77 Borough High Street. Tel (01) 407 2056. Galleried Dickens coaching inn. Mussels, sprats, cockles and jellied eels.

Grapes ♟
E14. 27 Narrow Street. Tel (01) 987 4396. Built C16th, now surrounded by tall warehouses. Overlooks the river. Music at weekends. Snacks.

The Gun ♟
Blackwall, E14. 27 Coldharbour Lane. Tel (01) 987 1643. This popular riverside pub serves snacks.

The Mayflower ♟
SE16. 117 Rotherhithe Street. Tel (01) 237 1898. Covered terrace with view of the river. The Mayflower ship was fitted out near here. Snacks.

The Old Justice ✕ ♟
SE16. 94 Bermondsey Wall (East). Tel (01) 237 3452. English cooking, snacks. LD by arrangement. Piano and sing-song every weekend ♟

Prospect of Whitby ✕ ♟
E1. 57 Wapping Wall. Tel (01) 481 1095. One of the oldest riverside inns, it has a long history of famous people who frequented the pub. LD 35s *until 22.00. Closed Sun.* Parking.

The Royal Pavilion ✕ ♟
North Woolwich, E16. 2 Pier Road. Tel (01) 476 2455. There is a garden overlooking the river where children are welcome. L *Mon-Fri,* snacks. *Fri-Sun* family entertainments are put on. Bar billiards, juke box, one armed bandit. Mooring along the pier.

Tower Room Restaurant ✕ ♟
EC3. 23 Tower Place. Tel (01) 626 0955. Sumptuous decor—velvet and a huge chandelier. L only (à la carte) *from 21s Mon-Fri until 15.00.* Licensed.

Mooring

Cherry Garden Pier. Landing by prior arrangement. Tel (01) 237 3498.
Johnson Draw Dock, Poplar, off Manchester Road.

Natural history

After the bombing the black redstart began to colonise London in 1941, nesting in nooks and holes left by the bombs. Rebuilding has driven them from the City but they are still breeding in dockland. On Walthamstow reservoirs is the nearest heronry to the centre of London. The herons went there when they left Wanstead Park in the First World War, disturbed by gunfire.
Surprisingly enough, there are many wild flowers in this area of dockland. On walls and derelict buildings two alien plants flourish: *Buddleja davidii* (butterfly bush), a native of China, has escaped from gardens, and quite large bushes seem able to live in cracks of old brick walls. In summer many butterflies are attracted to the long sprays of scented purple flowers in the heart of dockland; small tortoise-shells, red admirals and others. *Senecio squalidus* (Oxford ragwort), from the lava slopes of Mount Etna, was first recorded in 1794 from old walls at Oxford, and is now widespread on old walls and waste places, where its bright yellow flowers make a brave show. Its plumed seeds have spread along railway lines, aided by the wind caused by the passage of trains. The rare and beautiful *Sambucus ebulus* (danewort) a dwarf elder, covers over an acre of ground in Mill Meads on the River Lea. In July the mass of large, flat-topped heads of creamy flowers with purple anthers is an impressive sight. *Chamaenerion angustifolium* (rosebay, fireweed) used to cover acres of London's bombed sites with its tall spikes of magenta flowers; it still grows in masses on waste ground.

Fishing

Not fished, but it is known that there are several species of fish in the waters between Southwark and Blackwall Reach, notably roach, perch, bream and eels. Several kinds of sea fish have also been reported.

Tackle shops

Rangemore Sports
71 Watling Street, EC4.
Sowerbutts & Son
151 Commercial Street, E1. Tel (01) 247 1724.
Bernard's Sports
141 Salmon Lane, Limehouse, E14.

The Royal Docks *Port of London Authority*

North Bank: Places of interest

Island Gardens
Saunders Ness Road, E14
This small park at the south tip of the Isle of Dogs was opened in 1895 to commemorate the spot which Wren considered had the best view of Greenwich Palace across the water.

West India Docks
See East London. Here the east entrance opens out just before the Blackwall tunnel. To watch a ship negotiate the narrow gates into the basin can be a fascinating experience. In 1969 the Preston Swing bridge will open to allow vehicles to cross over the dock gates.

Blackwall Tunnel
See London Bridges and Tunnels.

East India Docks
The Dock was opened in 1806. The East India Company had achieved powers to build another dock following the increase in traffic and the success of the enclosed West India Docks. Ships to and from the East Indies and China were loaded and unloaded here. The granite gateway with its domed cupola makes a proud display. Beside the entrance to the dock stands the modern two-chimneyed Brunswick Wharf Generating Station, a landmark on the river.

Bow Creek
The creek provides the mouth to the River Lea. It connects with the canal network, and is therefore much used by Thames barges.

Royal Docks
The London and St. Katharine Docks Company opened the Royal Albert Dock in 1880, then the largest and finest in the world. It was an extension of the Victoria Dock, 1855, which was insufficiently deep. The George V Dock was added to the group in 1921. These docks are the largest of the dock groups. Three miles from end to end, they have berths for over fifty ships up to 775ft long. Over forty shipping lines use the docks. Fruit, butter and meat are imported; motor vehicles, machinery and steel exported. Mechanical unloading and sorting has speeded up delivery. On the south side of the Royal Victoria Dock are four large private flour mills with storage capacity of 138,000 tons. Bulk grain is discharged into silos.

Woolwich Tunnel
See London Bridges and Tunnels.

Woolwich North
Essex. The Royal Victoria Gardens on the riverside are a good place to while away the time whilst waiting for the Woolwich Free Ferry.

South Bank: Places of interest

Greenwich
SE10. The splendour of Greenwich's Royal and Naval past is witnessed by the magnificent riverside grouping of the Queen's House and the Royal Naval College. Their perfection is frozen, missing the environment for which they were originally conceived. Once a fishing village, Greenwich grew in stature after the building of the Palace of Placentia, favoured by the Tudor sovereigns. Little remains of the medieval period and the Queen's House and Naval College reflect the glories of the C17th and C18th. Inland, Greenwich is crowded and busy with traffic. There are some good antique shops.

Royal Naval College
Greenwich. The College was once the site of the medieval Palace of Placentia. Mary II decided not to live in the Palace, then already partly rebuilt by Webb. Instead she commissioned Wren to rebuild it as a hospital for aged and disabled seamen. Designed in the Baroque style, it was completed in 1705. The Painted Hall, or dining hall, has a swirling Baroque ceiling by Thornhill, one of the finest of its period. The chapel with details in the neo-classical spirit dates from 1789. In 1873 the Hospital became the Royal Naval College to provide for the higher education of naval officers. Hall and Chapel *open May-Sep (not Thur) 14.30-17.00. Oct-Apr 14.30-17.00 (not Thur and Sun)*

Queen's House
Greenwich. Framed and dominated by the Naval College, this delightful white house in the Palladian style was built for Queen Anne of Denmark by Inigo Jones, 1618. It is now part of the National Maritime Museum.

National Maritime Museum
Romney Road. Tel (01) 858 4422. The Museum is devoted to the history of the sea and is of exceptional maritime interest. There is an unrivalled collection of seascapes, many of which bring the naval battles they depict vividly alive. Naval charts, magnificent ship models of all periods, uniforms and navigational instruments are all here. *Open 10.00-18.00, Sun 14.30-18.00.*

Greenwich Park
The park was laid out for Charles II by Le Notre. It commands a magnificent view of The Royal Naval College and of the river. It contains thirteen acres of wooded deer park, a bird sanctuary and archaeological sites. To the west of the park is Crooms Hill, whose C18th houses flank the road up to Blackheath. At the foot of the hill is the new Greenwich theatre. On the site of the old music hall, the 400 seat theatre will include an art gallery and coffee bar. *Park open 7.00-20.00, winter 18.00 or dusk.*

Old Royal Observatory
Greenwich Park. The original Observatory, still standing amidst the group of C17th, C18th and C19th buildings, was built by Wren for Flamsteed, first astronomer Royal, in the C17th. Astronomical instruments and exhibits relating to the history of astronomy are displayed in the old Observatory buildings and the time ball which provided the first public time signal in 1833 can still be seen. The Caird Planetarium in the south building has educational programmes for schools in the term time and public programmes in the holidays. Apply at the National Maritime Museum. The Observatory is *open 10.00-18.00, Sun 14.30-18.00.*

Greenwich Pier
The *Cutty Sark*, one of the old C19th tea and wool sailing clippers, stands in dry-dock. Many hardships were endured by the crew in the clipper races between England and China or Australia. The history of the *Cutty Sark* is displayed in drawings and photographs, and she is *open 11.00-18.00 (17.00 winter), Sun 14.30-18.00* 2s. Close by *Gypsy Moth IV*, the yacht in which Sir Francis Chichester made his solo circumnavigation of the world, is·also open for public viewing. 1s.

Trinity Hospital and Chapel
Riverside Walk. The hospital was founded by the Earl of Northampton in 1613 but was much altered in the C19th. The chapel has fine Flemish glass and a fragmentary monument to the Earl of Northumberland by Nicholas Stone, C17th. It is dwarfed by the power station.

St Alfege
Greenwich. Church Street. Apart from the tower, 1730, the church is by Hawksmoor and James, 1711. All in the classical style, its portico is of giant Tuscan order supporting a heavy pediment. The Church was badly bombed in the war and has been restored.

Greenwich Town Hall
Royal Hill. Built in 1939 by E. C. Culpin & Bowers, the Hall, with its tall tower and stock brick, is a worthy municipal building of the late 30's. Its Dutch motifs were fashionable at this time.

Charlton House
SE7. Charlton Road. Tel (01) 854 1121. Apart from Holland House, this is probably the most important Jacobean house in the London area. Built by Sir Adam Newton in 1607, it has original plaster ceilings and fireplaces. The summer house is attributed to Inigo Jones. The grounds and gardens are open to the public, but to visit the house application should be made to the Town Clerk, Town Hall, Greenwich, SE10.

Greenwich Marshes
These dismal stretches are dominated by the buildings of the South Metropolitan Gas Works and the Power Station, both of which make a suitable impact on their surroundings.

Woolwich
SE18. The individual character of Woolwich has been swept away and inland it appears as a suburban extension of Greenwich. But amidst this amalgam, the Old Woolwich with its distinguished military and naval past can still be found near the river in the Royal Naval Dockyard and the Royal Arsenal. But these, too, will soon be demolished to make way for modern development and both are already closed. A plan is afoot to absorb the site of Royal Arsenal into Thamesmead, which is to be a 1300 acre community and residential centre stretching through the Erith marshes. It will utterly transform this sector of the Thames.

Emergency: see map 111

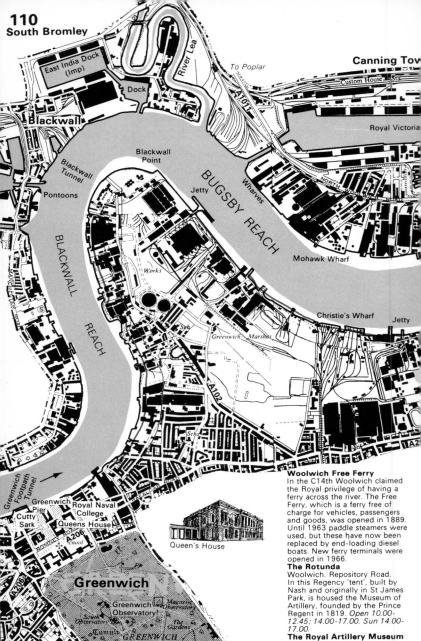

Queen's House

Woolwich Free Ferry

In the C14th Woolwich claimed the Royal privilege of having a ferry across the river. The Free Ferry, which is a ferry free of charge for vehicles, passengers and goods, was opened in 1889. Until 1963 paddle steamers were used, but these have now been replaced by end-loading diesel boats. New ferry terminals were opened in 1966.

The Rotunda

Woolwich. Repository Road. In this Regency 'tent', built by Nash and originally in St James Park, is housed the Museum of Artillery, founded by the Prince Regent in 1819. *Open 10.00-12.45; 14.00-17.00. Sun 14.00-17.00.*

The Royal Artillery Museum

Woolwich. Academy Road. The museum depicts the history of the Regiment of Artillery from 1716 to the present day—pictures, uniforms and models. Also see 'Rotunda' above. *Open 10.00-12.30, 14.00-16.00 weekdays.*

Royal Arsenal

Woolwich. Woolwich already had several military establishments when the Brass Gun Foundry, the first of the Arsenal buildings, was built in 1716. This building was probably designed by Vanbrugh as was the Model Room, 1719, which in 1741 became the Royal Military Academy. The Victorians enlarged the Arsenal to cover 1200 acres and in the 1939-45 war, 40,000 workers were employed. It is now closed and the site will soon be redeveloped as Thamesmead.

Places of interest

Royal Naval Dockyard
Woolwich. The dockyard, founded in the C15th, became the most important naval establishment under Henry VIII. In the C16th and C17th the *Great Harry* and *Royal Sovereign* were built here. The dockyard declined with the growth of Devonport and was closed in 1869.

St Mary Magdalene
Woolwich. Church Hill. This C18th church of no particular architectural interest occupies a commanding site overlooking the river. It has been put to original social use. The churchyard has been made into a public garden stretching to the river, the galleries have been converted into a lounge and restaurant, the crypt has become a discotheque and the Greenwich Council of Social Services has its office here.

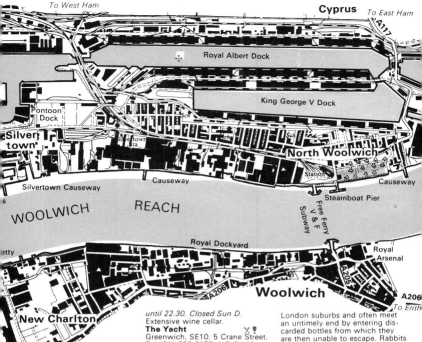

Sport
Swimming
Greenwich Baths. Trafalgar Road,
SE10. Tel (01) 854 0159. Turkish
and Russian vapour baths, foam
and brine baths.
Woolwich Baths. Bathway, SE18.
Tel (01) 854 8888.

Archaeology
Greenwich
A Saxon cemetery at Old Tilt Yard,
¼ mile from the river. In Greenwich
Park there are several Saxon
barrows. Also in the park the
remains of a Roman villa. It was
discovered in 1902.
Royal Albert Dock
A dug-out canoe discovered during
the building of the dock. Probably
Roman.

Eating, drinking &
accommodation
Gloucester Hotel ✕ ♥ BB
Greenwich, SE10. 1 King William
Walk. Tel (01) 858 2666. Opposite
the entrance to Greenwich Park.
5 rooms BB 30s. L from 8s
D from 10s *Mon-Fri until 22.00.*
Cold buffet and snacks *Sat-Sun.*
Folk-singing *Wed and Sat.*
The Pilot
Greenwich. River Way. Tel (01)
858 5910. Dating from 1660, this
inn is in the industrial part of
Greenwich, beside the river.
Snacks. Juke box, one-armed
bandit.
Spread Eagle Restaurant ✕ ♥
Greenwich, SE10. 2 Stockwell
Street. Tel (01) 858 5861. Once a
coaching house and now a
Victorian pastiche restaurant.
L 15s D 20s *until 22.30. Closed
Mon and Sun D.* Morning coffee.
Trafalgar Tavern ✕ ♥
Greenwich, SE10. Park Row.
Tel (01) 858 2437. The original
'Old George' of 1837 was rebuilt
in 1965, and renamed. LD from 35s

until 22.30. Closed Sun D.
Extensive wine cellar.
The Yacht ✕ ♥
Greenwich, SE10. 5 Crane Street.
Tel (01) 858 0175. L 7s6d *Mon-
Fri.* Snacks. Riverside terrace.
Galleons Hotel ♥
E16. Royal Albert Docks, off
Manor Way. Tel (01) 476 1706.
An old dockland pub. Snacks.
YMCA
SE18. Artillery Place. Tel (01)
854 1630.
Cutty Sark ♥
SE10. Union Wharf, Lassell Street.
Tel (01) 858 3746. Quiet
Georgian pub with wooden interior.
Near famous *Cutty Sark.* Snacks.
Whitebait suppers.
Waterman's Arms ♥
E14. 1 Glenaffric Avenue. Tel (01)
987 2821. Victoriana collection.
Local art exhibitions and music
hall evenings.

Boatyards
Ship Towage (London)
E16. North Woolwich Pier, Pier
Road. Tel (01) 476 1144.
Water, mooring.
Greenwich Pier
Short-term mooring only.
Tel (01) 858 0079.
Caldergate
Re-fuelling barge. Tel (01) 987
3122. Off Badcock's Wharf, Cubitt
Town. Diesel and lubricants.
Barge House Drawdock
West Ham, off Albert Road.
Bugsby's Hole Causeway
East Greenwich, off Blackwall
Tunnel Avenue.

Natural history
Greenwich Park has fallow deer in
an enclosure, and many very tame
squirrels and waterfowl. Crossbills
are sometimes seen here, and
among the breeding birds are
lesser whitethroat, spotted flycatcher, bullfinch, coal tit and
willow warbler.
There is a fine Sweet Chestnut
at Greenwich Park.
At Bromley by Bow Gasworks
there is a colony of rabbits, paler
than normal wild rabbits and with
a slightly darker back. Hedgehogs
also breed there. Woodmice live in

London suburbs and often meet
an untimely end by entering dis-
carded bottles from which they
are then unable to escape. Rabbits
live on the high rubbish tips which
are warm because they are always
burning deep inside.
Plants of waste places, which
spread because their feathery seeds
can fly a long way, are *Sonchus
oleraceus* (sowthistle), *Cirsium
arvense* (creeping thistle), *Cirsium
vulgare* (spear plume thistle) and
Conyza canadensis (Canadian
fleabane). *Oenothera* species
(evening primroses) also grow
here. They have large, pale yellow
flowers.
Charlton Sand Pit is of great
geological interest; it shows a full
section of the Lower London
Tertiaries. Moulding sand was
obtained from this pit, and this may
have been the reason for the siting
of Woolwich Arsenal. Permits are
necessary before visiting.

Fishing
The Blackwall and Woolwich
reaches have some different species
of freshwater and sea fish. Not
fished, but bream, roach, perch,
eels, mullet and flounders have all
been seen.
Bow Creek is the mouth of the
River Lea. There is little fishing on
the Lea below Tottenham, but at
Walthamstow the MWB reservoirs,
although not easy to fish, yield
specimen roach, bream and perch.
Above Tottenham as far as Ware
the fishing is varied. Notable
stretches are Cheshunt, Broxbourne
and St Margarets. The gravel pits
at Cheshunt are renowned for
specimen tench, pike and perch.
Metropolitan Water Board
See Hampton map page 89

Emergency
Police: 31 Royal Hill, Greenwich,
SE18. Tel (01) 858 6322.
Hospital: Memorial Hospital,
Shooters Hill, Greenwich, SE18.
Tel (01) 854 8811

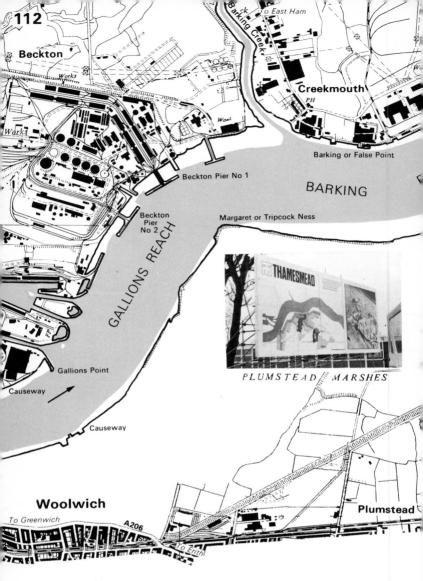

Beckton

Creekmouth

PH

Barking or False Point

Beckton Pier No 1

BARKING

Beckton Pier No 2

Margaret or Tripcock Ness

GALLIONS REACH

PLUMSTEAD MARSHES

Gallions Point

Causeway

Causeway

Woolwich

To Greenwich   A206

Plumstead

To Erith

Places of interest

Beckton
Essex. Dominating the riverside to the west of the mouth of the river Roding is Beckton Gas Works. This huge industrial complex is one of the largest gas works in the world. It uses over 5000 tons of coal per day.

Plumstead
An indeterminate extension of Woolwich, Plumstead is separated from the river by a wide expanse of marshland. During the 1939-45 war this desolate area was the ideal situation for a munitions factory.

Destruction has now given way to optimism, for the drained marshes will soon be the site of Thamesmead, the most exciting and revolutionary of London's new towns. At present the site is a mass of mud and cranes, but already the first houses are taking shape. These and the plans and models, give a refreshing feeling that this will really be a new town, not just an extension of London's suburbia. The town is designed to make the most of its valuable riverside situation. The plan includes a thirty acre lake, a fine riverside promenade with shops and restaurants and a large yacht basin. In all, 60,000 people will be housed. This exciting project will perhaps set the pattern for the development of other riverside areas such as Wapping, Fulham and Wandsworth, areas which have ignored the Thames since the C19th.

The road links with Thamesmead include a plan for a new tunnel to fit in with the London motorway box.

Cross Ness
Beside the river in the depths of the Erith marshes is Cross Ness, the largest sewage precipitation works in London. The sludge produced by the works is carried sixty miles out into the Black Deep by a fleet of six vessels, which work continuously, day in, day out. These vital but unappetizing vessels are nicknamed 'Bovril boats'.

Abbey Wood
To the west of Erith is Lesnes Abbey. Founded in 1178, the abbey is surrounded by a large area of woodland. Rising up from the Erith Marshes, these woods have many splendid walks. It is easy to forget the proximity of London. The abbey remains are largely of the medieval period.

Dagenham
This area is dominated by the two 487ft high pylons that carry power cables over the river. Sandwiched between Becontree estate and the Ford Motor Works, Dagenham has preserved elements of its earlier village existence. The largely C18th church is close to the C17th vicarage, and the Cross Keys Inn, a fine C15th timber-framed building.

The Thames frontage is entirely taken up by the Ford factory, established in 1928. This huge industry is virtually self-sufficient. Iron ore is taken in from the wharf at the rate of over 340,000 tons per year at one end, and over 60,000 completed vehicles per year roll out at the other end.

The factory has its own blast furnace, the only one in the south of England, and its own electricity generating station. The riverside is dominated by the huge, familiar Ford sign.

Sport

Swimming
Plumstead Baths. High Street, SE18. Tel (01) 854 0402. Excellent public baths, including Russian and Turkish.

Country crafts

Stephen Rickard
Plumstead. The Old Vicarage. Vicarage Park, SE18. Tel (01) 854 3310. One of the few remaining artist-engravers of glass. The designs are individually created on the finest quality crystal. Visit by appointment only. Prices from five guineas, by quotation.

Archaeology

Lullingstone
About five miles from the river south of Dartford. Lullingstone Roman Villa is an important building containing a Christian chapel and temple-mausoleum. It dates from C1st to C4th. Open to the public.

Barking
Stone Age and Bronze Age axes found in Barking Creek.

Camping

Co-operative Woods Camping and Caravan site
SE2. Federation Road, Abbey Wood. Tel (01) 854 8612.

Natural history

Marshes of this area, fast disappearing under factories and houses, once held a rich flora and fauna. *Phragmites communis* (reeds) grew in the dykes and ditches and reed warblers and reed buntings nested.
At Beckton Gasworks skylarks sing and small flocks of goldfinches feed on thistle seeds.
Sharks' teeth, fossils of the Eocene period, are numerous in the Blackheath Beds on which Abbey Wood stands. Remains of musk ox from the Pleistocene period have been found at Plumstead.
Typical butterflies of the area at its best are wall brown, comma, meadow brown, small heath, red admiral, painted lady, small tortoiseshell and brown argus. *Aster tripolium* (sea aster) and *Cochlearia anglica* (long-leaved scurvy-grass) grow on the salt marshes and *Melilotus alba* (white melilot) and *M. officinalis* (yellow melilot) on the waste areas. *Artemesia vulgaris* (mugwort, wormwood) and the more aromatic *A. absinthium* (absinthe), from which the liqueur is made, are common. *Colutea arborescens* (bladder senna), a poisonous Mediterranean plant, is a small bush with yellow pea-like flowers and inflated 'bladders' for seed pods.
At Lesnes Abbey ruins are two splendid walnut trees. In Abbey Wood behind the ruins thousands of *Narcissus pseudo-narcissus* (wild daffodils) are naturalised. There are also *Anemone nemorosa* (wood anemone). *Endymion non-scriptus* (bluebells); *Galeobdolon luteum* (yellow archangel, weasel snout) and *Viola* species (violets).

Fishing

Although the river from Woolwich to Erith reach is not fished it is known that there are bream, roach, eels and perch.
On the north bank the Chase at Dagenham is a 17-acre lake stocked with roach, rudd, bream, tench, carp and perch.

Tackle shop

G. E. Dunn
Dagenham. 169a Broad Street, Plumstead.

Emergency: see map 115

Old Man's Head

Rainham Shoot

Rainham Creek

Rifle Ranges

Rainham

Pier

Frog Island

Jenningtree Point

Pier

Mills

Chy

Works

Pier

Pier

ERITH REACH

Works

Pier

Works

Pier

Works

Coldhar

Coldharbour Point

Works.

Mills

Railway Pier

A206

Railway Wharves

To Bexley A220

Erith

Works

To Dartford

A206

Places of interest

Dartford
Kent. Set back from the river, Dartford is connected to the Thames by the river Darent, and is navigable by barges. The Darent runs into Dartford through a heavily built-up industrial area. An important centre for paper making, Dartford has developed more through the Dover road than through the Thames. In the Central Park is the Gateway from the Roman villa at Farningham, which was excavated in 1925.
The marshes separating the town from the river are important as an area of isolation hospitals.
All shops, banks and post office.

Slade Green
Between Dartford and Erith is Slade Green, a living reminder of what a new town should never be; a collection of the worst examples of 'council house' architecture with no understanding of social needs.

Wennington
Essex: A tiny village separated from the river by the firing ranges on Wennington Marshes. The largely C13th church has a good Jacobean pulpit, but a surprising lack of monuments.

Erith
Kent. Although its character has been destroyed by industrial development, Erith is still attractive by the river. Among the older riverside inns are the new indoor swimming baths, an exciting building with splendid views over the river towards Wennington. To the west of the town is the church, notable for its large desolate churchyard with fine C18th and early C19th monuments. General shops and post office.

Erith Theatre Guild
The Playhouse, High Street. Tel Crayford 25396. Repertory. Classic Cinema, High Street.

Rainham
Essex. Set back from the river. Because it has been by-passed by the A13, the older part of Rainham has survived virtually intact. The centre is dominated by the church, a complete late Norman building which was well restored between 1897 and 1910. Beside the church is Rainham Hall, a delicate, but rich early C18th building. Note particularly the porch and doorway.
The riverside at Rainham follows the usual pattern of heavy industrial development. All shops and post office.

Archaeology
Erith
Roman pottery and tiles indicate a riverside settlement.

Eating, drinking & accommodation

The Wheatley Arms Inn ♀
Erith. 2 Pier Road. Tel 32755. A pub with a riverside setting. Snacks. Bar billiards.

The Old Leather Bottel ✕ ♀
Erith. Belvedere, 131 Heron Hill. Tel 32066. Over 400 years old. Situated beside a wood. Overlooks the river. L from about 12s6d Mon-Fri. Snacks until 23.00. Bar billiards. Gardens. Parking.

The Running Horses ✕ ♀ BB
Erith. High Street. Tel 32669. A riverside situation. 3 rooms BB 30s. L 5s Mon-Fri. Snacks. Juke box, pin table. Parking.

Mooring
Erith Town Causeway. Landing is possible at all states of the tide. Erith Yacht Club.

Natural history

At Aveley Clay Pits fossils of fish teeth and other remains, including the bones of a mammoth have been found recently.
Magpies are becoming increasingly common in urban areas. Swallows and swifts are regular summer visitors, and sedge warblers and tree sparrows nest.
Alien plants at Great Coldharbour Ness include *Rumex cristatus*, a giant dock from Asia Minor, and *Verbascum phlomoides*, a woolly mullein from Western Asia. *Typha angustifolia* (lesser reedmace) grows on Dartford Marshes, and a rare sowthistle. *Sonchus palustris* (marsh sowthistle), with golden dandelion-like flowers $1\frac{1}{2}$ inches across, has been found near Dartford Creek.

To Rainham

To Rainham

Southall Bridge

South Run

A13

Easthall Lane

East Hall

B1335

Wennington Hall

P Sch

Wennington

Wennington

W

Gravel Pit (Disused)

Gravel Pit

WENNINGTON MARSHES

Purfleet Rifle Ranges

AVELEY MARSHES

To Gre

Purfleet

Saltings

Barracks

ERITH RANDS

Crayford Ness

A

Works

Dartford Creek

DARTFORD SALT MARSHES

Work

Works

River Darent

JOYCE GREEN HOSPITAL

Fishing
Erith Reach to Purfleet is not fished by anglers, but it is known to hold bream, roach, eels, and perch. Occasional sea fish have been reported.
Dartford Creek provides the mouth to the river Darent.
There are stretches of free fishing on this river, but in the upper reaches most of the water is held by clubs and syndicates. These areas are controlled by the Kent River Authority and a rod licence is required. Fishing is mainly for roach, bream and dace.
Kent River Authority
Maidstone. College Avenue.

Emergency
Police: 22 High Street. Erith Tel 38113.
Hospital: Erith Hospital, Park Crescent. Erith. Tel 30161.

To Rainham

Purfleet

Botany

Beacon
Hill

High
House

A126

A1090

Works

LONG REACH

Works

Dartford Tunnel

WEST
THURR

Deepwater P

Works

Marsh Street

STONE
MARSHES

Ellingham Ponds

A282

Works

Works

Works

School

Anglo · Saxon
Burial Ground

Old
Chalk Pit

Hall

Sch

Wks

Works

Quarry

Stone

Hospl

Works

Quarry

Horns
Cross

A226

Hospital

STONE HOUSE
HOSPITAL

Cobbs
Croft

my

To Dartford

A2

To Rochester

Places of interest

Greenhithe

Kent. An amazing survival, in
contrast to similar villages on the
north bank. Greenhithe is still an
C18th and early C19th village.
Apart from a new estate to the
north which borders Ingress Park
the village is intact. The strong
feeling of ships and of the sea is
reminiscent of an East Anglian
fishing village. The shape of the
village as a whole is very pleasing,
especially when seen from the end
of the causeway. The river is
dominated by the Thames Nautical
College Training ship *Worcester*.

Built 1905, this steel ship is a
replica of an C18th ship of the
line. Owing to the opening of a
new college at Greenhithe, the
future of the *Worcester* is now in
doubt.
Post office and stores.

West Thurrock

West Thurrock

Essex. In an area of total industrialisation, devoid of architectural

Boatyards

Esso Petroleum
Jetties below Purfleet. Tel 5841.
Every type of fuel and oil can be
bought if there is no large vessel
already berthed.

Shell-Mex & BP
Purfleet. Jurgens Road. Tel 6161.
Diesel, paraffin.

Greenhithe Conservancy
Greenhithe. Causeway. Tel Gravesend 67684.

Cross
Stone, 82 London Road. Tel Dartford 20789. Gas.

interest. The church, cut off by the
railway, is buried in the marshes.
Although dwarfed by factories, the
C15th tower is pleasing.
Shops and post office.

Stone
Kent. A curious scattered village
on the scarp overlooking the river.
The area is surrounded by quarries. Hidden among trees are some
interesting C18th and C19th
buildings. The well situated church
is largely C13th and is thought to

have been built by the masons of
Westminster Abbey. The propor-
tions are excellent.

Dartford Tunnel
See London Bridges and Tunnels.

Purfleet
Essex. An important oil town,

handling over 1½ million tons of
petroleum products every year.
The old part of the town is on the
river, breaking the continual line of
industry. In the town is the
Government Powder Magazine, an
C18th structure that was moved
from Greenwich after 1760. Note
the store-keeper's house and the
clock turret. To the west of the
town is the Royal Hotel, a fine
classical early C19th building with
a good view over the river.
All shops, banks and post office.

Darenth
About three miles from the river
south of Stone is the site of
Darenth Roman villa. Discovered
in 1895, the villa is one of the
largest in England. The site is
mostly covered but a few walls are
still visible.

Dartford
To the west of the new Dartford
by-pass is an Anglo-Saxon burial
ground.
In the same area, Roman pottery
was discovered in 1955.

Swanscombe
The gravel pits to the west of the
town revealed important Palaeo-

lithic remains. The famous Swanscombe Man was discovered here
in 1935. The gravel pit is now a
nature reserve.

Littlebrook Power Station

Eating, drinking & accommodation

The Brown Bear Hotel
Greenhithe. Tel 2133. Built in
1820 with later additions.
Garden. Darts.

The Lads of the Village
Stone. Elizabeth Street. Tel Greenhithe 2083. L Mon-Fri. Beer
garden, children welcome. Parking.

Emergency: see map 115

The White Hart
Greenhithe. High Street. Tel 2074.
Snacks.
The Royal Hotel
Purfleet. London Road. Tel 5432.
Excellent C19th hotel with garden
and river view. 25 rooms BB 40s.
English cooking. L 13s6d D 16s
daily until 21.30. Parking.
The Pier Hotel
Greenhithe. Tel 2291. From this
old pub on the river one can
watch ships being loaded and un-
loaded. Sandwiches. Juke box,
one-armed bandit. Parking.

Natural history
Dunnock, meadow pipit and linnet
are common here; yellow wagtail and whinchat are sometimes
seen.
Stoats, common lizard and grass
snake have been recorded on
Dartford Marsh.
Fish common on West Thurrock
Marshes include common goby,
pike, eels and 3 and 10 spined
sticklebacks.
There is chalk from Purfleet to
Grays and characteristic plants are
found. Grays Chalk Pit is of great
interest to naturalists: fossils
which have been found include a
brown bear. Unusual plants such
as *Hieracium aurantiacum* (devil's
paint brush), an orange hawk-
weed, and *Epipactis palustris*
(marsh helleborine) a tall and
beautiful orchid can be seen.
Swanscombe, in the Boyn Hill
Terrace Gravels, has a pit of such
geological importance that it is
a site of Special Scientific Interest.
Two parts of human skull of the
Pleistocene period have been
found in it.

Fishing

There is no fishing on the main
river but it is known to hold
bream, roach, eels and several
kinds of sea fish.
South of the Dartford tunnel are
the Ellingham ponds which can be
fished on permit from the Dartford
& District A.A.
It is essential to have a Kent River
Authority licence.
**Dartford & District Angling
Association**
Secretary: D. E. Reeve, 29 Berkeley
Crescent, Dartford, Kent. Tel
26728.
Kent River Authority
See page 115

Places of interest

Gravesend

Kent. EC Wed MD Fri. Situated on the last stretch of high ground beside the river. After Gravesend the marshes run unbroken to the sea.

Although greatly damaged by bombing and subsequent speculative building, Gravesend is still very much an C18th fishing town, the first port on the river for incoming vessels. The river front is particularly well preserved. Note the weatherboarded houses in the high street.

The early C18th church near the river is no longer used. It contains the tomb of Princess Pocahontas who died here in 1617 on her way back to America.

The Victorian town pier, now disused, is overlooked by the partly

C16th Three Daws Inn. At the top of the High Street is the classical town hall, built 1836. The grey stone pillars of this building are

imposing, but totally unsuited to its surroundings.

To the south of the town is Woodville Hall, a new civic centre in the style of the Royal Festival Hall. Gravesend is the headquarters of the Port of London Authority Thames Navigation Service. The new riverside building, opened in 1959, has radar and radio control over the Thames from Southend to Northfleet Hope.

To the east of the town is the old canal basin. Although derelict, the first lock on the canal is still visible.

There are good riverside walks, especially eastwards towards Shornmead. All shops, banks and post office. Parking.

The Chantry Museum

Fort Gardens. Roman and Early Saxon relics, including finds from Springhead. View by appointment through The Borough Librarian, Central Library, Windmill Street. Cinema: ABC New Road.

Tilbury Fort

Built 1670-83 as a defence against the French and the Dutch. A functional, but still attractive structure. The gateway is splendid:

a triumphal arch with heavy French-inspired carving. Much of the fort was rebuilt by General Gordon in 1863. It is scheduled as an historic monument by the Ministry of Public Building and Works. All around the fort are horses, roaming wild.

There are fine views across the river to Gravesend.

Tilbury

Essex. A late C19th town of no character that has grown up round the docks, opened in 1886. Although the early days of the docks were a financial disaster, the situation, 26 miles from London, is now a great asset. As the size of ships and the volume of traffic has steadily increased, so Tilbury has begun to take over from the other London docks. Today the docks are used by drive-on drive-off ferries, and contain the largest grain-terminal in Britain.

Recently a totally new port has been built for container traffic, a new system that will revolutionise the shipping industry as much as the change from sail to steam.

Northfleet

Kent. Built up on a ridge with sharp chalk cliffs on all sides. Although elements of its past survive, Northfleet today is the Bowater factory. This huge paper mill, built in 1926, has eaten up all the riverside.

In the town the most dominant building is the Roman Catholic church. The huge brick tower blends in well with the industrial surroundings. General shops and post office. Note the good sans-serif lettering on the post office.

Grays Thurrock

Essex. Although the old town exists south of the railway, it has been buried and forgotten by the council house architecture of the newer town. Grays is well named

Grays Church

A large cement factory to the west of the town throws clouds of grey dust over everything; grey grass, grey trees, grey cows, grey people. All shops, banks and post office.

Archaeology

Northfleet

The Springhead Site (Roman settlement of Vagniacae). The site, two miles from the river, is being excavated by the Gravesend Historical Society. Digs are organised at weekends and during holiday periods. Finds include temples, buildings, burials, wells, coins and pottery. Some finds are displayed in the Chantry Museum, Gravesend.

Eating, drinking & accommodation

Canal Tavern   ♟

Gravesend. Canal Road. Tel 2038. Overlooks the old canal basin. Snacks. Parking.

Clarendon Royal Hotel   ✗ ♟ BB

Gravesend. Royal Pier Road. Tel 63151. Once the Earl of Clarendon's residence. The hotel restaurants overlook a garden stretching to the river. Popular with river pilots. 30 rooms BB 53s. LD 15s *daily until 23.30*. Sat night dancing.

Hill Cafe   ✗ BB

Northfleet. 8 The Hill. Tel Gravesend 3043. 8 rooms (shared) BB and evening meal 21s. Hot meals *all day until 19.00. Closed Sat 12.00 and all Sun.* Parking.

Three Daws   ♟

Gravesend. Town Pier. Tel 2080. This inn is about 500 years old and has tunnels to the centre of the town (presumably for smugglers). 48 small rooms, once used by the river pilots on 24 hour call. Snacks. Children's room. Pin tables and juke box.

The World's End   ♟

Tilbury. Fort Road. Tel 2785. Built in 1639, it was once surrounded by marshes, and fre-

quented by watermen and wildfowlers. There are paintings and old prints of ships on the walls of this weatherboarded inn. Snacks, meals by arrangement the day before.

Ye Olde Leather Bottel   ♟

Northfleet. Dover Road. Tel Gravesend 2978. A weatherboarded inn situated above the paper mills with a view down to Tilbury. This was once a coaching station on the old London to Dover road. Collection of old guns and swords. Snacks. Parking.

The Thames & Medway Canal at Gravesend

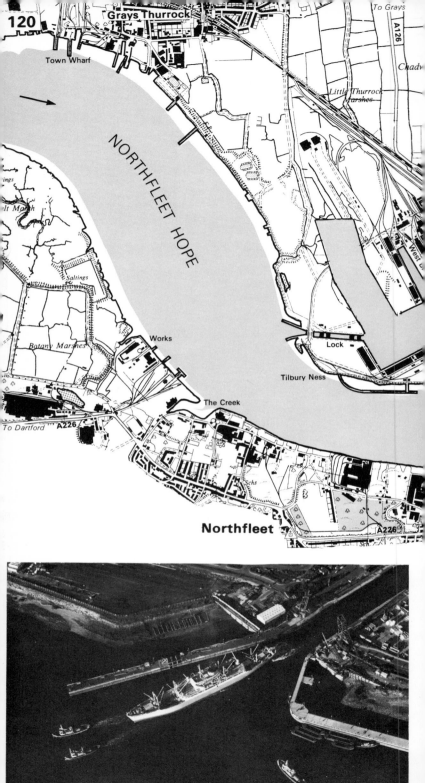

Grays Thurrock

To Grays

A126

Chadw

Town Wharf

Little Thurrock Marshes

NORTHFLEET HOPE

West D

lt Mouth

Saltings

Botany Marshes

Works

Lock

Tilbury Ness

The Creek

To Dartford A226

Schs

Northfleet

A226

Sch

Tilbury Docks *Port of London Authority*

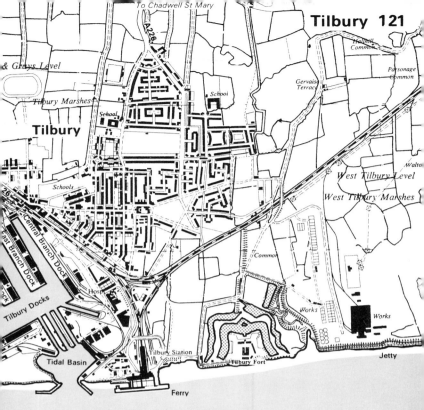

GRAVESEND REACH

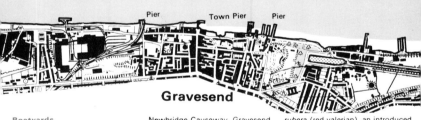

Gravesend

Boatyards

Clift Oil
Gravesend. Terrace Pier Wharf.
Tel 6495. Oil, 3 hours either side
of high water.

J. Collis
Gravesend. King Street. Tel 2283.
Gas.

Gravesend Sailing Club
Gravesend. Promenade East.
Visitors welcome. Fresh water. In
canal basin, entry according to
state of tide.

J. & R. Starbuck
Gravesend. 73-75 West Street.
Tel 3182. Oil, gas, paraffin, repairs, agents for British Seagull;
repairs, canvas-work undertaken,
chandlery. Towing contracted.

Mooring
Apply to Assistant Harbour
Master, Thames Navigation
Service Building, Gravesend.
Tel 67684
Thurrock Yacht Club.

Thurrock
Yacht Club

Newbridge Causeway, Gravesend.
Grays Thurrock Town Causeway,
Grays.

Ferry
Tilbury-Gravesend 2s return.

Natural history
Asparagus officinalis (asparagus)
grows in many places by the river.
Its bright red seeds are probably
spread by birds. Another herb still
used in cookery is *Foeniculum
vulgare* (fennel) with finely cut,
feathery leaves and small umbels
of yellow flowers. *Centranthus*

rubera (red valerian), an introduced
plant, has colonised old walls and
cliffs, covering them with its deep
red, or occasionally white, flowers.

Fishing
From Tilbury as far as Holehaven
Creek the main species reported
are eels, flounders, bass, mullet,
smelt, roach and bream.

Emergency
Police Orsett Road, Grays
Thurrock Tel 2201
Hospital Orsett Hospital, Orsett.
Tel 5100

Boats at Grays

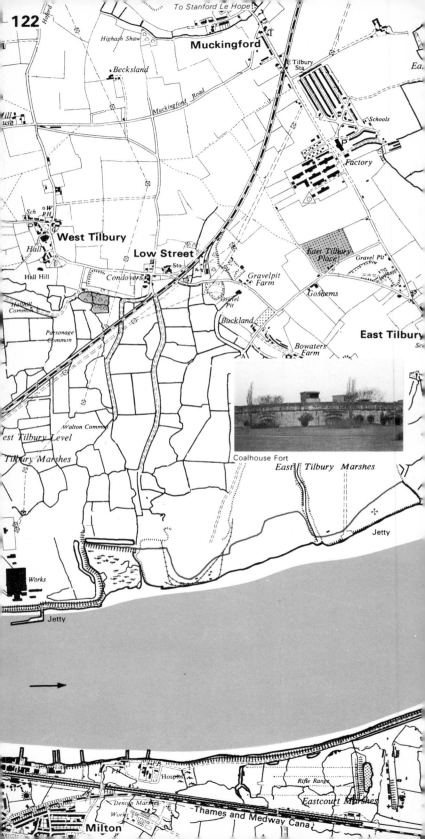

To Stanford Le Hope

Highash Shaw

Muckingford

E Tilbury Sta

Becksland

Muckingford Road

Schools

Factory

Sch
W
PH

West Tilbury

Low Street

East Tilbury Place

Gravel Pit

Hall

Sta

Condovers

Gravelpit Farm

Goshems

Hall Hill

Parsonage Common

Gravel Pit

Buckland

East Tilbury

Bowaters Farm

Walton Common

Coalhouse Fort

East Tilbury Level

East Tilbury Marshes

Tilbury Marshes

Jetty

Works

Jetty

Hospital

Rifle Range

Denton Marshes

Eastcourt Marshes

Works

Milton

Thames and Medway Canal

Lower Hope Point

THE LOWER HOPE REACH

East Tilbury Level

and Counter Wall

East Tilbury Marshes

Sea Wall

Coastguard Cottages

Pier

Wharf

Cliffe Saltings

Cliffe Creek

Jetty

Coal House Fort

Higham Creek

Coalhouse Point

Higham Bight

Shornmead

Higham Saltings

Saltings

Roman Remains
found AD 1953

Higham

Higham Marshes

SHORNMEAD
FORT

Common

Barrow
Hill

Beckley Hill

Works

Shornmead Fort

To Higham

Lower Hope Reach

Places of interest

Shornmead Fort
The Kent equivalent of Coalhouse Fort, built by General Gordon.
The fort is now a total ruin, but enough remains to give a romantic impression of its former glory.
Alone in the marshes, the empty gun emplacements look out over the most desolate stretch of the river.
The fort can be approached along the river wall from Gravesend.

Thames and Medway Canal
Built between 1801 and 1824, the canal ran from Gravesend to Strood, linking the two rivers. It passed through a tunnel 2½ miles long outside Strood. Badly conceived, the canal was a financial failure. It was closed and the tunnel was taken over by the South Eastern Railway. It is still in use.
The canal is not navigable, but the old canal basin is now the Headquarters of the Gravesend Sailing Club.

West Tilbury
Situated high on Gun Hill, East Tilbury has excellent views over the marshes to the river. Near the green the village has a C19th feeling, as little development has taken place. To the south, by the church, is a partly derelict farmyard complete with a pair of steam ploughing engines. It seems that work stopped for the day fifty years ago, and has never started again. General stores.

East Tilbury
Built on a hill overlooking the river. The large unrestored church is partly C12th. It has no tower, the suggestion being that it was destroyed during the Dutch raid of 1667.
The church looks down on Coalhouse Fort, one of the series built by the National Defence Committee under General Gordon. The massive grey stone structure is now derelict, but is so solidly built that it will remain as a permanent reminder of military crises of long ago. The marvellous riverside site around the fort has been turned into a pleasure garden by a very imaginative Council. It includes children's swings and public lavatories. There are good walks along the river, looking over to Shortmead Fort, the equivalent fort on the Kent Coast. Post office and stores.

Mucking
Essex. A remote, scattered village 2½ miles north of East Tilbury. The C19th church has fine views over East Tilbury Marshes. To the

south is the Bata Shoe Factory and Estate. Built in 1932, this model estate was designed to be a complete social unit. Apart from the factory and the housing there is also a hotel, shops and post office, a swimming pool and sports fields, and a cinema. In 1932 it must have seemed a brave decision to choose such a site.

Archaeology

Higham
Roman remains found on Higham Saltings in 1953 indicate a riverside settlement. This is borne out by the discovery of Romano-British huts on the opposite foreshore below East Tilbury. The largest was 20ft in diameter. Pottery finds suggest the C1st and C2nd.

Natural history

East Tilbury and Mucking
The salt marshes and mud flats here have many waders and duck, and there are green sandpipers around Coalhouse Fort. The bird population is similar to the Cliffe Marshes on the opposite bank.

Fishing

The main species recorded here are flounders, bass, mullet, smelt, eels and by repute roach and bream.

Tilbury Reach

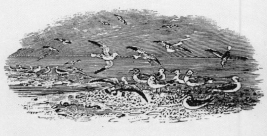

Emergency: see map 121

Thames Estuary

Insects

Among lepidoptera are silver moths, red admiral and painted lady butterflies. On freshwater ponds there are water sketers, and caddis fly and dragonfly larvae in the water. The magnificent adult insects can be seen on hot summer days.

Birds

Geese congregate on mud flats near the mouth of the river. Brent geese are the most common, but white-front and other species can be seen.

Shelduck, mallard, widgeon, pochard, teal, pintail, tufted duck, garganey, gadwall and shoveller feed here. Some species also breed. Waders, which can be seen feeding at low tide at Shell Ness and Allhallows, include huge flocks of oystercatchers, bar-tailed godwit, redshank, ringed plover, golden plover, snipe, jack snipe, woodcock, curlew, knot, dunlin and other occasional visitors. Mute swans are common and Bewick's swans have visited Cliffe.

On higher land there are large flocks of lapwing, crows and rooks. Skylarks, yellow wagtails, linnets, fieldfares, redwings, twites and bramblings can be seen. And of course gulls are everywhere.

Plants

Salt marsh plants include many with small or inconspicuous flowers: *Salicornia* species (glassworts), *Sueda* species (seablites), *Plantago maritima* (sea plantain), *Chenopodium* species (goosefoots), *Atriplex* species (oraches), and *Triglochin maritima* (sea arrow grass).

Some plants have more colourful flowers: mauve *Limonium* species (sea lavender), *Aster tripolium* (sea aster) and *Glaux maritima* (sea milkwort), a low-growing plant covered with tiny pink flowers. On the shore and the low cliffs there are many typical sea-side plants: *Daucus carota* (wild carrot), *Spergularia rubra* (sand spurrey), *Apium graveolens* (wild celery), *Smyrnium olusatrum* (alexanders), *Honkenya peploides* (sea sandwort), *Silene maritima* (sea campion), *Medicago arabica* (spotted medick) and bushes of *Tamarix anglica* (tamarisk) with feathery leaves and sprays of pink blossom.

On the hill behind Leigh are particularly fine bushes of *Rosa canina* (dog rose). On this high ground and in waste places grow *Potentilla anserina* (silverweed), *Amorica rusticana* (horseradish), *Sambucus nigra* (elderberry), *Linaria vulgaris* (toadflax), *Solanum dulcamara* (woody nightshade, bittersweet) and *Convolvulus arvensis* (field bindweed). Many reeds, rushes, sedges and grasses also grow here, and near Shoeburyness a few plants of the beautiful blue *Eryngium maritimum* (sea holly) have been found.

Shells

On Essex beaches there are shells of common mussel, common oyster, Baltic tellin, cockle, sandgaper, slipper limpet, common periwinkle and common whelk.

Sea animals

Common seal, dolphin and porpoise occasionally visit the estuary, and very rarely whales are seen.

Fossils

The Isle of Sheppey has a classic exposure of a cliff section of London clay with good fossils: sharks' teeth, bones of fish, turtle and other creatures of the Eocene period. There are also fossil seeds of the nipa palm, a tree that still flourishes in Malaya.

The Sea Wall of the Thames Estuary

A dominant feature of the estuary is the sea wall, especially on the Kent side. This is vital, as in many places the land is below sea level. Over the centuries the land around the Thames has slowly been sinking relative to the sea level. This is a continuous process and so the height of the sea wall has to be increased every hundred years or so. The land sinks about 12 inches every hundred years. The site of a Roman settlement at Southwark is now 6 feet below the present high tide mark, which indicates that London is probably 15 feet lower in relation to the sea than it was in Roman times.

The result of this process is that the flood risk increases year by year. The London floods of 1928, the Canvey floods of 1953 and the recent inundations in Molesey indicate these dangers, which incidentally are not confined to Britain. The water level in the Dutch canals has to be controlled to the inch, while Venice is slowly disappearing into the sea.

The present sea walls were largely started in the C13th, and have steadily become more vital and more dominant. At present the sea is often out of sight from behind the wall, and so the only sign that it is there may be the sudden, totally unexpected sight of a huge tanker apparently sailing through the middle of a field.

The other function of the wall is to separate the salt marshes from the fresh-water marshes. There are extensive fresh-water marshes on both sides of the estuary. Crisscrossed by wide ditches, they are largely pasture land for cattle and

horses. The marsh consists of about 8 feet of deposited mud overlaying a deep bed of salty sand — which explains the general lack of trees.

Lining the river banks on the other side of the wall are the salt marshes. These are often as much as 3 feet above the level of the flat mud banks, and are cut by creeks and tidal waterways. The marshes are covered at exceptionally high tides. The salt marshes are approximately 8 feet above the fresh water marshes. The sea wall is the bulwark between them, withstanding the full pressure of the high tide. Automatic sluice gates release the contained fresh water into the sea at low tide.

The Sea Wall Walk

Along the top of the sea wall is a path which offers a walk of unsurpassed interest. The walk is one of the loneliest and most windswept within 200 miles of London, and in winter can be a test of endurance. The walk has an unforgettable quality: cargo boats and river traffic on the fast tide, and the curious futuristic shapes of factories and refineries, the thousands of sea birds and the feeling of immense space make the walk a unique and solitary experience.

The natural history of the Thames estuary

An unusual and rewarding area. Very deserted and isolated marshland with extensive bird life of all kinds, unusual sea plants and abundant pond life.

Land animals

Moles, voles, shrews and mice. Identified best by remains in owl pellets. At Cliffe hares, rabbits and foxes can be seen.

Eastcourt Marshes, Shornmead

Works
School

Works
(Dis)

Herd
Farm
Bull Inn
(PH)
Corringham Hall

Corringham
(P)
Buckley
Hill

Old
Hall

Corrin

bots
all

Abbots Hall
(Site of)

A1014

Oak Farm

Rainbow
Cottages

Great
Garlands

Manor Way

Stanford Le Hope

arm

Broad Hope

Marshes

Saltings

Stanford le Hope

Saltings

Stanford le Hope Wharf
(Disused)

Saltings

Mucking Flats

Hard

Salt

Sea Wall

THE LOWER HOPE REACH

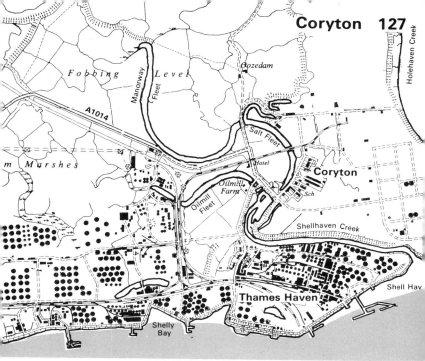

Holehaven Creek

Fobbing Level

Manorway Fleet

A1014

Oozedam

Salt Fleet

m Marshes

Hotel

Oilmill Farm

Oilmill Fleet

Coryton

Sch

Shellhaven Creek

Thames Haven

Shell Hav

Shelly Bay

Shell Hav

Places of interest

Stanford le Hope
Essex. A small town dominated by the tall tower of St Margaret's

church, which was added in 1883 during the major development of the area. The church contains good C19th glass, some by Kempe A good shopping centre suffused with the feeling of depression characteristic of many Essex towns. Post office, banks. Regal cinema.

Corringham
Essex. Although buried by new housing development the village centre around the green remains intact. The church has an early Norman tower, one of the finest in the county, while the interior is still largely C14th; the restoration by Gilbert Scott in 1843 was well restrained. General stores and post office.

Shell Haven & Coryton
Essex. A marvellous landscape formed on the marshes by the futuristic towers and spires of the oil refineries. The whole is exciting visually as all the abstract shapes are pure and sculptural without the normal brick or concrete cladding of industrial architecture. Flames burn against the sky while the gleaming towers are totally self contained; no human presence seems necessary. And incongruously, apparently wild horses roam around the marshes. Coryton is hidden in the midst of the Mobil refinery and only exists to serve it. Post office and stores.

Coryton Refinery

Archaeology

Stanford le Hope
Roman pottery was discovered in old gravel pits by Stanford Wharf in 1931.

Eating, drinking & accommodation
The Haven Hotel X ¶ BB
Stanford le Hope. Thames Haven. Tel 2116. 25 rooms BB 30s. L 10s6d D 12s6d *until 20.30 Mon-Fri. Residents only Sat and*

Sun unless booked. Snooker table. Miniature putting green.
Stanhope Cafe X
Stanford le Hope. 6 Corringham Road. Tel 3015. Good hot meals all day. L 5s. The sultana roll is excellent.

Fishing
The last bend in the river before it opens out into the estuary. Species here are mainly mullet, bass, eels and flounders.
Emergency: see map 121

Coryton Refinery

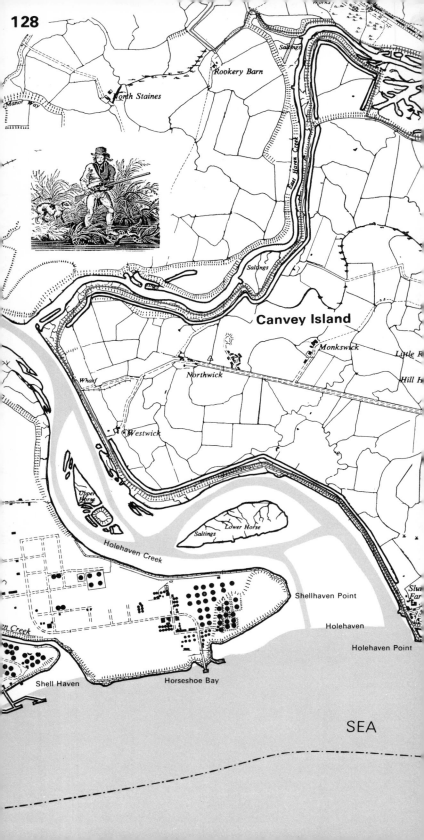

Rookery Barn

North Staines

Manor Way

Saltings

East Hava Creek

Saltings

Canvey Island

Monkswick

Little R

Northwick

Hill H

Wharf

Westwick

Upper Horse

Lower Horse

Saltings

Holehaven Creek

Shellhaven Point

Holehaven

Holehaven Point

Slui Far

n Creek

Shell Haven

Horseshoe Bay

SEA

Benfleet

Reeds Hill

Round Hill

Kersey Marsh

Benfleet Creek

HWMMT

Waterside Farm

Saltings

Saltings

Saltings

Old Fleet

Russellhead

Central Wall

Winter Gardens

head

Little Geppy

Southwick Farm

B1014

Charfleet

Sch

Canvey

Brickhouse

Thorny Creek

Deadmans Point

EACH

Places of interest
Benfleet
Essex. A bungaloid town with good shops. Part of the old weatherboarded fishing village survives beside the creek. General shops and post office.

Canvey
Essex. It was the first place in England to use natural gas, and was all natural by 1966. Terminals for methane gas from the Sahara. The whole of Canvey was reclaimed by Dutch engineers after 1620. Essentially it is an area of flat marshland bounded by a sea wall; generally the land is below sea level, a feature that only becomes apparent on climbing the wall. There is one road onto the island, via a swing bridge, which crosses the mud-flats where boats of all ages and styles lie side by side.

Until the C20th, Canvey was a deserted area of agricultural land with a few farms, and the C17th cottages of the Dutch engineers. Two Dutch cottages survive today, one containing a museum. *Open Whitsun-Sep, Wed, Fri, Sat 14.30-17.00.*

The C20th however has revolutionised the island. It is now an amazing suburban shanty town, the epitome of modern life. An endless and eternally varied pattern of random development, completely anti-architectural; houses of wood, houses of tin, houses of brick, and inevitably the ranks of caravans marching towards the sea, built apparently on the principle that a holiday estate should look just like the council estate back home. The sky is patterned with a wild confusion of telephone and power cables. Clearly nothing can be buried. There is a vast selection of shops, many no more than glorified market stalls lurking under a discoloured tin roof. Overall the feeling of decay and delapidation, and impermanence, as though the dykes will one day be removed and the whole island disappear under the sea once more.

The eastern tip is the holiday area; the caravans have almost engulfed the Haven Hole refinery, the most interesting structure on the island. They terminate at the Wild Mouse amusement arcade, a huge sad affair of peeling paint and past pleasures.

The largest and most splendid buildings are always the public lavatories of which there are an amazing number. There are fine views over the dyke towards Shell Haven. Shops for all needs, post office and banks.

Fobbing
Essex. On the hill overlooking Coryton and the marshes, Fobbing still has some village feeling. The C14th and C15th church is set away from the rest of the village. Post office and general stores.

Archaeology
Canvey Island
Numerous 'Red Hill' salt making sites from 75BC to 50AD. Many Iron Age and Romano-British finds, including pottery. This indicates fairly continuous settlement of the island until the land sank and the sea gradually encroached.

Benfleet
Site of a Danish camp. In 894 a battle between Hasten's Danes and an English army of the East. The Danes were routed.

Eating, drinking & accommodation
Canvey
One of the features of Canvey is the amazing number of Fish and Chip shops and Chinese restaurants; in one place there are two side by side.

The Lobster Smack
Canvey Island. Tel 3034. Licensed in 1563, this inn is beside the sea wall, but from first-floor windows one can see the estuary. Antique copper and brass, old four-poster beds. *Lunch Mon-Fri,* buffet, snacks.

The Monico
Canvey Island. Eastern Esplanade. Tel 3026. A modern pub, opposite a children's playground. Snacks. Snooker table, bar billiards, darts, football machine. Country & Western music on alternate Tue. Band all summer; Thur-Sun only in winter.

White Lion
Fobbing. Tel Stanford le Hope 3281. A C15th inn on the old

coaching route to London. Bargees used the inn about 150 years ago, but now the river has been drained off close to the pub to prevent floods. Cold snacks and salads. Parking.

Camping
Hole Haven Caravan Park.

Boatyards
The Dauntless Company
Canvey Island. Yacht and Boat Builder, The Bridge. Tel South Benfleet 3702. Petrol, diesel, repairs, agents for Stuart, BMC Seagull, Johnson; mooring, launching, storage.

Mooring
Lobster Smack Stairs, Canvey. Yacht Club.

Fishing
In the mouth of Hole Haven Creek, mullet, flounders, eels and some bass have been reported. Off shore these fish can also be caught by anglers in boats.

Places of interest

Hadleigh

Essex. Despite the ever increasing
sprawl that joins Hadleigh to the
bulk of Southend, a surprising
amount of rural landscape survives, especially around the castle.
Hadleigh Castle, built 1232-1370,
is well situated overlooking the
marshes and the sea. It was one of
the most important castles in
Essex but today only enough survives to give an impression of the
building. The remains are cared for
by the Ministry of Works who
charge 1s to look around. It can be
seen as well from outside the iron
fence. There are good walks·all
round in an area thick with black-
berries.
Hadleigh is a main road shopping
centre, apart from the church of
St James the Less, a complete

little Norman building. Only the
belfry is a later addition, making
the church a most unusual survival, especially for this part of
England. All shops, post office,
banks.

Leight on Sea

Essex. The municipal bulk of
Southend stretches now from
Leigh to Shoebury, as the various
independent parishes have been
swallowed. The High Street at
Leigh was effectively cut off by
the Southend railway, which made
development impossible. It has
thus been able to retain the
character of a pre-Victorian fishing
village. Apart from the visual
pleasure, this remoteness has
enabled fishing to continue.
The other side of the railway has
developed into a C20th commuter town, one of the more desirable suburbs of Southend.
The church of St Clement is well

placed high above the village, with
a long flight of steps leading down
to the river. The church of St
Margaret, built 1931 by Sir Charles
Nicholson, is interesting; the
interior is particularly good,
revealing Early Christian inspiration. All shops, post office, banks.

Archaeology

Hadleigh

Behind the castle is the site of a
Roman marching camp, or fortlet.
Not excavated.

Eating, drinking & accommodation

The Admiral Jellicoe ✕ ♥ BB
Canvey Island. Leigh Beck. Tel
3070. 7 rooms BB 40s. D to order,
12s6d. Parking.
Crooked Billet ♥
Leigh. High Street. Tel Southend
76128. Inglenook fireplace in the
smoke-room, and brass and photographs of old boats on the walls.
One can watch the cockle boats
being unloaded. Snacks. Shellfish
can be bought nearby in the
summer. Darts, dominoes.
Peter Boat ♥
Leigh. High Street. Tel Southend
75666. The new bar overlooks the
river estuary where cockle and
shrimp boats are unloaded. L
16s6d, D a la carte *until 22.00
(Sat 22.30 and summer later).
Closed Sun.* Darts. Electric organ
during the week. Parking.
The Smack Inn ♥
Leigh. High Street. Tel Southend
76765. An old pub with oak
beams, a terrace and sun lounge.
L winter only from 2s9d. Snacks at
the bar. Parking.
Mayflower Grill ✕
Leigh. 77 Leigh Road. Tel Southend 78137. LD 7s6d daily. Good
value. Home made pastries.

Boatyards

F. A. Turnidge

Leigh. Tel Southend 75134.
Sailmaker.

Mooring

Leigh. Occasional mooring along
Bell Wharf.

Fishing

Leigh is situated in the estuary of
the tidal reaches and the main
species to be caught are bass,
mullet, flounders and shad. The
offshore marks here are best fished
from a small boat.
In the Leigh area there are creeks
and inlets which offer interesting
fishing for flounders, eels, mullet
and bass. In this area the Ray Gut
channel, which runs between
Canvey Island point and Westcliff,
is noted for allis shad fishing, but
this mark is best fished from a
boat. The old part of Leigh is still a
fishing village. Shrimping boats go
out each day.

Emergency: see map 135

Belton Hills

Hadleigh Castle
(Remains of)

To Hadleigh

Hadleigh Marsh

Benfleet Creek

Saltings

Leigh Marsh

Saltings

Saltings

HWMMT

Hadleigh Bay

Tewkes Creek

HWMMT

Saltings

Saltings

Newlands

Saltings

Oyster Creek

To South Benfleet

B1014

Leighbeck
Point

Saltings

B1014

Sch

Leigh Beck

Chapman Lighthouse

SEA

Leigh on Sea

Westcliff on Sea

Chalkwell

Sta

Leigh Creek

Saltings

Saltings

Works

Bathing Pool

Chalkwell Oaze

Crow Stone

Marsh End Sand

Ray Gut

Clock Bank

Canvey Point

Chapman Sands

Leigh Middle

REACH

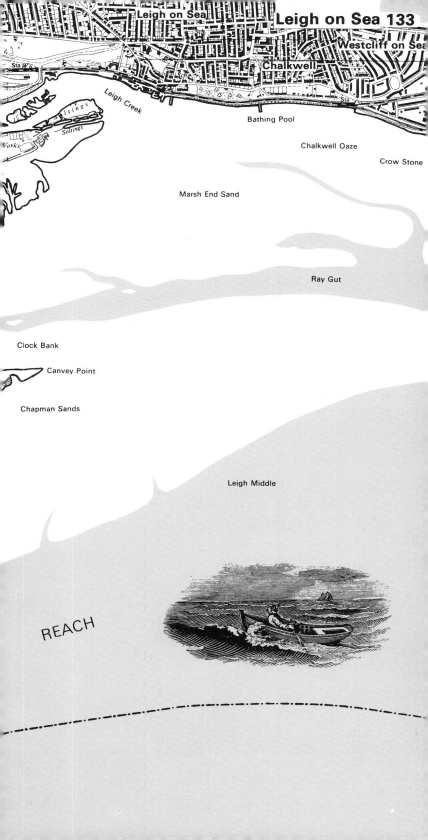

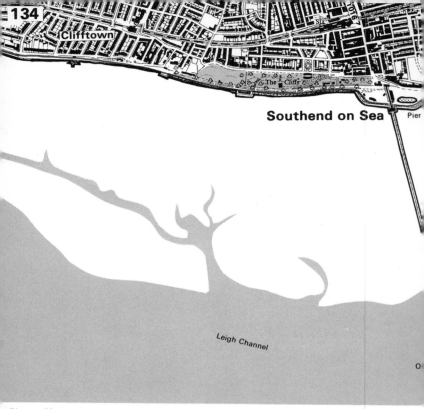

Cliftown

Southend on Sea Pier

Leigh Channel

Places of interest
Westcliff on Sea
Essex. Westcliff continues the commuter pattern of Leigh, but has no individuality or character. St Alban's church is by Nicholson, (1898-1908). Note the painted roof and the reredos.

By the river is the Cliff Pavilion, an imposing concrete building which serves as a concert hall, cinema, lecture hall and general cultural centre. Shops, post office, banks.

Southend
Essex. Southend is essentially a late Victorian fun town that owes its development to the coming of the railway. This background is still apparent. Prior to the C19th the area was a centre of oyster cultivation, although there was an attempt to develop the area as a resort in 1791. Royal Terrace, a fine regency

ment. The most obvious feature is the pier, built 1889-95. Over a mile in length, it is the longest pier in the world; there is a railway along it, and all the usual pier entertainments. The Kursaal, built 1902 by

Sherrin, is a typical fun palace but for its unlikely Wren dome. The town is overshadowed by Palace Court, 1901, a monumental characterless hotel, now divided into old people's flats. Away from the sea front the town takes on a more serious appearance which

The north part of the town is called Prittlewell. Little survives of the priory, founded about 1110, except the refectory.

The Southend Museum is in the priory park. Nearby is the church, no longer well situated, which is dominated by the large Tudor tower. Shops of every kind, including Keddie's department store, Warrior Square, and entertainment galore. Parking is difficult at all times, meter men are very keen, so use official parks.
Cinema: The Ritz.
The world famous Southend Illuminations are switched on in the Autumn.

Southend Municipal Airport
Southend. Tel 40201.

Eating, drinking & accommodation
Good Will Chinese Restaurant ✗ ♥
Southend. 55 Southchurch Road. Tel 67510. LD 15s *daily until 24.00.* Licensed.
New Karachi (Pakistan) Restaurant ✗ ♥
Southend. 36 York Road. Tel 63182. LD 15s *daily.* Licensed.
Offords ✗ ♥
Southend. 86 High Street. Tel 67295. Traditional English decor and cooking. L *daily* 12s6d D *Sat and Sun.*
Pied Piper ✗ ♥
Southend. Westcliffe, 96 The Ridgeway. Tel 76417. LD 40s *daily until 22.00.* Swiss night (fondue speciality) Mon, Gourmet Circle Thur. Licensed.
The Royal Hotel ✗ ♥ BB
Southend. Royal Terrace. Tel 42632. Victorian hotel with a view to the river. 25 rooms BB 45s. L 13s6d D à la carte, *daily until 22.00* Kon-Tiki Bar. 'Dance and dine for eight and nine.' *Mon-Fri 20.00-02.00, Sat 20.00-24.00.* Parking.

Royal Terrace, Southend

terrace reminiscent of Brighton, and the Royal Hotel are the only remaining fruits of this development. However, the true Southend is a glory of fish and chips, dirty postcards, rock and instant entertain-

contrasts strangely with the frivolity of the seaside. There is much new development, especially along Victoria Avenue; the 'Court House and the Crown office building are particularly pleasing.

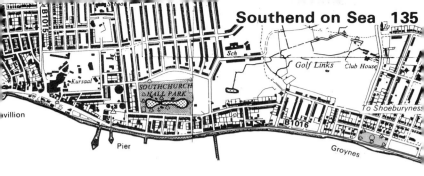

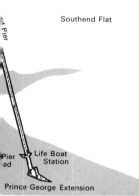

Southend Flat

Pier Head

Pier
ad

Life Boat
Station

Prince George Extension

Southend Pier   X

The Martinelli Shellfish Bar
Southend. Grove Terrace.
Excellent fresh shellfish, including
local oysters, cockles, shrimps.

The Sunray Bar   X
697 London Road. This cafe is
unique; the walls and ceiling are
entirely covered by excellent
Vorticist painting by the proprietor,
a mild friendly man who has a
valid, but totally unaesthetic
reason for choosing this style of
painting. Good meals all day.
L 6s6d. *Closed Mon.*

Boatyards
Wallis & Sons
Southend. 59 High Street. Gas.

Mooring
Southend Pier. Apply Berthing
Master at Pier Head. 5s per day,
£1 per week if available.

Emergency
Police. Victoria Avenue, Southend
on Sea. Tel 41212
Hospital. Southend Hospital,
Prittlewell Chase, Southend on Sea.
Tel 43383

Fishing

The pier at Southend is over a mile
long and fishing is allowed on one
side.
The area is noted for flounders,
but garfish, plaice, shad, mackerel,
bass, mullet, pouting and whiting
can be caught.
The best fishing is off shore where
cod may be taken. Further out in
the Thames mouth thornback rays
are to be found. All the sea fish
illustrated in this book have been
reported in these waters.
The lake in Priory Park, Southend,
offers fishing for roach, rudd,
mirror carp and crucian carp. Day
tickets and permits are issued by
the Southend Corporation.
Southend Corporation
Civic Centre, Victoria Avenue.
Tel 49451.

Tackle shops
The Angling Kiosk
Pier Head. Tel 43163.
Jetty Anglers
47 Eastern Esplanade.

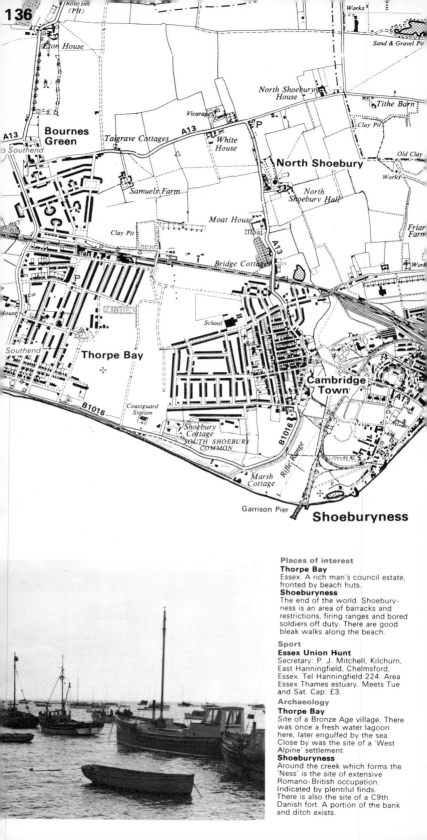

Map showing: Bournes Green, North Shoebury, North Shoebury House, Tithe Barn, Vicarage, White House, Talgrave Cottages, A13, Samuels Farm, North Shoebury Hall, Clay Pit, Moat House, Moat, Friar Farm, Bridge Cottages, School, Thorpe Bay, Cambridge Town, Southend, B1016, Coastguard Station, Shoebury Cottage, SOUTH SHOEBURY COMMON, Rifle Range, Marsh Cottage, Garrison Pier, Shoeburyness, Eton House, Rose Inn (PH), Sand & Gravel Pit, Clay Pit, Old Clay, Works

Places of interest

Thorpe Bay
Essex. A rich man's council estate, fronted by beach huts.

Shoeburyness
The end of the world. Shoeburyness is an area of barracks and restrictions, firing ranges and bored soldiers off duty. There are good bleak walks along the beach.

Sport

Essex Union Hunt
Secretary: P. J. Mitchell, Kilchurn, East Hanningfield, Chelmsford, Essex. Tel Hanningfield 224. Area Essex Thames estuary. Meets Tue and Sat. Cap: £3.

Archaeology

Thorpe Bay
Site of a Bronze Age village. There was once a fresh water lagoon here, later engulfed by the sea. Close by was the site of a 'West Alpine' settlement.

Shoeburyness
Around the creek which forms the 'Ness' is the site of extensive Romano-British occupation. Indicated by plentiful finds. There is also the site of a C9th Danish fort. A portion of the bank and ditch exists.

Great Wakering

Newtown

Wick

Samuel's Corner

New House

Morrin Point

The Cottage Crouchmans

Saltings

Nursery

W

Black Grounds

Poynter's Point

Saltings

Causeway

Suttons Road

Suttons

Pig's Bay

Causeway

Manor Ho

Shoebury Ness

Shoebury Boom

Maplin Sands

Danger Area

Eating, drinking & accommodation

Cafe Caroline   X
Shoeburyness. Rampart Terrace.
Inspired by the radio station. The
cafe serves hot meals until *24.00
daily*. Juke box, pin tables, etc.

Camping
Thorpe Bay Caravan Park.

Fishing
The tide recedes a long way at
Shoebury Ness but at high tide
flounders, mullet, bass, mackerel,
codling, eels and garfish may be
caught. From small boats cod,
whiting, plaice and pollack can
also be taken.
Shoebury Park Lake has fishing
for roach, rudd, perch and pike
on a day permit.

Emergency: see map 135

LOWER HOPE REACH

Lower Hope Point

Redham Mead

Mead Wall

Cliffe

Coastguard Cottages

Pier

Cliffe Salings

Cliffe Creek

Jetty

T

Higham Creek

HWMM

Quarry Cottages

Allen's Hill

Old Quarry

Manor House

We

Works

140 Cliffe

Places of interest

Cooling
Kent. At Cooling there is a return to the emptiness of the marshland which now stretches unbroken to the river. The church with its tall

tower contains monuments to the Comport family, the last great family to live in this part of Kent, they died out at the end of the C18th.

To the west of the village is Cooling Castle. Built in 1382, the huge chalk walls of this moated castle were to protect the inhabitants from the threat of French invasion. Today it is a magnificent ruin, with fingers of walls and towers reaching up into the sky.

The gateway is intact, owing to careful restoration, an incongruous survival in the flat landscape. A house has been built within the walls, with a marvellous out-look over the moat and the ruins. To the south is Cooling Court, a good

unrestored C17th building. Post office and stores.

Cliffe
Kent. On a hill above the marshes, Cliffe is dominated by the huge Blue Circle cement factory, a grey representative of the industry which has transformed the whole area. Cliffe Marshes have been turned into a huge inland sea by the search for clay, with only narrow spits of land separating the pits.

Further to the east the marshes were the site of the Curtiss and Harvey explosives factory which employed 2000 during the 1914-18 war. Trees were planted to minimise the effect of explosions and many survive today among the ghostly ruins of the factory.

Cliffe is an attractive town. Its situation is excellent, and there are marvellous views from the C13

C15th church. Note the magnificent C14th screen inside the church. The main street has several fine weatherboarded buildings which give a good picture of

the town in the early C19th. To the west lies the Manor House, a good timber-framed building largely of the C18th. The style is unusual for this part of Kent. General shops and post office.
Emergency: see map 115

Cooling Castle

Archaeology
Cliffe
A large number of Roman and Romano-British finds have come from the Cliffe area. Pottery fragments are often discovered in the marshes, especially around Rye-street Common to the NE. They indicate a settlement, or at least a pottery.

Natural history

Cliffe Marshes
Common sea birds may be seen on the narrow belt of mud flats but the area is notable mainly for the lagoons in the excavated clay pits on the fresh-water marsh. Great numbers of diving ducks and waders can be seen in winter.

Eating, drinking & accommodation
Black Bull
Cliffe. Church Street. Tel 278. About 200 years old. Snacks. Darts. Parking.
Horseshoe & Castle
Cooling. Tel Cliffe 237. Annual Vegetable Show for charity. Trapball, an old game for children, is played here. Snacks, meals by arrangement. Soup, coffee. Garden, bar billiards. Parking.

Fishing
The last bend in the river where it sweeps round Cliffe to open out into the estuary. Fishing mainly for flounders, eels, bass and mullet.

The Royal Albert at Cliffe

The barge *Westmoreland*, owned by the Thames Barge Sailing Club

The Thames Sailing Barge

At its peak the Thames Sailing Barge was one of the most efficient and economical coastal trading vessels ever made. Crewed by two men, the barge could carry between 80 and 250 tons of cargo from coastal port to coastal port, up shallow rivers, and for short journeys across the sea.

The barge developed initially from the lighters used for centuries to unload ships in the Pool of London. With the building of the docks in the early C19th, the need arose for a small self-propelled vessel to handle the coastal traffic. This need was answered by the sailing barge, which reached its final form in the 1880's.

The typical barge was a flat-bottomed, straight-sided vessel with a round bow and a transom stern. 80ft long and 20ft wide, it carried 120 tons of cargo.

The 70-80ft mast supported 3000 square ft of sail. It had many advantages over conventional sailing vessels. The square shape was easy and cheap to build, the cargo area was larger, the draught was shallower and the mast could be stepped, enabling the vessel to pass under fixed bridges. It was easy to sail in most conditions, leeboards giving it windward ability. Barges were particularly suited to carrying agricultural and building materials. Typical cargoes included hay and fodder for horses, grain, coal, chalk, stone, cement, bricks, manure, timber and London refuse.

Reaching its peak in about 1900 when 3000 were in service, barge construction was centred around East Anglia and the Kent coast and estuaries. Wood was the usual material, although steel was occasionally used.

The development of lorries and efficient road transport brought about a rapid decline in the number of barges, so that in 1939 only 600 were still sailing. After the war 300 remained, but only 140 were still under sail. The others were converted to motor barges.

In 1959 only seven still survived, and now the race is virtually extinct on a commercial level.

Many of the barges converted to motor power are still in service.

In order to preserve the Thames sailing barge from total extinction, the Thames Barge Sailing Club was founded in 1948. As well as researching into the art and history of the barges, the club maintains two boats in sailing trim to give members' practical experience in their handling. Following the club's lead, other people and organisations have preserved barges, and so, unlike so much of our industrial inheritance, the survival of the Thames barge seems fairly secure. Barge matches are now held four times a year (at Southend, on the Medway, the Blackwater and the Orwell) when as many as eighteen may be seen together.

Thames Barge Sailing Club
c/o National Maritime Museum, Greenwich, SE10.

Places of interest

St Mary Hoo

Kent. A remote, scattered village showing no development at any time. Throughout the C19th the population only increased by four, and it cannot have changed much since. The church is beautifully situated among trees away from the road. It preserves, unconsciously, a strong C19th feeling.

The Church, High Halstow

High Halstow

Kent. A village of council houses of all periods. It is important as it marks the edge of the marshland; the change from marsh to rolling wooded hills is breathtaking because so violent and unexpected.

Archaeology

High Halstow

By Whalebone Marshes, NW of High Halstow, a Roman pottery kiln was found in 1932.

Eating, drinking & accommodation

The Cleveland Garage
(R. M. Fuller & Sons) St Mary Hoo. Tel Allhallows 256. Hot meals are served *until 17.30*.

Natural history
High Halstow

Enormous numbers of duck and waders come to the mile-wide mud flats at low tide. The fresh water marshes have numerous whitefronts in January. Egypt Bay and various inner fleets offer good vantage points. Summer: heron, shelduck. Autumn: sandpipers, little stint, greenshank. Winter: whitefronts, pintail, shoveller, shelduck, widgeon, knot, curlew, redshank.

The Bird Sanctuary at Northward Hill can be deafening! As one comes inland from the marsh the noise of thousands of woodland birds can be heard from a mile away. The heronry further along the slope has over 100 nests. Entry by permit from the Royal Society for the Protection of Birds.

Fishing

In the main river fishing is mainly for flounders and eels. Blyth Sand is particularly good for flat-fish. In the creeks and bays, mullet and bass can often be taken.

Emergency: see map 147

Places of interest
Allhallows

Kent. Built on a slight rise, Allhallows has one of the best views in Kent. It is so placed that it overlooks the Thames, the Medway and back across the marshes into Kent. Today the marvellous expanse of marshland and skyline is broken only by the Grain refinery and the Kingsnorth Power Station. The landscape remains unblemished, as it has been for centuries. Only the possible siting of London's third airport on Sheppey is likely to alter this in the near future.

There have been many attempts to popularise this part of Kent, as it is the nearest seaside to London. The

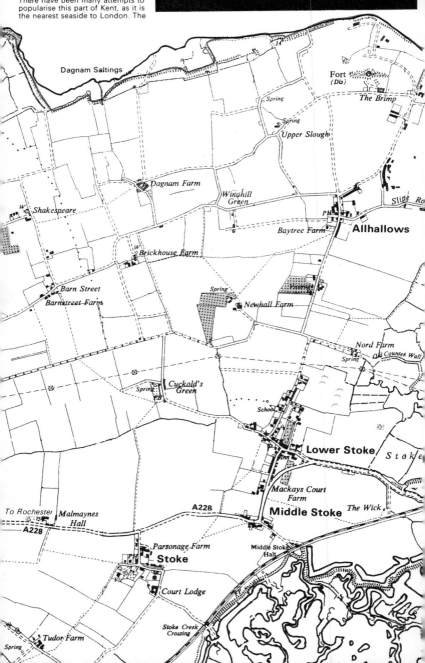

ghost town of Allhallows on Sea is a reminder that such ideas are doomed. All that remains of this resort, that never was, are a few huge blocks of buildings, looking like stranded whales. Even the railway station has been turned into a caravan park. In 1956 a new town of 25,000 people was planned, and then abandoned. Strood Rural District Council has laid out the whole of the riverside as a permanent chalet and caravan park. Although very well equipped, including a Chinese restaurant, this blemish on the otherwise empty landscape shows that the resort idea dies hard. A few shops and post office.

Stoke

Kent. Stoke grew up in the C19th because it was found that the saltings could be worked for clay and mud, vital to the new cement industry which was under development. This large scale removal of mud has left a permanent scar on the saltings. Only in mining areas can industry have had so devastating an effect on the landscape. Cement factories are still a feature of both banks of the estuary. A few shops and post office.

Eating, drinking & accommodation

British Pilot Hotel ✗ ❢ BB
Allhallows. Avery Way. Tel 243. 10 rooms BB 27s6d. L 12s6d, D residents only unless booked. Bar billiards. Parking.

Emergency: see map 147

Camping

Strood Rural District Council Holiday Estate
Allhallows. Tel 266. Chalets. Caravans. No tents. Chinese and English Restaurant.

Natural history

Yantlet Creek
Numerous duck and waders come to the mud flats which are a mile wide at low tide. Stoke Lagoon is excellent for waders, and Stoke Fleet to the south for duck and water rail.

Fishing

Off Allhallows, the fishing is mainly for flounders, mullet, bass and eels, but occasionally garfish and codling are caught.
In the creeks, and particularly in the Yantlet flats, there are good mullet, flounders and eels.

Places of interest

Grain

One of the bleakest villages in Kent, Grain is entirely dominated by the BP refinery. The huge industrial complex of pipes and spires and storage tanks glitters in the sun, looking like a futuristic mirage over the marshes, an oilman's dream. The whole area has the pungent smell of crude oil drifting over it, and yet there are large numbers of new houses. There are marvellous windswept

The Church, Grain

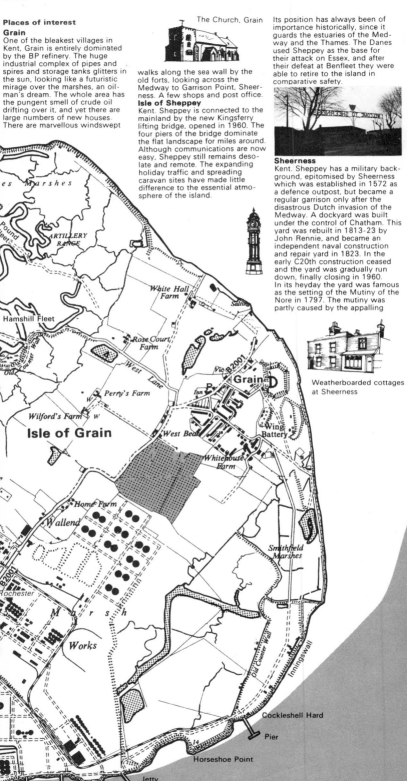

walks along the sea wall by the old forts, looking across the Medway to Garrison Point, Sheerness. A few shops and post office.

Isle of Sheppey

Kent. Sheppey is connected to the mainland by the new Kingsferry lifting bridge, opened in 1960. The four piers of the bridge dominate the flat landscape for miles around. Although communications are now easy, Sheppey still remains desolate and remote. The expanding holiday traffic and spreading caravan sites have made little difference to the essential atmosphere of the island.

Its position has always been of importance historically, since it guards the estuaries of the Medway and the Thames. The Danes used Sheppey as the base for their attack on Essex, and after their defeat at Benfleet they were able to retire to the island in comparative safety.

Sheerness

Kent. Sheppey has a military background, epitomised by Sheerness which was established in 1572 as a defence outpost, but became a regular garrison only after the disastrous Dutch invasion of the Medway, under the control of Chatham. This yard was built under the control of Chatham. This yard was rebuilt in 1813-23 by John Rennie, and became an independent naval construction and repair yard in 1823. In the early C20th construction ceased and the yard was gradually run down, finally closing in 1960. In its heyday the yard was famous as the setting of the Mutiny of the Nore in 1797. The mutiny was partly caused by the appalling

Weatherboarded cottages at Sheerness

conditions at the dockyard. There was no proper accommodation, the men having to live in old hulks, and epidemics were rife owing to the marshy land and the insanitary conditions. Similar hulks were used as prison ships in this area. Ships in quarantine were often forced to lie for months off Sheerness, the men unable to go ashore.

The most important feature of the dockyard is the Boatstore. Built in

1858-60, it is thought to be the first multi-storey building with a complete iron frame in the world. It combines great elegance and function in a surprisingly modern idiom. Until fairly recently it was thought to be a C20th structure. Designed by G. T. Greene, its historical importance is now recognised, as well as its aesthetic value.

Today the dockyard is a commercial port able to handle ships up to 450ft in length. It takes 250,000 tons of shipping per year and is much favoured by European traders as it avoids the delays and stoppages so characteristic of larger ports. Although the navy has left, Sheerness still retains the flavour of a naval town. Blue Town, the dockyard area, is now very derelict and decayed. Clearly its 'raison d'être' has disappeared. Only the dockyard itself is in a healthy state, and the many C18th and C19th buildings seem in a good state of repair.

By the east wall of the dockyard is Naval Terrace, a marvellous row of C18th officers' houses, complete with church.

Sheerness itself is still largely C18th and early C19th in the centre, but the outskirts have been

Naval Terrace
The Church

taken over by C20th naval and utility building.

On the front is a huge amusement park, complete with big dipper,

swimming pool, boating pond and putting green. Even this has the same atmosphere of decay and faded pleasure. The old cinema, looking like the bridge of a battle-ship, indicates how much the navy was the backbone of the town. All shops, banks and post office.

Eating, drinking & accommodation

Admirals Walk X ▼
Sheerness. Blue Town. Tel 4187. An interesting new building in an area of dereliction. The pub is fitted out like a ship inside. L *Mon-Fri* from 5s. Coffee, snacks. Juke box, football machine, pin table, one-armed bandit, darts. Parking.

Cat & Cracker X ▼
Grain. Tel Allhallows 205. The name derives from the name of a machine on the oil refineries nearby—a catalytic cracking machine. The inn sign puns on the name. LD 13s6d, D *18.00-19.00.* 5 rooms BB 35s. Fishing, garden. Parking.

Hong Kong Island Chinese Restaurant X ▼
Sheerness. 82-84 High Street. Tel 2466. L 5s D 12s6d *daily until 24.00.* Licensed.

The Royal Fountain X ▼ BB
Sheerness. Blue Town. Tel 2092. Built in the C18th. Lord Nelson is reputed to have stayed here. 17 rooms BB 40s. L 13s6d D à la carte daily *until 21.00.* Parking.

Station Cafe X
Sheerness. Railway Road. Hot meals all day *daily.*

Camping

Cheyney Rock Camp
Sheerness. 141 Marine Parade. Caravans.

Fishing

Sea and estuary fish are numerous in the Isle of Grain and Sheerness waters. Here flounders, bass, mullet, garfish, pouting and mackerel are common. Sometimes cod are taken. These are most frequent at the mouth of the River Medway. Cod of up to 20lb have been caught as far up river as Gillingham.

Tackle shops

Grain
Ironmonger's shop, Cat & Cracker's Inn.

Emergency

Police: Cross Street, Sheerness. Tel 2261.
Hospital: Sheppey Hospital, Minster, Sheerness. Tel Minster 2116.

The Tributaries of the Thames

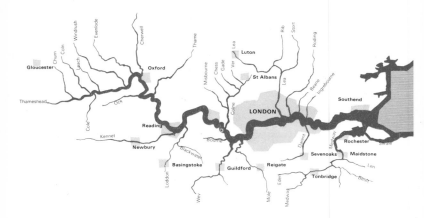

The Thames Tributaries

The Churn
The seven springs of the Churn
are a rival source for the Thames.
Rising south of Cheltenham, it runs
via Cirencester to join the Thames
outside Cricklade. The course of
the Churn is attractive, passing
sometimes through woodland.
Its reputation as a trout stream has
been destroyed by pollution from
the Cheltenham Road. A feature
of the woods by Rendcombe is
the Roman snail. Large and white,
this edible snail was introduced by
the Romans who considered it a
great delicacy. It has survived
because of its size. *The Churn
is not navigable.*

The Gloucestershire Coln
Rising six hundred feet above sea
level in the Cotswolds, the Coln
is a fast flowing trout stream.
It descends rapidly from its source,
joining the Thames by the
Inglesham Round House. It links
several splendid grey stone
villages, which are clustered right
on the river's edge, in the Cotswold tradition. Withington and
Coln St Denis are followed by
Bilbury. Here the C18th feeling of
the Cotswolds is replaced by an
earlier one; the Jacobean glory
of Bilbury Court and Arlington
Row. There is a trout farm above
Bilbury, which justifies the claim
that the Coln is the best breeding
river for the Thames. At Fairford
the C18th returns, gathered round
the church which dominates this
last plateau of the Cotswolds.
The Coln is not navigable.

The Leach
Fifteen miles long, the Leach rises
above Northleach. The splendour
of the church shows that Northleach was once an important wool
town with a flourishing export
trade. Sections are dry for most of
the year, the water travelling
underground to reappear a few
miles along the valley. Eastleach,
once famous for its watercress, is
distinguished by the two churches
and the clapper bridge. After
passing through Little Faringdon
Mill, the Leach wanders into the
Thames beside the Trout Inn,
Lechlade. *The Leach is not
navigable.*

The Windrush
A calm sedate river, rising in
marshes above Bourton-on-the-
Water. In Bourton the river is
bridged four times, in a variety of
styles. Passing through woodland,
the river reaches Windrush. This
part of the valley was once famous

for its freestone mines. The fine
white stone was used in the
building of Westminster Abbey,
Windsor Castle and some Oxford
Colleges. After Burford the river
flanks Wychwood Forest and
reaches Minster Lovell, one of the
most beautiful of Cotswold
villages. The Windrush is unusual
in having an industrial background; for over six centuries
Witney has been a centre of
blanket making. Before joining the
Thames at Newbridge, the Windrush flows through extensive
gravel pits. *The Windrush is not
generally navigable, except for
canoes. Start from Bourton-on-
the-Water. Many obstacles — wire,
mills and private fishing.*

The Evenlode
The last of the Cotswold rivers to
feed the Thames, the Evenlode
rises high above its name town.
Many villages cluster round the
river as it passes Wychwood
Forest. Now only 1500 acres of
woodland mark the site of one of
the greatest forests in England.
The only river town on the Evenlode is Charlbury. Before joining
the Thames opposite Wytham
Great Wood, the Evenlode runs
parallel with the old Cassington
Canal Cut to link Eynsham with the
Thames, the canal is now disused.
*The Evenlode is not generally
navigable, except for canoes — start
from Charlbury station — many
obstacles, but easy landing at
low banks.*

The Cherwell
The Cherwell rises above Charwel-
ton in Northamptonshire. It is the
only river linking the brown stone
of Northampton with the grey of
the Cotswolds. Passing the site
of the Roman village of Brinvarius,
the river reaches Edgcote House.
This site and the village of Cropredy
further along the river were both
important during the civil war,
the latter being the scene of a
battle. From Cropredy the river
runs beside the old Oxford to
Birmingham canal, which is now
disused. Banbury is reached, a
town that takes no interest in the
river, and after passing the famous
spire at King's Sutton the Cherwell
runs through meadows to William
Kent's mansion and garden at
Rousham. After Shipton and Islip,
the river approaches Oxford, with
Magdalen tower in the background.
The Cherwell's approach to
Oxford is the only unspoilt one,
culminating in the C18th bridge.
It is a pity the university has not

exploited the situation more.
*The Cherwell is navigable for
canoes only from Somerton — many
portages.*

The Kennet
The Kennet rises at the foot of
Silbury Hill, the largest artificial
mound in Europe. Leaving pre-
history behind the river reaches
Marlborough, an attractive town
that takes little notice of the
Kennet. A fine, peaceful stretch
leads to Chilton Foliat and out of
Wiltshire. Hungerford is the first
Berkshire town, where the river is
joined by the Kennet and Avon
Canal. This canal, opened in 1810,
runs from Reading to Bath, thus
linking the west of England with
London via the Thames. Built by
John Rennie, the canal includes
the Dundas aqueduct and the
flight of 29 locks at Devizes, where
the canal falls 250 feet in two
miles. Although disused, parts of
the canal are still navigable. There
are plans to reopen it. There is also
a trout farm near Hungerford,
which stocks the other tributaries.
After Hungerford the river passes
through Newbury, and then the
scenery that leads into Reading is
broken up by factories and gravel
pits. The final mile is the most
depressing on the whole river.
*The Kennet is navigable as far as
Tyle Mill Lock. Canoes can start at
Hungerford, but there are many
obstacles and portages.*
Apply British Waterways, Willow
Grange, Church Road, Watford,
Herts for a cruising licence. For
further details apply navigation to
The Secretary, The Kennet and
Avon Canal Trust, The Coppice,
Elm Lane, Lower Earley, Reading.
Tel 82149.

The Loddon
The Loddon, which gave its name
to the Loddon lily, rises in the
north Hampshire Downs. It soon
enters Berkshire, passing through
Swallowfield and Arborfield.
The upper Loddon flows through
meadows and pastureland, which
give it the slow, lazy character
for which it is famed. After
Twyford, the river enters St
Patrick's Stream, a backwater of
the Thames which it soon joins.
The Loddon is unusual among
tributaries in that it is fed by the
Thames for most of the year,
rather than the other way round.
*The Loddon and St Patrick's
Stream are not generally navigable
except for canoes from Swallowfield. Many obstacles and portages.*

The Ver and the Colne

The Ver, the true source of the Colne, rises near Redbourn in Hertfordshire. After passing the fish ponds of Gorhambury, it enters St Albans. The Roman remains of Verulamium (St Albans) include a theatre. Leaving the town the Ver flows swiftly through gravel pits, a feature of the landscape. However, its confluence with the Colne is very beautiful. Rising near North Mimms, the Colne is an indifferent river till it joins the Ver. At this point the combined rivers flow through unspoilt countryside towards Watford. After Watford development becomes extensive to Rickmansworth where the Colne is joined by the Gade, the valley of which is used by the Grand Union Canal. The river, gathering speed, flows along the Buckinghamshire and Middlesex border, and enters Uxbridge. By West Drayton and Harmondsworth the course of the river becomes more confused, but finally it rushes into the Thames at Staines, alongside the cinema. *The Ver and the Colne are not navigable.*

The Wey

Like the Thames, the Wey has two rival sources, one in Hampshire, one in Sussex. However, it is very much a Surrey river. The Hampshire branch rises at the foot of the downs beyond Alton. The river is invisible in Alton but the stretch between here and Farnham is deep enough for swimming. After Farnham the river passes Moorpark and the ruins of Waverley Abbey, and then joins the Sussex branch by the two bridges of Tilford.

The Sussex branch of the Wey rises on Blackdown, above Selbourne. It then flows through wooded country to Frensham, and passes Frensham Ponds. After Frensham the valley carries the river to Tilford, with the Hog's Back and Hindhead in the background. After the junction the river flows through parkland laid out by Capability Brown and reaches Godalming. Here the Wey meets the first stretch of canal. Opened in 1760, the canal made the river navigable as far as Godalming. It is now disused. Four miles of beautiful country separate Godalming from Guildford, the country town of Surrey. After Guildford the river is made navigable by the canal, the Wey Navigation. Built by Sir Richard Weston, the canal links Guildford with the Thames at Weybridge. After the village of Send, the fine weather boarded remains of Newark Mill are visible. The river then borders the Royal Horticultural Society Gardens at Wisley, passes through Brooklands airfield and joins the Thames in a confusion of locks and pools at Weybridge. *The Wey is navigable as far as Guildford, and sometimes as far as Godalming. For canoes one can start from both sources—from Farnham or from Frensham. A little portaging.*

Apply: River Wey Navigation, Guildford Wharf, Friary Street, Guildford. Maintained by the National Trust.

The Mole

The Mole rises in Sussex, in St Leonard's Forest beyond Rusper. Like the Wey, it is very much a Surrey river, however. After its wild origins in the forest, the river flows through the wilderness of Crawley. It passes Gatwick airport and Horley, and reaches the sharp heights of the North Downs by Dorking. There is a tradition that the Mole flows underground for three miles, having vanished through a series of swallow holes. The exact location is hard to find, but is thought to be in the area of Box Hill, so named because it is one of the few places in England where the box tree grows freely. Leaving the downs behind, the river enters Leatherhead. Here the river is crossed by a fine C18th brick bridge of fourteen spans. The Mole comes into its own when it reaches Stoke D'Abernon where the bank is dominated by the church and the manor house. Note the famous brass of Sir John D'Abernon in the church. The river meanders round Cobham, coming within a mile of the river Wey, crosses Esher Common and enters the town after passing Esher Mill. It then branches into two rivers, the right one being the Ember, but unites again as one before joining the Thames opposite Hampton Court. *The Mole is not navigable except for canoes starting at Leatherhead. (In wet weather from Horley.) Much private water.*

The Lea

The Lea rises in a stagnant pool north of Luton in Bedfordshire. It first appears as a river in the park at Luton Hoo which was laid out by Capability Brown. Below Luton the sewage purification works ensures that the river remains little better than a sewer, empty of fish. After entering Hertfordshire the river passes Harpenden, Welwyn Garden City and Hatfield. In the grounds of Hatfield House it feeds an ornamental lake once again. The rural countryside around Essenden is followed by Hertford, where the Lea, boosted by the waters of the Mimram, Beane and Rib, becomes navigable. Ware, which is the upper end of the barge navigation today, still has a fine C18th waterfront. The Lea is one of the few places where, with luck, a horse-drawn barge can still be seen. The river Stort joins the Lea at Rye House. It is navigable as far as Bishops Stortford. After Broxbourne and Waltham Abbey the river reaches Edmonton, where the outskirts of London begin. The last few miles into London are characterised by houses, factories and warehouses, and the inevitable rubbish tips. The river becomes tidal at Lea Bridge and finally reaches the Thames in two stages: the river stream wanders into the Thames by Blackwall in Bugsby's Reach, while the navigational section enters via a dock at Old Ford. *The Lea is navigable as far as Hertford.*

The Roding

One of the least known tributaries, the Roding idles through arable land for most of its length. This Essex river rises above Canfield. The first village of any importance is Fyfield, famous for eels in the 1920's. The river then flows through Ongar to Passingford Bridge, and to the C18th mill just beyond. Although narrow and shallow throughout its thirty-five miles, the Roding was once navigable as far as this mill. After Woodford, it borders Epping Forest, with the shadow of London in the background. It passes Wanstead and Ilford, the latter town marking the tidal limit of the river, and then wanders into Barking Creek, once a C19th fishing centre. From there the creek leads swiftly to the Thames. *The Roding is not navigable.*

The Medway

The Medway rises in a reservoir in Ashdown Forest, and meanders to Penshurst where it is joined by the Eden. The fine tudor brick of Penshurst Place dominates the village. On reaching Tonbridge the river becomes navigable. This pleasant market town is famous for the manufacture of cricket balls. Leaving Tonbridge the river wanders through meadows to Twyford, passing under the first of the series of excellent stone bridges. Between Teston and Farleigh the river passes through a fertile valley famous for its hops.

150 Canals

The Canal Link System

Navigable Canals
Navigable Rivers
Navigable in parts only

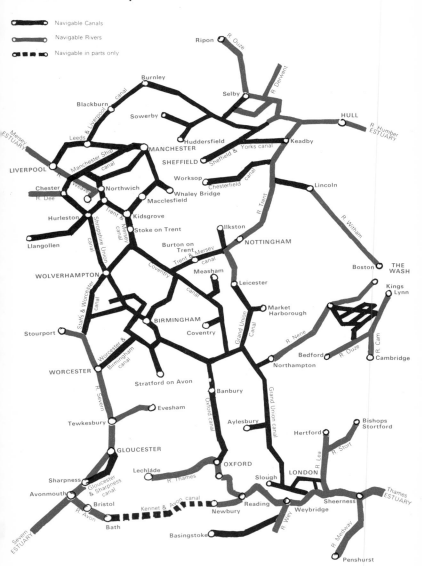

Carrion Crow

Rook

Jackdaw

Magpie

Jay

Starling

Goldfinch

Bullfinch

Chaffinch

Yellowhammer

Reed Bunting

Skylark

Yellow Wagtail

Pied Wagtail

Nuthatch

Treecreeper

Marsh Tit

Great Tit

Coal Tit

Spotted Flycatcher

Long-tailed Tit

Blue Tit

Willow Warbler

Reed Warbler

Blackcap

Whitethroat

Mistle Thrush

Song Thrush

Blackbird

Nightingale

Robin

Dunnock

Wren

Swallow

House Martin

Swift

Kingfisher

Green Woodpecker

Great Spotted
Woodpecker

Cuckoo

Tawny Owl

Turtle Dove

Barn Owl

Kestrel

Common
Buzzard

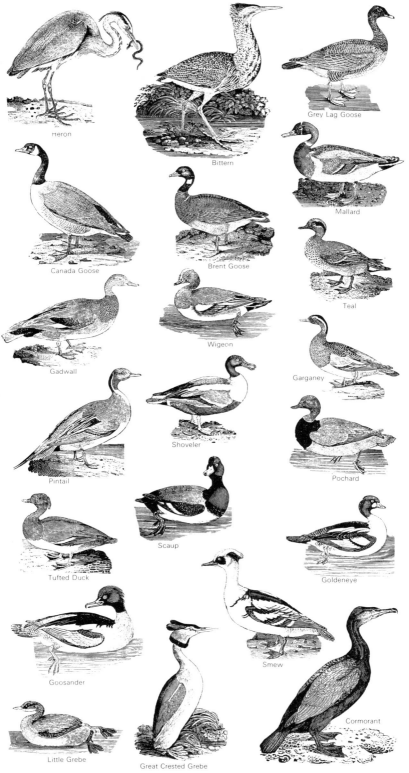

Heron

Bittern

Grey Lag Goose

Canada Goose

Brent Goose

Mallard

Teal

Gadwall

Wigeon

Garganey

Pintail

Shoveler

Pochard

Tufted Duck

Scaup

Goldeneye

Goosander

Smew

Cormorant

Little Grebe

Great Crested Grebe

Black-throated Diver

Godwit

Curlew

Snipe

Turnstone

Dunlin

Redshank

Greenshank

Golden Plover

Grey Plover

Lapwing

Oystercatcher

Black Tern

Common Tern

Black-headed Gull

Herring Gull

Great Black-backed Gull

Lesser Black-backed Gull

Coot

Quail

Barbel

Bleak

Common Bream

Bullhead

Common Carp

Chub

Dace

Freshwater Eel

Gudgeon

River Lamprey

Perch

Minnow

Roach

Pike

Ruffe

Rudd

Stickleback

Tench

Brown Trout

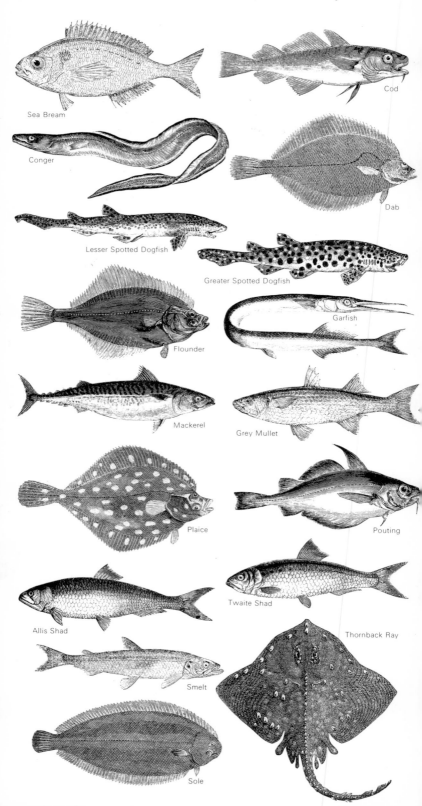

Sea Bream

Cod

Conger

Dab

Lesser Spotted Dogfish

Greater Spotted Dogfish

Flounder

Garfish

Mackerel

Grey Mullet

Plaice

Pouting

Allis Shad

Twaite Shad

Thornback Ray

Smelt

Sole

Other books about London and the Thames by Robert Nicholson Publications:-

Nicholson's Guide to the Thames	paperback	12s6d
	clothbound	25s
Nicholson's Guide to Thames Fishing	paperback	15s
	clothbound	30s
Nicholson's London Guide	pocket	6s
Nicholson's London Reference	paperback	9s6d

Obtainable from all booksellers or direct from the publisher.